For Peter —

OCEANS

APART

THE WANDERINGS OF
A YOUNG MARINER

Welcome to the monkey House !

by
Kevin McCarey

THE GLENCANNON PRESS

MARITIME BOOKS

El Cerrito
2016

This book is copyright © 2016, by Kevin McCarey.

Published by The Glencannon Press
P.O. Box 1428, El Cerrito, CA 94530
Tel. 800-711-8985
www.glencannon.com

First printing.

ISBN 978-1-889901-66-4

Library of Congress Cataloging-in-Publication Data available on request.

ACKNOWLEDGEMENTS

I would like to thank my fellow Maritimers Dave Ryan, George Lupo and George Schaberg as well as writers T.C. Boyle, Mitchell Burgess, Robin Green, Sam Gilston and Rosemary Daniell for their counsel and encouragement. I'm especially appreciative of publisher-editor Walter Jaffee, whose Glencannon Press is a treasure chest of maritime lore. Closer to home, I raise another glass to the brothers McCarey and sister Kerry too. And a glass to my own shipmate-for-life Fran McCarey.

And a very special thanks to the late Bob Fillare, a mariner with a heart as deep and wide as the seas we sailed across.

Authors note: This is a memoir, but also a sea story. Names have been changed, and the events, while true, have been dramatized to better serve the narrative.

Dedication

For Brett, the adventure continues ...

CONTENTS

To you alone, bold seekers, tempters, experimenters, and to all who ever went out on the terrible sea with cunning sails —
To you alone, you who were riddle-drunk and twilight happy, whose souls were lured by flutes to any treacherous chasm.
To you alone I shall tell the riddle that I saw.

— Friedrich Nietzsche

PROLOGUE

We were in the thick of the doldrums sailing west. Heat waves radiated from the sea, the ship's hull and our bodies. The wind was whisper light. Still, the easy roll of the ship produced a deep, resonate *bongggg*. The sound came from the nether regions of the vessel. It was loud enough and insistent enough to remind us that Suffering is the Human Condition.

I was third mate on a tramp freighter bound for Vietnam; a twenty-one-year-old greenhorn, fresh out of college. The SS *Green Wave* was carrying some 2,000 tons of warheads, nose rockets, mortars, depth-chargers, torpedoes, missiles and 500-pound bombs. The ship was a floating ammunition depot. And somewhere in one of the lower holds there was a loose bomb.

"Dis ship is bad from mornin'," said Carroll Flowers, the able-bodied seaman on my watch. "She bad from mornin'." Flowers was a black Honduran in his sixties. With more than forty years of sea time, he knew bad from mornin'.

The ordinary seaman, Wilbert Ebanks, was a huge garrulous black man from Cayman Brac. He had a booming laugh that annoyed the captain to no end. Captain Dunderborg was a dour Norwegian who strongly believed that laughter is a devilish wind.

"Can't you do something about that man?!"

"Sir?"

"I can hear him laughing even in my cabin."

"I can't stop him from laughing, sir."

The captain glared at me with an expression out of *Through a Glass Darkly*. "You are the officer of the deck, for god sakes! Don't you know how to give an order?"

"You want me to order him to stop laughing, sir?"

Truth is, I could see his point. With a bomb rolling around somewhere on the ship, a maniacal laugh did little to soothe one's nerves.

We first heard that haunting sound somewhere off the Pacific coast of Panama. We cut the ship's speed to dead-slow ahead, and sent deck crews into the cargo holds to search for the loose ordnance. But they found nothing. We couldn't risk being tossed about in a storm, so we headed south to the equator — and the doldrums — where the seas are notoriously calm. Almost too calm for the nerves.

> Day after day, day after day,
> We stuck, nor breath, nor motion,
> As idle as a painted ship,
> Upon a painted ocean.

About six months earlier, on Christmas Day, a bomb had come loose in the hold of another freighter, the SS *Badger State*. She was en route to Da Nang, Vietnam, carrying thousands of bombs and rockets. The runaway bomb exploded in heavy seas, blowing a hole the size of a billboard in its hull. The ship went down, and twenty-six crewmen were lost.

Even in peace time, countless freighters a year venture out into the Great Blue and are never heard from again. Yet the loss of a merchant ship and its crew rarely makes the news the way the loss of, say, a small private plane with a half dozen passengers would. The American merchant marine has simply fallen off our collective radar.

And yet, the sea still holds a special allure for many — especially budding novelists and poets, musicians and playwrights. In the early 1900s, the playwright Eugene O'Neill signed on one of the last of the merchant sailing vessels. The three-masted bark was bound for the Argentines carrying a cargo of lumber. O'Neill was escaping a failed marriage, and thought life at sea might help alleviate his chronic depression and alcoholism. Which is a little like throwing yourself off a cliff to help cure a fear of heights. He sailed on merchant ships for two years, drinking and debauching his way from Trinidad to Southampton, England. Later he would write a play in which his main character said things like "I hate dat ole davil sea, for make me crazy like dat!"

In 1923 at the age of twenty-one, the poet Langston Hughes joined the SS *West Hassayampa* in New York. "If I have to work for low wages at dull jobs," he wrote in a letter, "I might as well see the world." His first voyage was only forty miles up the Hudson River. The ship was then moored off Jones Point where it joined a fleet of ships in mothballs. There, it remained frozen in river ice for long months, where it inspired in Langston Hughes such wisps of poetry as:

> *Today like yesterday,*
> *Tomorrow like today*
> *the drip drip drip,*
> *Of monotony.*

But the young poet was still determined to see the world. "There were other rivers in the world to see besides the Hudson. And oh! so many dreams to chase." He quit the *West Hassayampa* and signed on the SS *Malone* as mess boy. The freighter steamed to West Africa. There in the Congo, crew members swapped shirts and shoes for exotic pets. Hughes traded for a red monkey he named Jocko. On the voyage home, a South Atlantic storm tossed the ship about, turning loose countless parrots and monkeys — screeching and howling and shitting where they pleased. The storm delayed the ocean crossing, and the ship quickly ran out of provisions. The crew subsisted on rank sardines and oatmeal infested with meal worms for the duration of the voyage.

There was a time when America's merchant fleet was the envy of the world. In the early nineteenth century, fast, sleek, and graceful clipper ships plied the world's oceans carrying spices, tea, passengers and mail. By 1861, the American maritime industry had become the world's largest. More than two-thirds of the ships trading in U.S. ports were American made and manned. But the Civil War took a heavy toll on the merchant fleet. And after the war, Yankee shipbuilders were slow to shift to the new propellant: steam. America's more humane treatment of mariners also contributed to the decline of the American merchant marine. Less enlightened American companies simply shifted their business to foreign vessels that flew the "flags of convenience."

But in times of war, the American shipping industry has always rebounded. And never more so than during World War II. Liberty and Victory ships, T-2 tankers and C-class freighters were built in record time by America's Rosie-the-Riveters. These were the merchant ships of legend. In one year alone almost 2,000 freighters were built. And more than 215,000 men went to sea in them.

Folk singer Woodie Guthrie was among them. In 1943, he sailed as messman aboard a black-hulled Liberty ship bound for Gibraltar. The ship was a part of a convoy of more than a hundred vessels. There was safety in numbers when running the gauntlet of German U-boats. Guthrie brought along his guitar, emblazoned with the words "THIS MACHINE KILLS FASCISTS." He entertained his shipmates with a foot-stomping version of a song he'd written at sea, "Talking Merchant Marine:"

> *Doorbell rung and in come a man.*
> *I signed my name, I got a telegram.*
> *Said, "If you want to take a vacation trip.*
> *Got a dishwashin' job on a Liberty ship.*

For actor Peter Falk, the merchant marine was an opportunity to contribute to the war effort, since having only one eye precluded service in the military. "There they don't care if you're blind or not," he once said. "The only one on a ship who has to see is the captain. And on the *Titanic* he didn't see too well either."

The egalitarian spirit of the "merch" allowed African-Americans to contribute to the war effort while maintaining the self-respect denied them in the segregated services. More than 24,000 served in the merchant marine in World War II. Seventeen Liberty ships were named after notable African-Americans, including George Washington Carver, Frederick Douglass, Harriet Tubman, Paul Dunbar and Bert Williams. Captain Hugh Mulzac, an African-American himself, commanded the SS *Booker T. Washington* which sailed with an integrated crew. The ship made twenty-two Atlantic crossings carrying some 12,000 troops to the war zone.

More than 7,000 merchant mariners lost their lives in the war. It was a higher casualty rate than the Army or Navy. But after the war, the maritime industry itself was a casualty — as American companies once again heeded the siren call of foreign-flag vessels.

It would take another war some twenty-five years later to revive the U.S. merchant marine. Vietnam. But this time, few new ships were built to meet the demand. Instead, aging freighters like the SS *Green Wave* were taken out of mothballs, scrubbed clean, and sent back to sea. But they were prone to suffering disrepair and corrosion, to foundering at their moorings. An apt description too of the men who sailed on them.

If the ships were the same ones that sailed in World War II, the seamen who manned them were a decidedly different breed. They were the flotsam and jetsam of a society that found them too eccentric, too incorrigible or too stoned to embrace. How these damaged souls managed to bring their ships — often laden with high explosives — across the not-so-pacific Pacific was nothing short of miraculous. But there were times when the gods failed them. And ships like the *Badger State* went down, taking many men with them.

There is the romance of going to sea — and the reality. Now on the SS *Green Wave*, I was living the reality. Our abandon-ship drill had been scheduled for this morning, and much to everyone's surprise, the captain decided to actually conduct it. Even though Coast Guard-mandated drills were required to be held on a weekly basis, this was rarely done. One would simply enter into the logbook: "No boats lowered due to inclement weather."

But somewhere far to the north of us there was indeed some inclement weather. It had generated huge swells that traveled more than a thousand miles and were now arriving at Latitude 2 degrees north. Our latitude. The SS *Green Wave* slowly rolled up one side of a liquid slope and down the other. Tilting now to port, now to starboard. Setting back into motion whatever heavy ordnance was loose in a lower hold. The captain decided that an abandon-ship drill might be prudent after all.

The ship's alarm sounded. I threw on my life-jacket, and headed to lifeboat No. 3, which would be mine to command should the ship actually go down. I looked over the motley crew that would be my boat-mates. There was Sparks, the radio officer, a paranoid schizophrenic and font of countless conspiracy theories. And Andy, the day man, a kleptomaniac — he'd had a finger cut off in Saudi Arabia for stealing a handful of figs. And Mohammed, the wiper, who always smelled of hashish. And Tony, the bedroom steward, afflicted with Communication Addiction Disorder — that is, he was a compulsive talker. Even now he was babbling on about wallpaper designs.

Then I gazed out at the horizon. Pewter skies, dead calm, not a whisper of life. The ship slowly rolled up one mound of Jello and down another. And there was that ominous sound again: *bongggg*. Like a death knoll. Or as Woody Guthrie sang:

> *Ship's loaded down with TNT,*
> *All stretched out across the rollin' sea,*
> *I stood on the decks and watched those fishes swim,*
> *Prayed them fishes weren't made of tin.*

In times like this, you may ask yourself: well, how did I get here? Perhaps I had read too much Mark Twain. "Twenty years from now," he wrote, "you will be more disappointed by the things that you didn't do than by the ones you did do. So throw off the bow lines. Sail away from the safe harbor ... Explore. Dream. Discover."

PART ONE:

CHILDREN OF THE SEA

1

GHOST SHIPS

I am haunted by waters.
— Norman McLean
A River Runs Through It

There were nights in the Valley when the mist was thick as treacle, and you could hear the foghorns of freighters on the Hudson River, the deep pained moans so loud the ships might be steaming down the brook that trickled behind the little white bungalow we called home.

The McCareys were tenants on a perpetually fallow potato farm owned by two perpetually feuding brothers. There were six of us: father James, mother Maggie and the four boys. I was the oldest, followed by Garrett and Brian and Neal. Actually we were seven, including my grandmother, Bridget Mooney, a square-jawed Irish peasant with merry eyes and a great heart.

We had moved here from Brooklyn when I was very young. My father aspired to be an artist, a cartoon illustrator in the tradition of Hal Foster whose comic strip Prince Valiant was his inspiration. Prince Valiant had reinvented the genre with its epic sweep, rich illustrations and elegant prose. In the early 1950s Jim McCarey, whose nom de cartoon was MacDara, seemed poised for success. For almost two years a comic strip he wrote and illustrated appeared weekly in the *Irish Advocate*, an Irish-American newspaper with a fairly decent circulation. The comic strip was called The Red Hand of Ulster and featured the exploits of the 16th Century chieftain Shane O'Neill. O'Neill was an Irish Prince Valiant. But the strip never quite caught on. When the series was abruptly canceled, my father was crushed.

It was clear to James McCarey that the demands of success were singularly unfair, even outrageous. They called for hard work, grit, courage, determination. Resolve in the face of defeat. To the Artist it was better to pack up one's hopes and dreams (and one's family) and retreat from these daunting requisites for accomplishment.

And what better escape than to Rip Van Winkle country where one could sleep and dream through the remainder of one's life? Maybe pick up a bookkeeping job now and then to feed the yawping mouths. Here in the Hudson Valley one could work at one's own pace, sketching, drawing, and inking in one's own creations: knights and cowboys, knaves and pirates. Here in the country one could fail on one's own terms.

The town which we called the Valley actually consisted of two valleys nestled in steep hills rife with rock: Piano and Granite Mountains, Tinker and Prospect and Candlewood Hills. The land was thick with stands of birch and hickory and oak. In winter, when the sun was low in the sky, the stark hills were illuminated barely five hours a day. In summer, they were shrouded in dense vegetation. To some this made the Valley as comforting as a cradle. To others it was as confining as a crypt: hemmed in by walls of granite in winter and buried by tangles of greenery in summer.

There was water everywhere. Dripping from rocky outcrops, rushing down mountain streams, rippling in countless lakes and ponds, sitting placidly in lush wetlands. Eventually the water found its way to the rivulets that defined our world: Roaring and Oscawana and Peekskill Hollow brooks, Adams and Sunken Mine and Canopus creeks. The streams flowed to the southwest joining Annesville Creek, which broadened and slowed as it approached the mighty Hudson River. There the waters spread out onto a wide marsh dotted with cattails and wild hemp. The waters seeped ever so gently, so quietly into the river, which was brackish even this far north. Its waters took two paces downriver, one pace upriver during every tidal cycle.

Thus, all the waters of the Valley led inexorably to the river and thence to the sea.

To escape the pressures engendered by actually having to work to support his growing brood, the Artist took his boys on long hikes in the woods. Look at him: yes, he is a darkly handsome man — some say a dead ringer for F. Scott Fitzgerald — but he is wearing this ridiculous cap with ear flaps — fit for a six-year-old perhaps — and a seedy tweed jacket, the elbow patches peeling off, and wingtip shoes encased in rubbers that squeak when he walks. I was twelve — too old to be following this absurd gander anywhere, but there I was on a rocky trail leading up the south face of Anthony's Nose, a granite headland that loomed a thousand feet over the Hudson River. It was early spring, the trees barely in bud, and snowmelt had made the trail a soggy mess. Each of us — even the wee ones — had his own crooked walking stick — essentially a branch found on the forest floor.

"Do you know why they call it Anthony's Nose?" asked the Artist.

"Nooo," said the boys — Garrett, eight and dark haired and rail thin — and Brian, six and tow-headed and round as a muffin.

"It was named after a sea captain in the days of sail. He had a great big schnozz." He pointed to a stream of water spilling over a ledge. "And do you know what they call that?"

"Nooo," said the boys.

"The snot from Anthony's Nose."

Just below us, Bear Mountain Bridge gracefully spanned the Hudson. This stretch of the river was marked by dramatic curves.

To the north, it swept around Storm Mountain. To the south it flowed around Dunderberg Mountain then veered around Stony Point, the last big bend in the river, before it straightened out at last, reconciled to its duty to go to sea.

We were sitting on a huge slab of bare rock streaked red with iron ore. We passed around an old Army canteen filled with hard, viscous Valley well water. To the south was Haverstraw Bay. There was a thick patch of morning fog on the waters, and we could see a forest of ships' masts jutting up through a gray blanket. "The Ghost Fleet," said the Artist. We could just make out the gray hulls of countless merchant ships moored tightly together. During World War II they had made daring runs across the Atlantic to Liverpool, Murmansk, and Archangel, and across the Pacific to Leyte, Sidney and Guadalcanal.

"During the war they turned out one a week," said the Artist. "Now they're just sitting there, waiting for the next one." Little did he know that next war was just on the horizon. The ghost ships would soon be dusted off and taken out of mothballs. And the skinny twelve-year-old the Artist had just passed the canteen to would be standing on the bridge of one of them bound for places like Cam Ranh Bay, Da Nang, and Saigon.

Once while perusing the McCarey family library, I found wedged between *The Great O'Neill* and *I Follow Saint Patrick* a weathered copy of the *American Merchant Seaman's Manual.* For Seaman by Seamen it was subtitled. At first glance, it looked like a Sea Scout manual with instructions on how to tie knots and splice lines, how to rig cargo slings and batten down hatches, how to use signal flags and read charts, how to give artificial respiration and sail a lifeboat. The pictures were few: seamen splicing lines or positioning a cargo boom or manning the helm, but there was poetry in the prosaic. I had always loved the sea stories of Jack London, but this was the real thing.

> A line under extreme tension may creak, make snapping sounds and may smoke. If it parts, it will snap back fast and can take off a leg or a head.

To the landlubber, marking the anchor chain may appear unnecessary, but after being on the focsle when the anchor has been dropped, trying to see through clouds of rust and to hear over the clatter of the anchor chain, it will make more sense.

Bowsprits were known as 'widow-makers' because many good men were lost when the ship dipped into a deep swell.

Venereal diseases can be prevented. The best method is:
1. Immediately get up and wash with soap and hot water.
2. Urinate.

For Seamen by Seamen. A guide book to a real world of adventure, danger, romance. What was it doing in the McCarey library of all places? When asked about the book, the Artist exhaled deeply and loudly. This often preceded yet another Tale of Lost Opportunity. There was a time, he said, when he'd thought about going to sea. "Gauguin went to sea, you know." So the young artist James McCarey decided he, too, would ship out. He knew nothing about ships, so he picked up the *American Merchant Seaman's Manual* and studied it every night after his bookkeeping job. Things never worked out, of course, and he recited the litany of excuses: a proclivity to seasickness, a root canal operation, a misplaced application form — ending with the Root Cause of All His Failures: "and then I met your mother."

But he did go to sea. In his imagination. He would often tell us stories of the SS *Tropical Breeze* which he sailed to the island of Zanzibar. It was a land of balmy winds and turquoise waters, and the air was filled with the scent of wild spices. There he met a native girl named Cinnamon — and what a wild spice was she! — and it was all a lie of course — but somehow this imagined adventure seemed more true than his real life as a landlubber.

The only true sailor in the family was my late grandfather, George Reynolds. He aspired to be a movie actor, having appeared briefly as an extra in the silent classic *Les Miserables* carrying a torch. Awaiting the call from Hollywood, he supported himself as a deck hand on a Hudson River ferry. When the ferry sank, so did any chance of George Reynolds becoming anything other than a freeloading souse. I have an old sepia photo of him sporting a rumpled seaman's cap, whiskey bottle in hand, leering drunkenly at the camera.

As for the Artist, the Valley was the farthest he had ever ventured from his place of birth in Brooklyn. Fifty miles up the river. Granted, this is considerably farther than European peasants traveled during the Dark Ages, but then their thatched roofed cottages were not chock full of travelogues and language books (French, Italian, German and *Irish?*) and old *National Geographic* magazines and maps, maps and more maps: tacked to the walls, spread across the kitchen table and stashed next to the toilet for a little light reading. Road maps and topographical maps, U.S. Geological Survey maps and nautical charts. A huge globe stood in the living room, the equator ring peeling off and Ireland effectively rubbed out from being touched too often ("You know we're going back some day"), the whole country worn away like the statuary of saints touched by centuries of penitents. Everything in the house said go. But no one went anywhere.

In fact no one in the Valley went anywhere. There was no need to. There were sixteen taverns for less than 1,000 year-round residents. House of O'Connor, Hollowbrook Inn, Murphy's, Frenchy's, Shamrock House, Alpine Inn, Spruce Hill Inn, Lakeview Tavern, Oscawana Inn, Hilltop Lodge, Oasis, Grasshopper, Cimarron, Brookside Inn, the Glockamorra, Roaring Brook Inn. A tavern for every dozen families. Every weekend and most week nights they were filled with men, women and children.

There they were: the Greatest Generation, arses planted on bar stools, ranting about politics, reviling other races, colors and creeds, ridiculing each other's foibles. Then to soothe bruised feelings they burst into song, everyone singing loudly and off-key along with Peggy Lee on the juke box:

> *Is that all there is?*
> *If that's all there is my friends,*
> *then let's keep dancing,*
> *Let's break out the booze and have a ball*

And there was Maggie McCarey, downing a whiskey sour and telling of one of the countless bawdy jokes she was known for. "Did you hear the one about the cross-eyed seamstress?" she said. "Lucky girl. She couldn't mend straight. Menstruate, get it?!" Raucous laughter all around, none louder than hers. Maggie was a striking brunette with a slender figure that belied the fact that she'd already had six children — two died in infancy — and there was another on the way.

It was my mother who defined our moral world and who instilled in us the guiding principle that would inform every decision of our lives: Don't get caught. She was our Fagin. Imminently skilled at stealing eggs from the henhouse of the Feuding Brothers, slipping whole roasts from the grocery store into her handbag, and — a holiday tradition for us — swiping Christmas trees from the lot near the hardware store. Maggie was nothing if not resourceful. Having run out of drink one Halloween night, she put on some heavy mascara, made an eye patch from a black sock, wrapped a kerchief around her head. Now a pirate wench, she knocked on the neighbors' doors, extended an empty whiskey tumbler and chirped: "Trick or Treat."

It was Maggie who taught us how to crib on our term papers — *it's all bullshit anyway* — how to skip school — *I like having you boys around* — how to forge the Old Man's signature on report cards — *what he doesn't know won't kill him*. Don't get caught. But if one does get caught there was another adage to fall back on: *C'est la vie. C'est la guerre.* To which she added: *C'est la* goddamn *vie.*

My mother was raised in the same orphanage that her mother Bridget was raised in and later worked for: St. Thomas's on Manhattan's East Side. Every summer of Maggie's youth was spent in the lakeside camp in Bear Mountain run by the orphanage. Those were the happiest days of her life, full of camaraderie, games, pranks, and songs. She brought that same camp spirit to the House of O'Connor, my parents' favorite tavern, favored because it was only a short stagger down the road from our house.

No movie house. No theater. No library. No restaurant. No pizza parlor. No bowling alley. No miniature golf course. No country club. No swimming pool. Sixteen taverns. Why go any-where?

There was also no high school. Once we graduated from the ninth grade in Valley Central we were bussed across the county line to one of two high schools. One was in the dying River Town, the other in suburbia. In the former, we were called "farmers." In the latter, "animals." But the resident students were not re-ally sure who we were. In our red-and-black plaid hunting jackets and surplus Army boots, we looked like hunter-gatherers. But we talked like Lenny Bruce. Our verbal dexterity never ceased to amaze them. It was a biting wit learned from our elders in the sixteen bars and taverns.

Once I met with the guidance counselor, Mrs. Shapowitz, who was going over my aptitude tests and psychology exams and academic records. Kevin is a bright boy but he "fools around in class." Scores well on the aptitudes, but with poor grades due to "too many unauthorized absences." Seems sociable enough but has "repeatedly expressed desire to get away."

"So where do you see yourself, Kevin. Say five years from now. After college. You have applied to college right?"

I fidgeted.

"You haven't applied to college?"

Should I have told her the Artist's investment in his own wob-bly futures market precluded contributing to his children's college educations? As well as the purchase of fresh milk and eggs, gas heat in the winter, an automobile that runs, school clothes that fit, visits to a dentist, barbershop haircuts, a television without snow and the local newspaper? ("Christ," railed the Artist, "who needs the paper? There's nothing in that rag but Help Wanted Ads.") No, I decided. Let's not go there.

"I just haven't got around to it yet," I offered.

She studied me for what seemed an eternity. Hmmm. This is a challenge. Obviously not college material. Perhaps a trade.

Or a government job. He is from the Valley. Maybe work for the town. That's what they do there. Everybody works for the town. "You know," said Mrs. Shapowitz brightly, "not everyone has to go to college."

Rippy's one-room cabin was set on a wooded slope overlooking the Hollow Brook. This was where my friends and I came to socialize and philosophize. Rippy was the quintessential Valley lad: a horseman, a fisher, a hunter. He knew every brook trout and Johnny darter, every mussel and elver, every tadpole and caddis-fly in the Hollow Brook. Rippy was the most popular kid in Valley Central School. He could dance the Lindy Rock, scoop groundballs at shortstop, and jump fences on his Palomino horse. But in high school he became something of a recluse. He would never move from the two hundred acres of rock, stream and pasture he was raised on.

The friends and I were up in the cabin taking swigs from a bottle of scotch lifted by Davey from his father's liquor store in the River Town. Davey was a conflicted young man. His mother, Dorie, our third grade teacher, was a Midwestern woman who, when she made a mistake, would say things like: "Oooh, I pulled a boner." Which led to a barely audible "Well, could you pull mine too?" from Davey's friends. Dorie exuded an irrepressible cheeriness that said life is rich, wonderful, full of possibility. Davey's father Oscar, on the other hand, was a dyspeptic Jew who routinely skewered his wife's sunny world view, as well as the hopes and dreams of his son and the pretenses of his son's friends. The result was that Davey — the spawn of two completely different species — was a kind of mythological creature — half bird, half tree — a winged creature but with roots instead of talons — roots that would forever prevent him from taking flight.

Guy was here too. He was our leader. Even as a teenager he had the savoir faire of a connoisseur. He introduced us to exotic foods — avocados, goat cheese, anchovy stuffed olives. Guy knew the precise word for everything in the world: from "ice augers" to "cunnilingus."

In our cabin-in-the-woods, I broke out the Sears guitar and played the half-dozen chords I knew to a Hank Williams tune. No one spoke to my teenage pain and passion more than Hank Williams. And I was deeply pained. I was infatuated with a young girl with raven hair, dark eyes, saint-white skin. Her name was Jane and she was too young for me. So I told no one — not her, not even my friends — about my feelings for her. Only through Hank Williams could I express the pain of this unrequited love. "Long Gone Lonesome Blues" "Take These Chains From My Heart" "I Can't Help It (If I'm Still in Love With You.)"

It was good to be here in our own secluded cabin cloaked with wild grapes and bearberry — the night chill warmed by a wood burning stove — fine scotch — free scotch! — Hank Williams and even better friends. We're a reasonably happy lot. Why go anywhere? And yet ...

It was a fine Spring morning and the striped bass were running up the Hudson. A good day to skip school. Just like the first day of grouse hunting season. Or deer hunting. Or trout fishing. We kept our own holiday calendar in the Valley. And now the friends and I were tossing bloodworms to stripers from a rocky shore on the river while our schoolmates in the River Town and suburbia were solving quadratic equations in overheated classrooms.

With two fat stripers in the cooler, I broke out a thermos of hot chocolate, and eased myself down on a rock. I then noticed something curious happening across the river. Tugs at work among the Ghost Fleet. They were separating a freighter from the anchorage as one might an old cow from the herd. Ever so slowly. Now the ship was mid-river. Suddenly a great billow of smoke spewed up from the ship's stack. They had fired up her engines. She appeared to be moving under her own power. And the old Victory was heading downstream. Heading back to sea. But to where? What ports of call? I wondered. Buenos Aires? Shanghai? Zanzibar? The other ships, stuck at anchor for almost two decades, must be envious, I thought.

And I was envious too.

2

The Roar Of the World

The boy in the family who wants to be a sailor is usually a source of more trouble in the present and more trouble in the future than all other boys put together.
  — William Henry Riding, "The Boy Who Wants to be a Sailor," *Scribner's Monthly*, 1878.

Except for the uniform — neatly pressed khakis, spit-and-polish shoes — he was an unprepossessing young man. He was sitting at a folding table in the high school gym, a student recruiter from a small college desperate for students. There were representatives here from many colleges, and students were crowded around tables stacked with brochures and manned by slick-tongued reps. But there was no one at the table of the young man in khakis. His name was Aldo Salmon and he was a cadet at New York Maritime College, one of a handful of schools that produces officers for the American merchant marine.

"It's not the Navy," said Cadet Salmon, "It's not the military. The merchant marine is privately owned cargo ships like tankers, freighters, passenger ships. You've heard of the SS *United States* right?" I was sure he'd had to recite that countless times, since few in America know what the merchant marine is. But he seemed enthused, so I didn't have the heart to tell him I'd known about the Merch since I was a kid. Cadet Salmon yammered on.

"The good thing about Maritime College," he said, "is that you come out with a bachelor's degree, a commission in the Naval Reserve and a third officer's license in the merchant marine — any oceans, any tonnage."

"It sounds interesting," I said.

"If you want to travel. To see the world and get paid for it. You can't beat it," said Cadet Salmon. I asked for a brochure but there were none. "People find out about us by word of mouth," he said. I liked a school that couldn't afford to publish a brochure. Perhaps they could afford me. In fact, as Cadet Salmon explained, they could. Students were given monthly stipends from the Maritime Commission that covered room and board. State scholarships often covered tuition. "Which really takes the financial pressure off the parents." Thank God. Wouldn't have wanted the Artist to suffer unduly. Student loans would cover the rest of one's expense, he offered. "You know" — wink-wink — "like dating the girls you meet on the cruises."

Girls? Cruises? Oh, yes, he explained. On the training ship, *Empire State IV*. Every summer the T.S. *Empire State IV* embarked on a cruise to Europe. This summer, he said, she was bound for Bremerhaven, Antwerp, Naples and Palma de Majorca. Palma! I had read about Palma in a *National Geographic* magazine. It was an island off Spain where Catalonian beauties, hibiscus flowers in their hair, strolled arm-in-arm down cobblestoned streets or sipped sherry in outdoor cafes. A magical place with cerulean waters and olive groves and mysterious caverns. "Life here is delicious," said Chopin.

Founded in 1874, New York Maritime College was the first of its kind in the U.S. With the decline of the merchant marine after the Civil War, Congress worried that there would be a lack of professional officers should the need for them arise again. A retired naval vessel, the USS *St. Mary's*, was offered to what was then called the New York State Nautical School to serve as a training ship. She was a classic three-masted sloop-of-war that had served during the civil war, prowling the Pacific Coast for Confederate raiders. Students lived and studied aboard ship. It wasn't until 1938, that the school — renamed the New York Merchant Marine Academy — had a land-based campus, Fort Schuyler on Long Island Sound where it remains today.

After World War II, the nautical school became a fully accredited college and was a founding member of the State University of New York System. SUNY Maritime was a military school where students could earn a U.S. Coast Guard license as Third Mate or Third Engineer, as well as a degree in Marine Engineering, Nuclear Science, Meteorology and Oceanography, or Marine Transportation. The school could boast of alumni such as John W. Anderson, longest serving master of the SS *United States*, Edward Villella, the acclaimed dancer and choreographer, as well as Ross Marvin, class of 1902, who accompanied Peary on his expedition to the North Pole. There, he fell (or was pushed?) into a hole in the ice and was never seen again.

"The boy who wants to be a sailor," wrote William Riding in 1878, "is what Mark Twain would call an example of the composite order of human architecture — a contradictory being, positive in some ways, negative in others, blending in his effusive disposition a varied assortment of vices and virtues; the merry plague of all who surround him."

I wanted to be a sailor. That night I filled out the application forms. There were some potential stumbling blocks. The Naval Reserve Officer program had a weight minimum that no McCarey boy could meet. Further, a candidate's teeth needed to be cavity-free. If I took a second summer job, I could afford the dentistry. But the weight requirement was another matter. Maybe if I stuffed myself with bananas all summer. Oy. But Palma — think about Palma.

I told no one in the family about my plans to apply to Maritime College, but simply forged ahead, enduring endless bouts with the dentist's drill and consuming countless bananas and milk shakes. Still when it was time to take my Navy physical, I was four pounds under the minimum weight for my height. "Drink water," said Guy." A quart of water weighs two pounds. Drink two quarts of water before they weigh you. And you're in."

On the train ride down to Manhattan and the Naval Recruiting Center, I consumed a half-gallon jug filled with water. The train arrived at Grand Central Station, and I waddled into a drugstore on 42nd Street and weighed myself on a penny scale. One hundred-twenty-and-a-half pounds. I was a half pound over. Kidneys bursting, I contemplated relieving myself of a pint or so to ease the pain. But no — couldn't take the chance.

At the Navy recruiting office, I waited with other recruits on an endless line that led down a long corridor, then snaked around a corner to what? The weighing station, I hoped. Please let it be the weighing station.

The line, of course, did not lead to the weighing station. It led to a chain-smoking Navy lifer who reviewed my medical history forms. Nor did the next line, where another chain-smoking Navy lifer examined my dental records. Nor the next, where one was probed and groped by a mutton-chopped Naval physician. By now, real tears were flowing down my face; the body was desperate to expel fluids by any means possible. But no line led to a weighing station. There was no weighing station. The weight check, I learned, would come in four years — upon graduation — just before being inducted into the Naval Reserve, the assumption being that underweight cadets would gain enough weight during the four years at Maritime.

It is one of those miracles of human physiology that for every ounce of water consumed, the body produces a gallon of urine. The long train ride home was spent in the closet-sized toilet — the train vibrating and lurching so persistently, so violently that one's urinary marksmanship was severely challenged. I would have cleaned up the piddle but there was no paper. And I was embarrassed to know that those who used the toilet next would think:

"Jesus, what a pig! Must be that skinny kid who's been in and out of here every five minutes. Oh my God, it's on the walls too."

In any event, the die was cast. New York Maritime was the only college I applied to. And if they didn't accept me then I was not sure what I would do. Maybe set out for the Yukon territory. Claim my one-square-inch plot of land from the Klondike Big Inch Land Company. The deed had come in a box of Quaker Puffed Rice. It was legitimate.

But I did get that acceptance letter from Maritime College. Time to tell the family. Maggie was thrilled. Nanny Bridget was thrilled. The boys were thrilled. And the Artist was infuriated. He ranted about the waste of my "precious god-given talent." What talent? I wondered. For drinking and shoplifting? "Jesus Mary and Joseph," he said, "why can't you go to a real college instead of some trade school, for chrissakes." That attending a real college might have required some sacrifice on his part never occurred to him.

That night, the old man planted himself before a crackling fire in the stone fireplace by the brook. He was cradling a bottle of Seagrams 7. Stewing and getting stewed. Fireflies flickered. A chorus of frogs chirped. It was a thick night. Someone upstream had opened a dam to flush their swimming hole and the brook was roaring.

"Jim hasn't eaten all day," said Nanny Bridget to my mother.

"He knows where the kitchen is," said Maggie.

Bridget was persistent: "Kev darling, go ask your father if he wants something to eat."

I went outside, dreading the confrontation.

"Nanny wants to know if you want something to eat."

He looked up — and it was a strange look — and I knew that this time what I had done had triggered something deep inside him.

"Oh, it's the sailor." He turned back to the light-show of fireflies flickering over the brook.

"Tell the old bag I'll eat when I feel like eating."

"You don't have to take it out on her," I said. A long beat. "The thing is I just want to go somewhere. I just want to travel. The school has training cruises to Europe every summer."

He inhaled long and loud through his nose. Unlike the Sigh of Lost Opportunity, the inhale was the Sniff of Smugness picked up from an old James Cagney movie.

"Oh, the sailor wants to go somewhere."

"Yes, I do. I don't want to just hang around here all my life like some slug."

"Who are you calling a slug?"

"He's calling you a slug," said Maggie. Another county heard from. She was walking a bit wobbly herself, half-spilling a glass filled with Seagrams. "And you are a slug."

"I'll show you a slug," he said shaking a fist at her.

"Ah, go scratch your middle ass."

"I could have gone anywhere I wanted to if I hadn't been saddled with you," he said.

"Yeah and if the dog hadn't stopped to shit he would have caught the rabbit." Classic Maggie. "Kevin's got his own life to lead."

"In a pig's ass. He doesn't know what the hell he's doing."

"He knows he doesn't want to be a failure like you."

"Oh, I'm a failure am I? Who the fuck pays the rent around here?"

"No one. We're months behind. We don't have a pot to piss in!"

"Yeah and who's fault is that?!"

"You figure it out."

"So I'm a failure am I?" He looked to me now. "You think I'm a failure?"

I said nothing. Maggie was not so reticent:

"You don't even know how to screw."

That did it.

"You want to see failure?" he said. "I'll show you failure!"

He rose up from the chair — the cheap aluminum thing with half the slats missing so anyone sitting in it appeared to be truly half-assed. "I'll show you failure!" he bellowed.

He stumbled past the two of us — "I'll show you failure!" — staggered up the back steps and into the house. We looked at each other — my mother and I — and she laughed.

Minutes later he was coming back down the steps, his arms full of crumpled sheets of sketching paper, inking paper, tracing paper. "I'll show you failure!" They were sketches of his latest creations: "Harvey Caddoo and his Sister Sue" and "Shannahy, the Teller of Tales" and "Moe the Schmo." One by one, he tossed them into the fire and whooof! — they burst into flames — "I'll show you failure!" — and then he staggered back into the house again.

Maggie settled into the aluminum chair — she always loved a good fire. Then I heard Nanny's voice: Ah, Jimmy no. Bridget was a woman who had seen white cats presage death. She had heard the howls of banshees. She had felt the spirit of her own dead mother brush across her face. But this was too much: the Devil had vexed her son-in-law. And — Jaysus no! — here comes the Artist again stumbling down the back steps with another armful of the McCarey oeuvre. When these went into the fire I could see it was the work from his Blue Period: "Grace O'Malley, The Pirate Queen" and "Murdoch, the Outlaw Cowboy" and "Joe Dugan, Sea Captain."

The boys came outside to watch the show. And Nanny Bridget too. She was rocking baby Kerry in her arms and saying "Ah Jimmy no" over and over as the Artist carried out yet another armful, and it was the countless early sketches of horses and trees and naked women, as well as his research notes, his writings.

He fed them all into the fire, until only a single sheet hovered in the updraft like an autumn leaf. It was the Kilmer poem. A poem the Artist had hand-lettered with an elaborately-drawn calligraphy in the style of *The Book of Kells*.

The roar of the world is in my ears,
Thank God for the roar of the world!
Thank God for the mighty tide of fears
Against me always hurled!

Now it was done. He'd burned it all. Every line he'd ever drawn, every caption he'd ever written, all gone, gone up in flames. He'd shown us failure all right.

But the drama of the evening was not over. He was leaving us too. Just to show he meant business, he put on the goofy hat with the flapped ears — he was taking off for good now — and he lurched towards the ancient 1951 black Studebaker — the one shaped like a submarine — and got behind the wheel — fumbled with the keys — dropped them — got out and felt around the gas pedal for them. Found them — thrust the key into the ignition. *Rrrrrr-rrrrr-rrr. Rrrr- rrrr- rr. Rrrr. Rr. r.*

The battery was dead. The old man stared blankly ahead.

The next morning found him still behind the steering wheel. Sound asleep, his face pressed against the horn. In a U-boat going nowhere but down.

Over coffee and toast, my mother and I discussed my future.

"I hate to see you go," she said.

"I know, Mom."

"But you've got to get out of here."

"I know."

3

SEA FEVER

Wasn't that the best time; that time when we were
young and at sea; young and had nothing, on the sea that
gives nothing, except hard knocks and a chance to feel
your strength.
— Joseph Conrad, *Youth*

New York Maritime College is situated on the narrow spit
where the East River meets Long Island Sound. Classes
were held in Fort Schuyler, a granite pentagon built before the Civil War to protect New York City from attack by sea.
The fort now sits directly under the heavily trafficked Throgg's
Neck Bridge.

It was a military school. Khakis were worn in the spring and
fall, navy blues in winter. We had number patches on our shirt
sleeves, indicating whether we were first, second, third or fourth
classmen. The latter were also known as "Mugs" — the acronym
for Mariner Under Guidance — and subject to the traditional haz-
ing of freshman students in military schools everywhere.

There were rules and regulations. A thick regimental handbook containing them had to be memorized. There were punish-
ments for transgressions: standing for hours "braced up" — chin

pressed against the chest: "Chins! I want to see chins, Mug!" Or confinement to quarters: "Forget the outside world, Mug, you're all ours!" Or for those who had racked up too many demerits: expulsion.

The dorms — a short march away from the fort — were spare, form-follows-function buildings. And we lived in monastic seclusion. No television, newspapers, game rooms. Who had time for games anyway? We carried a full academic load — English, economics, engineering, mathematics, and the physical sciences, as well as the courses required for our profession: navigation, piloting, seamanship, cargo handling, radar plotting. We read things like the *International Regulations for Preventing Collisions at Sea.*

> Every vessel coming up with another vessel from any direction more than two points abaft her beam, that is, in such a position with reference to the vessel which she is overtaking that at night she would be unable to see either of that vessel's side lights, shall be deemed to be an overtaking vessel, and no subsequent alteration of the bearing between the two vessels shall make the overtaking vessel a crossing vessel within the meaning of the rules in this part, or relieve her of the duty of keeping clear of the overtaken vessel until she was finally past and clear.

When we were not plodding through such dense nautical verbiage, we were engaged in military drills. Formations, inspections, watch standing, pass-and-review — oh, the monkey wrapped his tail around the flagpole. We barely got five hours of sleep a night. We called it Rack Time. And we were obsessed with it. Held in the highest esteem were rack artists who could steal forty winks during a lecture on admiralty law or while standing smartly at parade rest or while staring diligently at a ship's radar screen. If we had a cry of protest it was "Give sleep a chance."

The training ship, T.S. *Empire State IV,* was docked at a long pier on the East River. With her looming gray hull, some 500 feet long — she was a dominating presence on campus. And one with an intriguing history. She was built in 1941 as a banana boat for the United Fruit Company. But with the outbreak of war, the *Biloxi* was purchased by the Army Transport Service, and renamed the USAT *Henry Gibbins* after a quartermaster of the Army. The ship was crewed by merchant mariners, many of them survivors of ships that had been sunk by German U-boats. Her first runs, in early 1943, were to the Pacific, carrying troops to staging areas in Bora Bora and Australia. In September of that year, she was transferred to the European Theater of Operations. There, she made countless runs from New York to the ports of Naples, Cherbourg, Marseilles, LeHavre and Southampton.

Then in 1944, President Franklin D. Roosevelt sent the *Gibbins* off on a secret mission. From the earliest years of the Nazi oppression, refugees seeking asylum in the U.S. were told they could not enter America. The quotas were filled. And while Congress dithered over whether to increase the number of immigrants, millions died. President Roosevelt decided to take matters into his own hands. He issued a special order to bring 1,000 refugees to the U.S.

The gaunt and traumatized men and women boarded the *Henry Gibbins* in the Bay of Naples. Many of them had just been liberated from slave-labor camps. Others had spent years hiding out in the hills or in the attics and cellars of sympathizers. They came from eighteen different countries including Italy, Spain, Greece, France, Germany and the countries of Eastern Europe. While most, by far, were Jews, there were also Catholics, Protestants and Greek Orthodox Christians — including many who had risked their own lives for providing refuge for Jews. The ship also took on board some 1,000 U.S. soldiers who had been wounded in the battles of Anzio and Cassino.

As the sun set on a bright August day, the *Henry Gibbins* raised anchor and steamed towards the Atlantic. The Mediterranean passage — rife with German U-boats — would be the most dangerous leg of the journey. The ship joined a large convoy of troopships and freighters, accompanied by sixteen warships. One night, the passengers were awoken by machine gun fire, as a squadron of Nazi fighter planes soared overhead. Another night, the engines were silenced; all lights were extinguished — a submarine had been detected. But the ship made it through the straits of Gibraltar unscathed and out into the Atlantic. It was a smooth ocean crossing, with no threats of attack. But as the *Gibbins* approached New York Harbor, there were storm warnings; a hurricane was closing in on them. As Ruth Gruber wrote in her memorable account, *Haven*:

> By midafternoon the rain stopped, but the sky remained ominously overcast, so that we saw almost no land until we moved into the bay. Suddenly she emerged, the green mythic figure. The Statue of Liberty. The thousand refugees waved at her joyously, tearfully, as if she were a granite mother welcoming them to a new homeland.
> "The greatest day of my life," a bearded old man wept.

The refugees were sent to an internment camp in Oswego, New York, where they remained for some eighteen months. After the war, they were granted U.S. citizenship.

The USAT *Henry Gibbins* later served during the Korean War, where she transported men and equipment to ports in the Caribbean for eventual deployment to the Pacific. She continued serving as a troop transport ship during peacetime, shuttling between the U.S. and its foreign bases — most of them in Europe.

In the late 1950s, the training ship for N.Y. Maritime College was a former hospital ship, the USS *Mercy*. The *Mercy* had won two battle stars while serving the Fifth and Seventh Fleets in the Pacific Theater of War. In 1956, she was transferred to the Maritime Adminsitration and renamed the *Empire State III*. But in just a few years, it became apparent she was too small to accommodate the growing student body. She was also somewhat battle-worn and prone to breakdowns. So when the *Henry Gibbins* became available in 1959, the college quickly acquired her. And the legendary troopship became the T.S. *Empire State IV*.

When winter winds stirred the waters of the river and the sound, the ship would creak and moan and pull at her mooring lines, as if restless to set sail once again. And we cadets were just as anxious to join her. Every summer, the training ship would sail to ports in Northern Europe and the Mediterranean — places long familiar to the ship but strange, new and exotic to us.

The first time we were out of sight of land was a mesmerizing experience: the horizon empty except for sea and sky, blue on blue. A few days later, the ship was in the middle of nowhere — a thousand miles west of the Azores — when the T.S. *Empire State IV* stopped its engines and glided to an easy halt. It was time for our baptism. We lined up at the open side-hatch — skinny kids in Navy-blue swim trunks — and dove into indigo waters two miles deep. A hundred cadets bobbed around in the open seas — splashing, cavorting, goofing around — while up on deck the officers — ex-Navy men mostly — watched out for deep-water sharks.

The Gulf Stream is exceptionally salty, making it easy to float in. And I was on my back — face to the sun — drifting, drifting — and I was thinking: Can you believe it? Floating around in the very middle of the fucking Atlantic Ocean! Drifting, drifting. God, this is wonderful! The water warm as breast milk, and the ripples rocking me gently. Drifting, drifting. Far from the ship.

Suddenly, one of the ship's officers spotted a large fin cutting through the waters. "Shark! Shark!" Now everyone was in a tizzy. The swimmers quickly scrambled up the netting to the side hatch. But I had drifted too far out to hear the whistles and shouts. "Hey, you! Hey, cadet! Hey! Get your ass back here! Who the hell is that, anyway?" Urgent blasts from the ship's whistle cut through my reverie. I looked for the ship and could barely see it. The wind had kicked up and the ripples were now wavelets, and the gray hull was dipping in and out of sight. Then there was a frisson of anxiety — they know I'm out here, don't they? They're not leaving me, are they? I swam frantically towards the ship. And it was a long exhausting crawl — fueled by the fear of being left alone. I was closing in on the ship now. And I could see an officer staring down at me from the open hatch. I was the last one up the ropes.

The man was livid. "You're on report, Mug," he said. Oh, well, as my mother would say. *C'est la vie, c'est la guerre. C'est la* goddamn *vie.*

Unlike many of my shipmates, I was blessed with an iron stomach and never got seasick. It was the result, no doubt, of being weaned on the culinary offal of the sixteen bars and taverns. "Have another pickled egg, Kev. They go good with the Slim Jims and beer nuts and pig's feet."

I also found a curious joy in the shipboard tasks that others called tedious. I loved the scrub-downs in the pre-dawn light. The work was honest: wearing dungarees and white gob hats, we hosed down the steel decks with warm ocean water, then, shoulder to shoulder with our mates, long-handled brooms in hand, swept the sooty waters down the scuppers.

The salt-water environment feasts on metals. And the T.S. *Empire State IV* was all metal. We would spend hours chipping the decks and bulkheads with hammers and jackhammers, then rolling on red-lead primers and battleship-gray enamel paints. Once, I was sent aloft to grease down the thick wire shrouds. I was hoisted up in a boatswain's chair — about the size of the seat of a playground swing — higher and higher, until my shipmates below were the size of toy sailors. The easy roll of the ship would send mast, shroud and me hovering over dark-blue waters. Then back again over the main deck. It was the ultimate carnival ride, and, caught up in the thrill of it, I dropped gobs of grease on the watch officer below. It would be years before anyone figured out that all those greases, primers and paints were carcinogenic.

I also loved standing bow-watch, especially at night. The ghost-like appearance of dolphins. The eerie luminescence of the bow's wake. It was one of the few places on the ship you could be alone with your thoughts. And if you leaned far out over the bow rail, it was just you, sea and sky. One night, the ocean was flat as a pond, the sky perfectly clear, the stars huge fiery explosions out of Van Gogh — so brilliant they were reflected on the surface of the sea. There was no horizon line, creating the illusion I was soaring through a starry, starry night.

And I loved navigating by the stars. Out on the bridge wing in the crepuscular light, sextant in one hand, finding in the mon-ocular a tiny spot of light that was Polaris or Vega or Arcturus and marrying it in the split mirror to the horizon line so they just kissed. What a miracle, I thought, that distant stars, millions of miles away, could tell you where you were on earth.

Attending Maritime College was like living an article in *Boys Life* magazine. Except when it wasn't.

4

A ROGUE WAVE

*I hope you see things that startle you. I hope you
feel things you never felt before.*
                    - F. Scott Fitzgerald

It was called **M.I.A.P.S.** — Military Instructions and Practical
Services. An acronym for what was essentially menial labor
and prison time. For every transgression of the rules and regulations, demerits were given out. One was "bagged," as the saying went, for a variety of transgressions. Ten demerits were given
out for minor offenses such as wearing scuffed shoes or failing to
make one's bed or showing up late to class. Twenty-five demerits
for sneaking out of campus during the week. Fifty for more seri-
ous charges such as public drunkenness. A hundred demerits for
stealing or fighting or for something called "moral turpitude."

For every ten demerits, one was restricted to campus for a
weekend. Since we were not permitted to venture out during the
week, and had pass-and-review formations on Saturday mornings, this additional confinement time was rather onerous. The
Portugee earned 100 demerits for painting "FUCK" in large red

letters on a boathouse roof — an offense that led to half-a-year's worth of confinement. Fortunately for the Portugee, the boathouse belonged to our rival school, the U.S. Merchant Marine Academy across the sound at Kings Point, or he would have been expelled.

The "military instructions and practical services" involved performing menial tasks such as picking up litter, answering phones, manning the guard station. The real punishment was confinement to campus — being stuck on that lonely, wind-blown peninsula, week after week, or, for a few unfortunates, month after month. It could get to you after a while.

It got to one first-classman who was just a few short months from graduation. He'd been restricted to campus for some minor offense, but somehow managed to get a hold of some booze and get drunk. Some time in the middle of the night, he had a nicotine fit. He broke into the canteen area and when the cigarette vending machine ate his change, he punched the glass in. Blood spurted everywhere. And he went berserk. He toppled other vending machines, and tossed tables and trash bins about, cracking a glass partition. No amount of morning-after *mea culpa*s would spare him. He was promptly expelled — or, as we used to say, he got the death penalty. Which, because of events rapidly unfolding on the far side of the world, was not that far from the truth.

On an August night in 1964, there was a skirmish between North and South Vietnamese patrol boats in the Gulf of Tonkin, off the coast of North Vietnam. The USS *Maddox*, a naval destroyer, was sent north to monitor the situation and to "show the flag." There was a brief exchange of fire with North Vietnamese gunboats but no casualties. Days later and in low visibility, the *Maddox*'s radar picked up the signals of what appeared to be gunboats firing torpedoes at them. The *Maddox* returned fire; the targets disappeared from the radar and were presumed sunk. There were conflicting reports on whether the two exchanges took place in North Vietnamese territorial waters or in international waters — and whether the second engagement actually occurred.

Still, the incidents provided what President Lyndon Johnson had hoped for: a justification for increasing American involvement in what was then a civil war in Vietnam. Congress passed the Tonkin Gulf Resolution by a vote of 416-0 in the House, and 58-2 in the Senate. It authorized the President to deploy conventional military forces in Vietnam without a formal declaration of war. It would lead to a rapid escalation of the war, and the eventual drafting of more than 650,000 young men.

Young men scrambled for deferments. The most common deferment granted was for students attending college as an undergraduate. But the Draft Board gave you no more than four years to finish your degree. This made switching colleges difficult, because credits from one college were often not accepted by another. This was especially true for students from N.Y. Maritime College. The odds of another school accepting credits for courses such as Nautical Science 101 or Introduction to Marine Navigation were nil. So those who flunked out or who were expelled from Maritime usually met a singular fate: the draft. And the likely prospect of a stint as a grunt in Vietnam. The "death penalty."

It was mostly upperclassmen who dished out the demerits. For some, it was simply a way of maintaining order, of supporting a military system they sincerely believed in. After all, no one was drafted into Maritime College. We were there by choice, knowing full well it was a military school.

The cadets at Maritime sorted themselves out into one of two groups. One group consisted of studious, spit-and-polish officer material. God, Duty, and Country seeped from every pore. The *Regimental Regulations Manual* was their own Good Book. Their guiding principle: "Men and officers must obey. Obedience to orders, instant and unhesitating, is not only the lifeblood of armies but the security of states." Thank you, Stonewall Jackson. Those cadets were destined for great things. As first-classmen they would become "rates," that is, cadet officers in charge of platoons, companies, battalions or the regiment itself. They wore their spotless officer caps tightened pancake-flat.

But there was another group whose future was far more dubious. They were the Rogues — the fun-loving, raucous, rebellious gang. Their creed: "Why do today what can be put off until tomorrow?" These cadets were destined for long months of confinement on the Rock. And they too were distinguished by their caps: weathered and rumpled like Humphrey Bogart's in the World War II flick, *Action In the North Atlantic*.

Filario and Rays and Wishbone and Roadblock and the Porpoise were Rogues. As was Maharrey.

I can't even remember how "McCarey" became "Maharrey," but were it not for the spirited company of the Rogues, I could never have endured the four years at Maritime. Filario was my closest mate, a tall red-headed kid with a Brooklyn accent as thick as the fog on Sheepshead Bay. I called him "Filario" because he seemed like he stepped out of an Italian comic opera. He was a generous soul: "Hey, Maharrey, wyoncha take dese tree dollahs and buy youse-self a new friggin' tie and trow dat ratty ding away."

Rays was pure Buffalo New York: slow, easy going and with a drawl rife with flat A's. He earned his nickname from his penchant for lying in the sun and soaking up its rays. Like most of us, he was from a large working-class family, and, like some of us, had a difficult youth — including a stint in an orphanage when his father bailed out on the family. He was also a man who asked deep philosophical questions. We were sitting in a club on the Reeperbahn in Hamburg. On stage, nude women in a glass bathtub were doing obscene things to each other with rubber duckies. "Maharrey," he asked, "Why are we here?"

And there was Wishbone, eminently attuned to the music of the spheres. He played a fine saxophone and also dabbled in piano and guitar. In my freshman year, I managed to scrape together enough money to buy a scratched and battered Fender Stratocaster. One day Wishbone asked to take it to his Jersey home for the weekend. Something about wanting to accompany his sister's singing on the guitar. His older sister played the piano and had a beautiful voice. But when he returned to the Fort that Sunday night it was sans guitar. "Wishbone," I said. "My guitar?"

"Guitar?" he replied, as if I'd asked about a dirigible. "Oh, guitar. Sorry, Maharrey. I'll bring it back next weekend." Well, one weekend followed another. Still, no guitar. And always the same reply and always with same dazed expression. I was beginning to worry more about him than my axe. A concern that quickly dissipated when he finally did return it. The guitar was barely recognizable. That is, it looked brand new. Every weekend he had carefully sanded it down, then given it a fresh coat of varnish. Every weekend meant another light sanding, another coat until he was satisfied that my Fender Stratocaster would be worthy of its name. That was Wishbone.

Then there was Roadblock — a lanky Lithuanian with a brooding, sardonic presence. RB was a military brat who'd spent his formative years in places like Rota Air Force Base in Spain. Thus he spoke fluent Spanish. He was also a star athlete — a baseball pitcher with a smoking fastball. And a gifted student — straight-A's his first year. RB had all the makings of officer material. But alas — like most of the Rogues — he carried within him the seeds of rebellion. Perhaps they were planted by the One-Eyed Jacks, the rock 'n roll band we had formed that was our salvation. He took his nickname, in fact, from the guitar instrumental he had composed as the band's theme song, "Roadblock."

The band kept us sane. Roadblock played lead guitar, I played rhythm, Cozy Cole played drums and the Crayman played bass. We rocked out in waterfront bars, Irish taverns and seedy local joints. Now and then, we'd make the trek upstate to Cornell University where Rippy would book us for a Saturday night party at his frat house.

The Porpoise was our manager. He was like an oversized cherub with fat, rosy cheeks and an infectious laugh. The Porpoise was an upperclassman who eschewed all trappings of power, happy to befriend whomever shared his passions for sailing or a decent high. He was the Daddy of all Rogues.

The One-Eyed Jacks would practice in a storage room in the basement of our dorm. While the tight-assed military junta ruled above us, we were happily rocking out, out of sight and out of mind. We grooved on the early Rolling Stones: "Gotta get away ..."

And get away we did ... That is, when we could.

For even when we were confined to campus — as we Rogues frequently were — we would find ways to escape — even if just for a few hours in the dark of night. The main entrance to Maritime was well-guarded. But there was another way out. We would slip down to the boat shed and lower one of the Monomoy lifeboats into the water. The Monomoys were wooden-hulled, double-ended whaleboats. They carried six to eight passengers comfortably. Designed for rowing, they could be sailed as well. And we would sail away, risking even further detention if caught. But that's what Rogues do.

Sometimes we'd head out on the East River towards the heart of the city. The river is actually a tidal strait, salty not fresh, and a foul potpourri New York City effluent. It was a tricky sail because, as the strait narrowed, the tidal current intensified. Also should we decide to tie up somewhere and hit one of the local bars, we'd be more likely to run into an upperclassman which would put us in even more hot water. So more often by far, we would head east, out into the blue waters of Long Island Sound.

One night in late Spring, the Troll, Filario, Boomer and I were chafing at the bits, having been confined to the Rock for one fuck-up or another. Boomer was an ardent motorcyclist, a fine clarinetist and a superb sailor. He pursued all his diversions with passion and intensity, but never more so than when riding out heavy seas in a sailboat. The Troll too was a born sailor. On land, he was a bit daft, but in a sailing dingy he was sure and quick and focused.

It was an unseasonably warm night, almost balmy, as we ventured down to the dock. Stars peeked in and out of cumulonimbus clouds. An oval moon was rising. With a following wind, and a slack tide on the cusp of flooding, we hoisted sail and headed northeast on a broad reach. Soon we were passing under the shadow of the Throggs Neck Bridge. Willets Point lay to starboard. Willets Point was an industrial wasteland of scrap yards and waste processing sites.

The glittering lights of City Island soon appeared just off the port bow. The lights were from the many seafood restaurants and bars that lined the waterfront. City Island had all the visual charm of a New England coastal village, but one that was inhabited by boisterous, obnoxious New Yorkers. We weren't up for City Island this night.

On our starboard beam, we could see the lights of the U.S. Merchant Marine Academy at Kings Point, where everyone wore their officer's caps as tight as a drum. Many of my classmates had applied to Kings Point, but weren't accepted. The Academy had the same stringent admission requirements as Annapolis or West Point, including a recommendation from one's congressman. I had never applied — and not because there was little chance I would have been accepted anyway. I liked what N.Y. Maritime offered instead. Cadets at Kings Point sailed on actual merchant ships with no way of knowing where they would end up. Bahrain? Bombay? Mombassa? No, thank you. True, they gained much more practical and valuable experience than we did on our training ship. Our cruises were a joke. But what a delightful joke! Especially knowing you were guaranteed to visit ports like Oslo or Lisbon or Villa France or ... Palma!

Boomer lashed an oar to the bow; it would serve as a makeshift bowsprit so we could set the genoa. With the larger jib, we picked up some speed. Now we could venture farther into the Sound than we usually dared. Still, reading the wind at night is an art. By day, one reads the lines of breaking waves, or in calmer seas looks for patterns in the ripples. Sometimes the play of sunlight on the sea will reveal the direction of wind on water. But in the soft light of the moon, the sea plays tricks on the eye. We would have to depend on tell-tales — strands of yarn tied to the shrouds — to read the wind.

We also had to keep a weather-eye out, as sailors say, for the blinking lights of buoys. A night sail on Long Island Sound requires careful navigation; the channels are narrow, and outside the channels there are countless rocky islets, most of them unmarked by beacons or buoys. One such danger area is aptly named Execution Rocks for the countless boats that had been "executed" before a beacon was finally installed.

Soon we were sailing past a notorious graveyard for vessels, the Stepping Stones. On the chart, the waters east of the Stepping Stones were littered with asterisks labeled "rky" or "rks" or "wk." "Wk" stood for "wreck" and the sound was littered with them. Yet all of these hazards were marked only by a single green flashing light, which was now off our starboard beam.

For all the hazards of a night sail, the rewards more than made up for them. There was little other boat traffic, especially the loud motorized kind for which Long Island Sound is notorious. All was blessedly silent — except for the soft *shhhhhh* of the bow cleaving the waters, the gentle clanging of the rigging, the occasional flap of sail. The night air was exceptionally clear; the stars brilliant, the stars of poets. We spoke little as we sailed. Even Filario, chatterbox that he was, simply gazed at the heavens and savored the night.

Usually we would veer off to the north at Hewlett Point towards the buoy at the southern tip of Hart Island than head home.

"If we turn around now," said Boomer, "we can make it back to the Fort by midnight. Who wants to turn around?"

No one raised a hand.

"Why don't we check out Hart Island?" said Filario. "I always wanted to see what it's like dere."

"Are you fucking nuts?" said the Troll.

Hart Island is an eerie place with a dark past. It has the largest potter's field in the world. Some 850,000 are buried there in unmarked graves and trenches. The homeless, victims of infectious diseases, children of the poor. At one time or another, it had also served as a Civil War internment camp, a work house for poor children, a reform school, a women's lunatic asylum, a tubercular ward, and a prison.

"Hey, why not?" said Filario.

"Because we just escaped from there," I said.

And so we turned east, past the sunken wrecks and rocks marked by buoy No. 29, flashing green, and into a world that was strange in its own right. Manhasset Bay was lined with elegant homes bathed in moonlight. One glorious mansion after another graced the shore — just as they had in the golden years described by F. Scott Fitzgerald. Some sat on high bluffs, others hugged the waterline — all had magnificent views of the bay and the equally-resplendent homes of their social counterparts on the opposite shore. It was here that the Great Gatsby gazed across the waters, fixated on the green light at the end of Daisy Buchanan's dock.

As we sailed past Plum Point, we could hear the sound of music coming from somewhere beyond. It was a jazz combo — Boomer's favorite kind of music. He steered the boat towards the music, and soon we were entering a large cove. The wind died in the lee of the point, and the sails luffed. We dropped the jib, raised the centerboard, and let the tide carry us closer to shore — and the music.

"I've got the world on a string, I'm sitting on a rainbow, got that string around my finger." Boomer put a fist to his lips and kazooed a jazz accompaniment.

The boat drifted slowly along the arc of the cove, past a party of Swells. "In his blue gardens," wrote Fitzgerald in *The Great Gatsby*, "men and girls came and went like moths among the whisperings and the champagne and the stars." The lawn was dotted with Chinese lanterns. Guests were gathered around a huge three-tiered fountain festooned with balloons. It was a casual affair. A birthday party, perhaps. The men wore button-down blue shirts and khakis. Not an ascot in sight. The women wore spring dresses. They were an older crowd for the most part.

Waiters circulated among them. We had drifted so close to shore that we could almost reach out and grab an *hors d'oeuvre* from a tray (I'll take the paté, thank you.) or join in on a conversation (He was a splendid gelding. We hated to part with him.) There were quizzical looks from the gentry as we drifted by (Who are those ... those guys?!) It occurred to me that in our jeans, dark pea-coats and black watch-caps, we looked more like burglars than sailors. Or at least the kind of dress-white yachtsmen, they were used to seeing. But then, a sailor is always the guest who shows up unannounced and uninvited — and in inappropriate dress. No worries, folks, our stay will be short.

The boat continued its drift along the arc of the cove past snatches of Mid-Atlantic accents — the clinking of cocktail glasses — heads cocked to one side — forced smiles — gloved hands — blue hair — cigars — what a swell party this is! — to where a long dock jutted out into the waters. There were no boats tied up alongside. No doubt the family yacht had been shuttled south for the winter — to Palm Beach, perhaps. At the end of the dock, we could see a clutch of young Daisy Buchanans talking quietly among themselves. They seemed disinterested in the party — bored, even. Perhaps it was a generational thing. Or maybe they had come down to the dock for a glimpse of their own Jay Gatsbys on the opposite shore. Instead they were treated to the sight of us.

"Mermaids," sighed the Troll. We all knew what he meant. Beautiful, but elusive creatures. Only these wore mascara and mini-skirts.

"Strange children should smile at each other," wrote Fitzgerald, "and say 'Let's play.'"

So we smiled. As — to our delight — did they.

"Where are you from?" shouted one of the girls. She was a slender beauty who sported a wide-brimmed hat.

"Brooklyn," said Filario.

They giggled. Surely he was joking. Nobody was from Brooklyn.

"Nice night for a sail," said another in a scalloped mini-skirt.

"Sure is," I said.

"Well, stay dry," she said.

"Not if we can help it," said the Troll, raising his can of beer.
The girls laughed and raised their cocktail glasses.

"Chin-chin," they said. Chin-chin? Oh, yes, this is another country.

"Chin-chin!" we said. When in Rome ...

"You guys are from Kings Point, aren't you?"

"Oh, yeah," said the Troll. "Kings Point. That's us." It was only a white lie. Surely they'd never heard of N.Y. Maritime.

"I thought they never let you guys out," said a perky lass in a ruffled mini-skirt.

"Prison break."

"Well, don't get caught."

"We're like da guys in da Great Escape," said Filario.

"They got caught," I reminded him.

"Oh."

"Hey," said the Troll. "Wanna hop aboard? We got plenty of room." Not a bad idea, I thought, since there was no way we could crash that party.

"Where would we go?"

"How about the Azores?" I said. "They're just a short hop across the pond."

"Why the Azores?"

"Mountains and Madeira wine and fado music."

"Sounds enticing. How long would it take?"

"2100 nautical miles. At four knots, about fifteen days," said Boomer.

"Hmm. We're not really dressed for it."

"Hey, no dress code here," said the Troll. "This is the Love Boat." Don't get the Troll started, I thought.

"How about a short, sweet sail on the bay, then?" I offered.

They giggled among themselves.

"Moon, stars, a fair wind. We've got it all tonight."

Furtive glances back towards the party. Then muffled counsel among themselves. Could we? Should we? Oh, it would be a pisser. But what about the Chandlers? And our mums? No, we couldn't. We shouldn't. A collective sigh of disappointment. Then: "Maybe next time?"

"Okay. Next time, for sure." Though we all knew there would be no next time.

"Well ... chin-chin," they said.

"Cheers!" we said.

By now we had drifted almost out of earshot. The girls fell silent, looking crestfallen as we drifted away. They watched us until we were well beyond the cove. And I wondered if they were more imprisoned than we were.

The breeze picked up again, the boom swung to leeward. We hauled in the mainsheet until the wind filled the sail. Then we raised the genoa and sailed back out into deeper waters. And farther and farther away from the world of F. Scott Fitzgerald.

And this, I would learn, is what life as a mariner is all about: an endless string of brief encounters. A life of sketches and vignettes. Sailing in and out of alien worlds, but never staying long enough to become truly part of them. Strange people, foreign languages, exotic foods, unfamiliar customs, alien religions, and — more frustrating, perhaps — mysterious mating rituals. But it's what makes sailors such a tolerant breed. To exist among strangers, one must quickly discover common ground, shared values, the universal essence of their humanity. Which makes the sailor, I believe, more tolerant and less judgmental of others. And also one who is forever enchanted by the "inexhaustible variety of life," as Fitzgerald wrote.

We sailed on. "And as the moon rose higher, the inessential houses began to melt away until gradually I became aware of the old island here that flowered once for Dutch sailors' eyes ..."

5

MERMAIDS

Roaring chanteys as they swagger,
They were elbowing the bar,
While they wink at waiting wantons
Who were fairer than the stars.
                    - Anonymous, "Sea Wraiths"

In 1946, the T.S. *Empire State IV* — then sailing as the USAT *Henry Gibbins* — was assigned the task of transporting war brides from Europe to the U.S. Three decks of cabins and lounges, and two formal staircases were installed. Bathroom amenities were upgraded and dining areas were spiffed up. One can imagine the war brides chattering in the lounges and dining areas or simply standing at the railings, gazing out at the horizon, and longing for their new husbands. Thus, despite years of scrubdowns by cadets, the ship was permeated with the scent of female pheromones, afflicting those who sailed her with a certain randiness.

Whenever we first hit port, most of us — young and full of jism, heads spinning from the long crossing, hormones raging from inhaling the pheromones the war brides left behind — headed straight for the dockside bars and the promise — nay the guarantee — of female companionship — if only by the glass. The "B-girls" made their living hustling drinks.

Filario, whose generous spirit made him an easy mark, would soon find himself surrounded by women eager to become his personal welfare project. "Dese ladies are okay, Maharrey. Dey just need a friggin' break, is all." Wishbone, too, would buy them endless rounds of drinks while describing in loving detail how he rebuilt the V-8 engine of his '54 Ford. "So I put in a four barrel Holley carb. You know what a Holley carb is, right?" They wouldn't understand a word, of course, yet they seemed perfectly content to listen to his sonorous voice.

We loved the bar girls and they loved us. Still, most of us longed for a genuine romantic encounter. They were hard to come by. Too few days in port. Too many cadets flooding the streets. Too few women enamored of the sight of an American in uniform. Some of us got lucky though. It was easy to spot the cadet who had had an affair to remember. The object of his affection accompanied him back to the ship to see him off. And then she did what no hooker would ever do. She would kiss him goodbye. Sweet, simple, chaste, it was the most envied of kisses.

In Paris — where else? — I met Mary Jones, a delightful Welsh girl. I had travelled there with a contingent of cadets by train from Le Havre — the bleak port city where the *Empire State* was docked. After a couple of days of sightseeing I decided to take a late-afternoon cruise on the River Seine. There I met Miss Jones of Wales. She was from a town called Llanbradarnfwar, which, she said, was near Aberystwyth. Oh, that Llanbradarnfwar.

As the tour boat chugged through the heart of the city, Jane provided a whimsical commentary, "translating" what the guide was telling us in French. As we passed the Louvre, she said: *this may look like the Louvre but it is actually the Loo ... the largest loo in the world in fact. Seats thousands.* We passed the Eiffel Tower. *So named because it is certainly an eyeful.* We circled the Isle de la Cite and Notre Dame Cathedral. *Ah oui, it was right up amongst the gargoyles that Charles Laughton rang Maureen*

O'Hara's bell. Whilst she pulled his rope, of course. This is a woman who could clearly hold her own in any of the Valley's sixteen bars and taverns.

Later in a café, we were talking about music: the Beatles and the Stones and the English Beat. But what she truly loved, she said, was country music: Ernest Tubb, Faron Young and yes! Hank Williams. And then we talked movies: she couldn't get enough of the old Hollywood musicals. *Black and white on the telly but so grand. And so corny they make me cry.* Still, she said with a sigh, she felt culturally deprived. There was no movie theater in her home town. No museum. Not even a library. Just dozens of pubs. I reached for her hand. A soul mate, at last. And the night was young.

But alas, not young enough. We cadets had a night train to catch for Le Havre. The *Empire State IV* was sailing on the morrow. Mary Jones was a wonderful lass — funny, ebullient and sane — all that a lad could hope for. But before you could say Llanbradarnfwar she was gone from my life.

The Holy Grail of romantic encounters was an affair with a Scandinavian girl. The beautiful, free-spirited women of Copenhagen and Gotenberg and Stockholm and Bergen and Oslo. But these were the most elusive beauties of all.

It was a gray day in Oslo, and I was in a beer garden sipping a frothy Rignes and nursing a hangover from the night before. It had been a long strange night spent among the ruins of an ancient monastery on a thickly forested island in the fjord. Wild-haired women everywhere, writhing sensuously to music. If only I could have joined in.

I'd been fighting off a cold and had downed some codeine pilfered by the Porpoise from the ship's medicine locker.

"How many bottles of codeine you want, Maharrey?"

"Bottles? I just need a few teaspoons to get rid of this cough."

"Hey man, there's no success like excess. This stuff'll give you a real nice buzz. Here finish the bottle."

"The bottle?"

"Trust me," said the Porpoise. "It's a gentle high."

That evening, with no particular agenda, I wandered along the fisherman's wharf in Oslo where they sold fresh steamed shellfish in paper cups. I sat on the dock happily munching pink colored shrimp and sipping plum-colored cough syrup. Nearby, music was blaring from a ferry boat.

The ferry landing was crowded with young Norwegians milling about, waiting to board. I struck up a conversation with a tall lanky lad with the happy slobbering demeanor of a Great Dane. His name was Rudi Topp. The boat, he said, was going to Hovedøya. It was a small island in the fjord — yah — vhere dey haf music and dancing — yah — and ve vill haf some fun. He was going with his two friends, and he pointed out two girls chatting near the gangway: Nina, a gray-eyed blonde in skin-tight jeans and Lene, a Nordic pixie with dark hair cut in a delightful bob. I fished around for the twenty kroners fare.

The boat set sail about 9 P.M. Dusk lingers late in the Norwegian summer, and the ochre light played beautifully on the crystal waters and the gray-green islands and alabaster faces of the Viking women who were everywhere on the boat, sipping beers, laughing, the sea breeze tousling their yellow locks. The salt air was like an electrolyte charged with possibility. I could feel it. And I could also feel the gentle high of the codeine slowing kicking in. I had taken the Porpoise's advice and finished off the bottle.

Rudi asked if I would take a picture of him and his two friends on the stern of the boat. He was an amateur photographer and he showed me a snapshot of a moose taken somewhere in the hinterlands, and as much as I tried to feign interest — "Yeah, that's a really cool moose, Rudi" — I couldn't help but glance over to Lene, the pixie, who returned my look with an inviting smile. I took a picture of Rudi, Nina and Lene. Then he asked if I would take a picture of him and Nina — and now I got it — they were the couple. Then Rudi took a picture of me and Nina and Lene. And I was hoping that by the time the evening was over he'd be taking a picture of just Lene and me. But for now we were all just one big happy foursome on our way to an evening of music and dance under the sub-Arctic stars and amongst the ancient ruins and the fragrant evergreens of Hovadøya. Isn't it good, Norwegian wood?

Rudi bought us a round of Rignes beer. Skols all around — the pixie was still giving me the eye. I took a long swallow, wiped the suds from my lips and turned to say something to her. My mind reached for something that would transcend mere small talk about the boat ride. Something with a touch of poetry to it. About the lonely sea and the sky, perhaps. And she was looking at me — at my mouth on the verge of uttering something — and she nodded in anticipation — yah? But no words came out.

What came out instead was a long hideous spurt of purple liquid. Somewhere in my gizzards alcohol had met codeine. The result was like something out of The Exorcist. The first volley hit Lene squarely in the bosom, splattering her white blouse with violet-colored puke. She shrieked, and feeling another retch coming, I turned to throw up over the side, but I was too late and another vile spurt splattered against the lifesaving ring — much to the shock and disgust of the passengers who had gathered to have their picture taken against purple skies not purple puke. I then leaned over the rail and threw up pints of it.

At last it was over and there couldn't have been a single dram of liquid left in my gut. I wiped my mouth with a handkerchief and tossed it over the side and turned to the gathering crowd and saw them staring at me as if wondering: What sort of alien being is this guy?

Rudi, good natured soul that he was, put an arm on my shoulder and asked if I was all right. I tried to explain that it was only cough medicine.

"*Hoste, yah?*" he said.

Yes, I said. I had a cough.

"I see," said Rudi, but I could tell he was a bit leery of me now. "Maybe you go back to Oslo with the boat?"

I shook my head no. I would be all right. "Is Lene okay?" I asked.

"The girls are washing the blouse, yah."

"Please tell her I'm sorry."

"Ach!" said Rudi, dismissing my concern.

"I think I'll to go up to the bow," I said, "to get some air."

"Yah! Go to the bow."

I saw neither Lene nor Nina nor Rudi for the duration of the ride. But when the boat docked I caught a glimpse of them hurrying ashore and casting furtive glances behind them as if hoping they weren't being followed. At last I too went ashore but I was still a bit whoozy. Just need a little more time to get it together, I said to myself. I veered off the main path and followed a narrow wooded trail that led up a hill to a jumble of ancient stones that overlooked the courtyard of the old monastery.

I eased myself down on a blanket of moss, and my whole body felt like a foot that had gone to sleep. Below, the bacchanalia had begun and I caught a glimpse of Lene dancing with Nina. Lene tossing her bobbed hair this way and that to the music of Sam the Sham.

Matty told Hattie: that's the thing to do
Get you someone pretty to pull the wool with you.
Woolly Bul-laaay
Woolly Bully

Everyone was dancing wildly, like Nordic gods and goddesses. There were many more women than men — every sailor's dream. But dream is all I would do this night.

Woolly Bully
Woolly Bully
Woolly Bully.

The next morning I woke to the screech of ravens staring down at me from a stone perch. The ancient ruins were blanketed with a chilling mist. I shivered a bit, then coughed — a hacking cough. There was no sign of life in the courtyard below.

Later, I caught a ride back to Oslo on a ferry that took families out to the island for Sunday picnics. Foul and unshaven, I found my way to the beer garden for a bite of the dog that bit me. A few glasses of Rignes and I slowly came back to life. But it was a recovery fueled more by the desire for revenge — like Captain Ahab. I will find the Porpoise wherever he is, I vowed. I will thrust a harpoon into his heart. I will cut the blubber from his body and render it into oil and cook his liver in it. I will cut the meat from his muscle and lay it out to dry in the sun and feed it to the wharf rats. I will carve scrimshaw from his bones.

My other prospects for romance were no less ill-starred. I met Randi, a cute squirrel-cheeked blonde, at Frogner's Park in Oslo. The park is filled with giant stone figures sculpted by Gustav Vigeland in a style called "erotico-primitive." When I first saw Randi she was sitting on a bench absorbed in a life-sized statue of a naked little boy throwing a temper tantrum. I sat next to her and soon we were chatting away.

She told me she was from a coastal village about 100 kilometers north of Oslo. Her father was the village minister. They also raised Angora rabbits for their wool. The rabbits were nasty creatures, she said. "Mean, yah? Bad bad bad." I told her about my own rural upbringing — the Feuding Brothers raised sheep — and how the rams took a sadistic pleasure in tormenting brother Brian when he was a toddler — singling him from the other children and ramming him in the butt. She smiled — what lovely dimples! — and there was this country-girl wholesomeness about her that reminded me of the fresh-faced girls of the Valley.

I told her I missed the Valley sometimes. But she said she never missed Skudeshaven. In fact, she could never go back. We strolled the park together, passed a huge granite sculpture of naked bodies all intertwined up the column. I whistled something from The Sound of Music not realizing I was about to enter a Bergman film.

It began with the seagulls. They were perched on a granite sculpture of this very fat, very naked couple who appeared to be wrestling. Suddenly Randi began shouting at the birds, cursing them: "*Fokking mohkes! Fokking mohkes!*" Fucking seagulls! And she flapped her arms at them until they took flight. My first thought was that they must have been shitting on a favorite statue and she just wanted to shoo them away. But soon it became clear this was a personal vendetta. She hated seagulls.

We took a seat on a stone bench before a granite sculpture of two naked children riding an enormous naked woman who was on all fours. Randi was still distraught over the birds. At last, she told me why she so hated the fokking mohkes. She hadn't always felt that way. Once she had even loved them. Once they were her friends. Her best friends. Her only friends. As a young girl, she said, she used to hang out at the fishing dock at Skudeshaven, and she and the gulls would spend long hours just talking about everything. Soon she was confiding in them, telling them her deepest secrets. But the sea gulls betrayed her. They spread rumors about her, and told others in the village about the secrets she had shared with them. She knew this because of the way the people of the village began to treat her. As if she were — well — crazy. But we all have secrets, don't we? she said. "What if someone told other people your secrets? They think you are crazy too, yah?"

And I couldn't disagree. They would. They most certainly would. We were now sitting in a quiet corner of the park by a fountain, a massive bowl overflowing with water held up by sculptures of four butt-naked Norwegians. She pointed to another sculpture: a nude little girl flying through trees of stone. "That is my favorite statue, said Randi. "She is flying, yah? She is flying." We sat there in silence for the longest while. There were no seagulls around, but Randi was still on the lookout for them. Eyes darting furtively about. She was a vigilant young woman. And I imagine she is still there today, a dotty old crone railing against the seagulls in the erotico-primitive world of Frogner's Park.

Then there was Tatyana, a Russian beauty. She had cat's eyes — blue-gray eyes slanted like a Tartan's. And raven hair, dark as a winter night. And she was bright, very bright. She was a university student from Leningrad, majoring in literature and she spoke English fluently. We were sipping dark coffees in an outdoor café in an amusement park in Gothenburg, Sweden. The café was across from a merry-go-round where towheaded children were riding carousel horses — and we were discussing Faulkner — whom I'd never read because the sentences are too long. Still, I nodded knowingly as Tatyana went on and on about "the black peoples" and Faulkner and how he was "blind to the oppression — blind to it!"

After Faulkner, we discussed Henry James whom I'd never read either (though I'm sure he was a nice old lady, as Hemingway said). But to Tatyana, Henry James was a giant. "A giant! And much more influenced by the impressionists than people think. But he was homosexual and so he was unappreciated in his own country — which is a tragedy — a tragedy!"

Then it was on to Dos Passos. I believe his books run to a thousand pages or so — a very long read and so I hadn't quite gotten to him yet either — though I didn't let on, but simply nodded in agreement as she ranted on about Dos Passos' great trilogy, and how it captured "the soul of America — the very soul! but it also captures the repression of socialist values. It is so sad. So very sad!"

About now I was wondering if we could lighten things up a bit. I took her on the roller-coaster. On the merry-go-round. On the silly ride where you sat in mini-cars shaped like lions or tigers or bears that whirled around in circles. We were entertained by clowns. By strolling musicians. By mimes. All around us children were laughing and shrieking with joy. But Tatyana never cracked a smile. I had no idea why she had come to an amusement park. But I do know that in her presence I'd seen more clouds of gray than any Russian play could guarantee.

After a long day's journey into night we took quiet leave of each other by a kiosk plastered with gaily-colored posters. Peck-peck on the cheeks and oh, yes, let's write. She was holding the balloon I bought her.

It was bright. Red.

6

THE PATRON SAINT
OF LOST THINGS

Not all who wander are lost.
- J.R.R. Tolkien

When the *Empire State IV* sailed into the port of Livorno in 1965, the city was still in the throes of rejuvenation. Livorno was a bustling port city where the golden plains of Tuscany met the blue Ligurian Sea. During World War II, it was heavily bombed by the Allies. Most of the historic buildings were destroyed – including the magnificent Duomo, St. Francis Cathedral, built in the 17th century in what was once one of Europe's largest and most beautiful plazas.

Now smoke stacks from new factories, chemical plants and refineries spewed the Fumes of Progress. And though the great Duomo was being rebuilt, Livorno was still a drab, war-torn industrial town. I decided to venture off to Florence – Firenze, the City of Lilies – to savor the works of Michelangelo or stroll the Boboli Gardens with its flowers, fountains and birds. And leave the Eternal Quest for Female Companionship to my shipmates.

My plan was to hitchhike to Florence on the new Livorno-Firenze Autostrada. The trip itself would be an adventure. By all accounts the highway was a demolition derby for zippy little Fiats driven by Italian anarchists.

I asked a taxi driver to take me to the nearest entrance ramp to the Autostrada. Why do you want to go there? he asked suspiciously. I told him the Plan. He looked incredulous. Hitchhike to Firenze? On the Autostrada? *Pazzo! Pazzo!* Are you crazy? He offered to drive me to Firenze instead. I told him I couldn't afford it — no denaro. Grumbling under his breath, he beckoned me into the taxi.

The battered old hulk wound through the maze of streets that was Livorno. Here and there, I saw buildings with their walls pocked and scarred from the long-ago shelling. The wounds seemed fresh though they had occurred more than two decades ago. During the war, the allied commanders were convinced the Italian Campaign would be over in a matter of weeks. Instead the Germans dug in their heels, and it took 275 days with the loss of more than 125,000 lives.

Livorno was an energetic city, but one drained of color — a neo-realist film shot handheld in black and white. Young women wearing dark tight-fitting skirts pedaled furiously on bicycles. Young men in white sleeveless t-shirts scooted by on Mopeds. Old crones — dressed in perpetual black — scurried about on foot. Everyone was in a hurry. *Fretta! Fretta!* There is still a big mess to clean up after. *Una pasticciare!*

Quite a contrast to the outskirts of the city which we were now driving through. The countryside was as sedate as a Modigliani — he haled from Livorno — and a *pasticcio* of colors. Lush green stands of pine, golden fields of wheat, brilliant swatches of red and yellow tulips and stunning rows of lavender. Even the sky itself — swept clean of smoke and smog — was a brilliant morning glory blue.

Are we near the Autostrada? I asked the driver. He dismissed my question with a gesture I'd never seen before. He shaped his hand like the head of a goose and pecked at me. *Pazzo pazzo Americano.*

He pulled off to the side of a country road and flashed fingers for the number of lira I owed him. I got out and took in the surroundings. The road was lined with cypress trees. I saw an olive grove of gnarled ancient trees with silver-green leaves. And a small pasture with a few head of cattle. A buzzard soared overhead. There were no other signs of life.

Dove la Autostrada? I asked. He pointed to a narrow lane across the road. Follow the lane, he said. It is a short ways. I gave him a skeptical look. *Ascolte!* he said. Listen. I listened. And yes, I did hear the steady drone of traffic coming from somewhere over the hill. I asked if he could drop me off there, but he shook his head vigorously. Autostrada? No, he wouldn't go near it. He wasn't that crazy. He flashed his fingers again to pay up. And I forked over a wad of lira. He didn't even count them. The taxi peeled out, leaving me in a cloud of Tuscan dust.

I walked up the lane — vineyards on either side. The air was redolent with the thickly sweet smell of overripe grapes. When I reached a rise in the road, I could see Livorno below. The tiled roofs were a sea of amber — the golden spires of churches and the green dome of the cathedral jutted up like islands. A post-card view, yes, but one curiously devoid of the Autostrada. I could hear the sounds of a highway. But where exactly was it?

A young girl herded goats across the lane. I waved hello, but she didn't wave back. Instead she shooed her goats with renewed urgency. I realized what an odd sight I must have been: a pale young man in a strange white uniform — a ghost, perhaps.

I followed the lane upward to a village of stone houses clustered tightly together. On the far side of the piazza stood a tiny church with a steeple shaped like a huge dunce cap. The fountain in the piazza was supported by bare breasted caryatids. I approached a cluster of small round tables. Seated there were three men, faces burnished from the sun. Grandfather, father and son perhaps. *Nonno, padre, figlio.* They were sipping coffee and conversing Italian style: as if life were One Long Argument. But they were not listening to each other — their attention had shifted to this *spettro bianco*. This apparition in white.

Buon giorno, I said. *Buon giorno*, they replied in unison. I asked if the Autostrada might be nearby. *Si si si*, they said in unison and each pointed to where I'd just come from. The old *nonno* tugged at his ear lobes. *Ascolte*. Listen. Follow the sound. Now all three were tugging their ear lobes. *Ascolte. Ascolte. Ascolte.*

But where is your auto? the *nonno* asked. I don't have an auto, I said. They turned to each other, quizzically. Did he say he has no auto? *Si si si*. He has no auto. Then why is he looking for the Autostrada? Who knows? Does it make sense to you? Not if he doesn't have an auto. The *nonno* turned to me and asked: why — if you have no auto — are you looking for the Autostrada? In my stilted Italian I told them my plan to hitchhike to Florence. I might as well have said that I was heading to the Roman Circus to throw myself into a pit of lions. *Santa Maria! Autostoppista en la Autostrada?! No no no! Pericolo! Pericolo!* Danger! Danger!

A woman poked her head out of an upstairs window. What's going on? And the three of them shouted back up to her: *Pazzo pazzo Americano*. He wants to hitchhike on the Autostrada. The woman shook her head. *Pazzo pazzo*. Villagers were now emerging from every nook and cranny. Someone wants to hitchhike on the Autostrada? *Si*, it is him. That *pazzo Americano*. Now they were all yelling at me — a dozen faces pressed close to mine, hands gesticulating wildly, showering me with spittle as they talked. The gist of it seemed to be: Why do you want to do such a thing? Have you no mother who loves you? The old *nonno* had a tight grip on my arm. *Figlio mio* — listen my son — I'm holding you back for your own good.

An enormous bejeweled woman approached and everyone hushed in deference. Hair streaked in magenta, she was the Mayoress or something. She quickly sized up both me and the situation. *Mama mia*, look at him, she said. *Scremato*. So skinny. The poor boy must be hungry. Why else would he want to do such a crazy thing? Everyone nodded: *si*, of course. With a little food he'll be able to see the error of his ways. The Mayoress asked if I would like something to eat. *Tante grazie,* I said. But you see I have a long way to go. *A Firenze.* And if I don't leave now ... But her look made it quite clear she'd made an offer I couldn't refuse. She turned to the proprietress, a cheery woman shaped like an eggplant and said: Zola! *Pasta di pecorino e mandorlas!*

I soon found myself before a plate of steaming pasta smothered with a creamy chestnut sauce. The café table was tilted so the food had slid to one side of the plate. But the pasta was wonderful as was the *vino tinto* — my glass filled and refilled by the *nonno.*

The villagers pulled up chairs around the table to watch me eat and to pepper me with questions. You have been to New York? *Sì,* I said. I live in New York. Nods of approval all around. You have been to Brooklyn? *Sì sì,* I said. I was born in Brooklyn. This generated a real buzz. Perhaps he knows Angelo Bustafaccio. Ask him. You know Angelo Bustafaccio? asked the *nonno.* He is from here, from Montesanantonio, but he is living in Brooklyn now. No, I said, I'm sorry. I don't know him. Sighs of disappointment. He doesn't know Angelo Bustafaccio. But perhaps he knows his son. You know Carmen Bustafaccio? asked the *nonno.* He is your age. No, I'm sorry, I said, I don't know any Bustafaccios. Brooklyn is a big city.

I finished the pasta and the *nonno* asked if I liked it. And I said yes it was delicious. And Zola asked if would I like some more. And I said, no grazie, I'm really full. Then the *nonno* said: See — he didn't like it. The Mayoress loomed over me: You didn't like it? I said yes I liked it. It was delicious. *Delizioso!* I insisted. Then why don't you have some more? Zola, bring him more. He liked it!

As the sun arced across the piazza, they asked me about my ship and what it was like to cross the great ocean. They asked me about America and did I like Connie Francis and was it true we eat food that is frozen. This they had heard from Angelo Bustafaccio. They asked me what I thought of Italia (*Bravo!* I said) and what I thought about their village (*Bravissimo!*) It occurred to me that I was perhaps the first American in uniform to visit this village since the war. It was like stepping into an episode of the Twilight Zone.

You should come here for the Fiesta *padronal*, said the padre. Our patron saint is San Antonio. It was here in Montesanantonio that the saint first appeared as a vision, he said, to a man who had stolen someone's *Book of Psalms*. The man was so frightened by the saint's appearance that he promptly returned the book. And that is why San Antonio is called the Patron Saint of Lost Things. Perhaps it was San Antonio, adds the *nonno* with a wink, who led you here.

Now the sun was low in the sky. We were all having caffé *macchiatos* and I passed around a pack of Marlboros. It was the least I could offer since any payment for the meal was adamantly refused. Each took a cigarette with a florid expression of gratitude. When I asked them the best way to return to Livorno, they seemed especially delighted.

They waited with me by the bus stop, and when the battered old rig arrived, the villagers — speaking all at once — recounted to the driver the story of this *pazzo Americano* who stumbled into their village looking for the Autostrada — even though he has no auto! — and their success in dissuading him from his crazy Plan. The driver assured them he'd watch out for me. Then it was time for *arrivederci*s and embraces and kisses on the cheeks.

As the bus wound down the country road, the Tuscan sky was just beginning to catch fire, and the wheat fields were turning burnt sienna. I caught a glimpse of a sign pointing back towards where I've just come from. It said: Autostrada. No matter. I'd spent my day lending credence to an old Italian proverb:

There's no form of madness that a plate of pasta cannot cure.

7

THE RED HAND OF ULSTER

I arise today through the strength of heaven
Light of sun, brilliance of moon
Splendor of fire, speed of lightning
Swiftness of wind, depth of sea
      - St Patrick

My first stop upon returning home from a training cruise was always Nanny Bridget's apartment in Manhattan. My grandmother's eyes were gray with cataracts; her left arm shook a little. She'd had a stroke. Had a stroke and dropped baby Kerry on her head. So she was banished by the Artist from our house in the Valley. Now she lived with her middle-aged daughter, Georgiana, in an apartment not far from the 59th Street Bridge and her old neighborhood.

We sipped hot tea — plenty of milk and sugar — and dipped toasted soda bread in it. She had my postcards and photos from Ireland spread out on the table. "Oyr-land" she called it — a place she hadn't seen since she was three years old — when in 1896, Bridget Mooney left Tipperary with her maiden aunt on the SS *Britannica* bound for Ellis Island.

She pointed a shaky finger at a picture of the Giant's Causeway — step-like pillars of volcanic rock on Ireland's northeast coast. I told her how they were set in place by the giant Finn MacCool so he could walk across the Irish Sea and throttle a Scottish giant who had insulted him. "Really, true and honest, Kev?" Really, true and honest, Nanny.

And there was a photo of me by the castle of the great Shane O'Neill. "Do you remember him from the Red Hand of Ulster? The old man's comic strip?"

"Ah, Jimmy," she sighed. "Burnt them all, didn't he?"

"Yes he did."

"Ah, but he didn't mean it," she said. "It was all that whiskey."

All that whiskey indeed, and a touch of that Celtic urge to self-destruct that has haunted us since the time of the Red Hand of Ulster. Even the symbol itself speaks to it. Accordingly to legend, two young princes vied to be heir to the kingdom of Ulster. It was agreed that the kingship would be decided by a race from the sea to the land in skin-covered curraghs. The first prince to touch shore would be named king. It was a close race but as the two boats approached the beach, the prince of the O'Neill clan saw that he was about to lose. And so he raised his battle axe and chopped off his own hand, then tossed the bloody red thing onto the shore. Thus he was proclaimed the first to touch shore and won the kingdom of Ulster.

In the 16th century, the symbol of the Red Hand would inspire the O'Neill clans in their war against the English invaders. *Lámh Dhearg Abú* was their battle cry — Red Hand to victory! Alas it was not to be so. The native Irish were ultimately defeated, yet the battles have raged on in Ulster right up through modern times.

Northern Ireland is comprised of six counties of the ancient province of Ulster. And Belfast, its major city, was our port of call. But I spent little time there, preferring to explore the countryside instead. Belfast was an industrial city like those of northern

England — a drab, dull, "dirty old town" as the Dubliners sang. But our last night in port, I found myself in a small pub not far from the shipyards of East Belfast. It was called The King Dick. As in local hangouts the world over, the entrance of a stranger in their midst quelled conversation and elicited curious stares. I had no sooner settled on a stool and ordered a pint, when an older man with mutton-chop whiskers, a ruddy face, and light-blue eyes — "piss eyes" Maggie would have called them — sidled up next to me. He stood there staring at the row of whiskeys on the shelf and eavesdropped as I ordered a pint.

"Yank?" he said hearing my accent.

"Yes, sir."

He contemplated this a moment, scratched a mutton chop, then nodded and turned to the others.

"Aye, shall we welcome the Yank?"

The others raised their pints.

"Welcome, lad."

He signaled to the barman that the pint was on him. "Ach, your money's no good here, son. Put it away. Put it away. Dat's a good lad."

He invited me to join him and his mates at the table. And the place was filled with banter and blarney once again. Their accent was so thick — a blended spirit of Scottish and Irish brogues — that I found myself nodding like an "eejit" at things I barely comprehended.

If they kept me in stout, I kept them in "fegs." Fags. Cigarettes. "A feg for me and a feg for him and feg for Kilty-Caul-Bum," they'd say. Whatever that meant. Not surprisingly they had more words for "inebriation" than the Eskimos have for "snow." "Stocious" and "steamin'." "Hammered" and "half-cut." "Right-blocked," "right-clabbered" and "full as a boot."

And the good-natured insults flew. "Shut yer bake ya wee header!" "'Tis a face like a scalped arse, ye have." "Aye, yer sech a minger!" "Ach, what are you on about?! I'll draw me hand across your hoop ye bloody shite!"

I asked them what they did for a living, and they told me they all worked in the shipyard, Harland and Wolff, one of the world's oldest.

"'Twas we who built the fooking *Titanic*, you know."

"Aye, shut yer gub! That's not something we brag about."

Right now they were framing in what would be the first supertanker built in the UK, the largest vessel ever launched down a slipway. Which was grand, they said, because they'd been on hard times for more than a decade. They asked about me about the state of the American "marchant navy," as they called it. And I told them that with the escalation of the war in Vietnam more and more ships were being taken out of mothballs. I told them about Operation Rolling Thunder — the bombing of the North, and the landing of the marines in Da Nang and how U.S. troop levels now topped 200,000. An escalation that many found worrisome.

But they seemed less interested in the war, and more concerned about something else. Something I found amusing at first ... then disturbing. It was Muttonchops who, pulling his chair up close to mine, and asked me in a low conspiratorial voice a worrisome question: what did I know about the impending marriage of President Johnson's daughter Lynda, to a Mr. Charles Robb. I looked at him blankly. "Is it true?" he went on, "that Mr. Robb is a Papist?" I shrugged. I didn't know if he was Catholic or not. Who cared? I wanted to say. But to lads in the King Dick Pub this was apparently a matter of grave concern.

"'Tis Rrr-romanism," said Muttonchops with a wagging finger. "Rrr-romanism!" Or as he and his mates saw it, the first step in the Roman Catholic take-over of the United States. The others grumbled and nodded in agreement. "Ye'll be having a Pope for President, lad. Aye, as sure as these lamps can see," he said pointing to his eyes.

I hadn't realized the pubs in Northern Ireland were segregated by religion. And I had wandered into a pub full of Prods. I should have taken a clue from the sign I saw just a few doors down from The King Dick. "Prepare to meet thy Maker." I was just glad that no one asked me about my own faith — such as it was.

A stone's throw from our house in the Valley stood the Church of the North American Martyrs, known as the Indian Church. It was built by our landlords, the Feuding Brothers, some time after World War II. The church was shaped like an Iroquois long-house with a half-cylindrical roof tar-papered green, and siding made of thick logs. Carved totems stood watch outside. Inside the church, the Stations of the Cross were painted on tom-toms. Christ and the apostles were rendered with Indian features. The benches and kneel boards were of hardwood and without padding, so for the boney-kneed McCarey boys the rituals of Mass — sit, stand, kneel — were an especially painful experience — made no less so by the croaking of the ancient choir mistress whose singing tortured the eardrums.

Some time after receiving Confirmation — I had now reached the Age of Reason — the doctrines of the Church began to seem, well, less credible to me. Yet one could not live in the Valley and witness the wonders of Nature through the seasons and not contemplate the possibility of a Grand Design wrought by a Great Spirit. Autumn colors, yes, but the colors too — the iridescent colors — of dragonflies and rainbow trout and sun dogs in the winter sky. The hoarfrost inching across the faces of stones in intricate interlaced patterns. The lilting concert of birds. And in summer: the glittering lightshow of fireflies. And so — in the tradition of Franklin, Jefferson, Paine, Thoreau and Lincoln — I became a Deist. Deists believe that a divine spirit created the world but then left humanity to its own fate and foibles. God is an apostle of divine indifference. Or in the words of another Deist, Robert Frost:

God once declared he was true,
And then took the veil and withdrew.

This personal revelation came just as I was finishing the 10th grade in the River Town. It happened at a time when I was considering transferring from the high school there to the one in Suburbia. I had to fill out a transfer application and parental consent forms and next to "Religion" I entered "Deist."

Upon seeing this, the Artist flew into a rage. Oh, you're a Deist are you, boy? Too smart for your own fucking good is what you are. He ranted on: I was spitting in the face of the Catholic martyrs — and worse — of the Irish Catholic martyrs who had suffered for centuries under the Protestant English heel just so ingrates like me would be free to worship in the One True Holy Catholic and Apostolic Church. Deist?! What the fuck is a Deist anyway? And if I kept running around calling myself a fucking Deist for chrissakes then he would never ever permit me to set foot in the Church again. No more sacrament of the Mass for you, boy!

I knew the grim fate that awaited those who abandoned the faith. I had read James Joyce on Hell:

> Every sense of the flesh is tortured and every faculty of the soul therewith: the eyes with impenetrable darkness, the nose with noisome odours, the ears with yells and howls and execrations, the taste with foul matter, leprous corruption, nameless suffocating filth, the touch of red-hot goads and spikes, with cruel tongues of flame.

Still, a month of Sundays without Mass became a year of Sundays, and still I hadn't seen fit to recant my heresy and return to the One True Holy Catholic and Apostolic Church.

I rather enjoyed my Sunday mornings now. Reading the funny papers, tossing Spalding balls against the barn wall, waving goodbye to the little brothers all dressed up in their wrinkly white shirts and red ties and blue pants as they trooped across the two-plank bridge behind the house, then marched — like prisoners of war — up the overgrown path to the Indian Church — and the long hour of tedium and pain and grating music that awaited them there.

But the rift over religion would forever set my father against me. And it all came back to me that night in the Belfast pub. When the clock struck 10 P.M. — the legal closing time — its patrons ordered two or three rounds and carried the pints into the back room. It was an all male crowd, and soon the little room was filled with cigarette smoke and loud craic, as the Irish say, meaning good conversation. Much to my surprise a couple of Catholics joined us, as indicated by the gentle ribbing they received. "Alright me Papist muckers, fancy a pint?"

And I remembered the classic Celtic curse: "May those that love us love us; and those that don't love us may God turn their hearts; if He can't turn their hearts may He turn their ankles, so we'll know them by their limping."

The Catholic lads worked at the shipyard alongside the barkeep's son and so were welcome in the pub — no need for God to turn their ankles. There was no more talk of Romanism. Nor was there any talk of soccer — football — a subject that was sure to raise the hackles of all. How curious that from their looks, their accents, and their senses of humor, there was no telling Papist from Proddy-dog.

Yet in just a few years hence — in the time of "the troubles" — these same genial lads — Christians all — would be at each other's throats in the name of their own version of the faith. More than three thousand innocents would die in beatings, shootings and bombings. No place would be safe; not a school, not a marketplace, not a pub.

But in the King Dick Pub this night all was tranquil. It was time for some music, and someone shouted "Aye, give us something sweet, Dermot." The dapper gent tipped his tweed cap, slowly rose from his chair and cleared his throat. I waited in anticipation for some classic Irish song. Instead he belted out "I Left My Heart in San Francisco." Though he did Tony Bennett justice, I might add. There was a round of applause, and then another man was coaxed into singing. ("Get up off your arse, Tommy, and give us a tune.") It was Elvis time, a lovely rendition of "One Night with You." So much for Irish traditional music. I gathered it was house rules that everyone contributes a song, and soon I heard "Let's hear something from the wee Yank." I gave them my rendition of Hank Williams' "Mansion on the Hill."

Tonight down here in the valley,
I'm lonesome and oh how I feel ...

And for a moment, I was back in the Valley. In O'Connor's Bar and Grill among friends and family. In any event, I could see where our tradition of music and laughter and, yes, belligerence came from.

It was near the witching hour when a big burly man rose to sing — "Ach, Mr. Downey, at last!" — and the men fell silent in anticipation. From the lilting opening refrain, they listened with rapt attention as he sang a classic song from the turn of the century "I Hear You Calling Me." Years ago, I'd heard a version of it on a scratchy 78 record played on Nanny Bridget's vintage record player. It was sung by the great Irish tenor John McCormack. Now in the smoky backroom of an Irish pub in Belfast, I would hear Mr. Downey's rendition, and it was just as moving — if not more so — as a live performance often is.

I hear you calling me
You called me when the moon had veiled her light
Before I went from you into the night
I came, do you remember
Back to you ...

It was a fine performance — as were all those that had preceded it. And I thought: what beautiful voices! If only they could learn to sing in harmony.

8

LISBON IN THE FOG

Only the gusts of winds
Make lyrical sounds
on the sails of windmills.
Only the things touched
by the love of other things
have a voice to sing ...
       - Fiama Hasse Pais Brandão,
       Portuguese poet

I spent the few weeks between the summer cruises and the resumption of classes back home in the Valley. The Artist avoided me as much as possible, exiting with the Sniff of Smugness whenever I entered the room. I would have loved to have told him about Shane O'Neill's castle, and the Giant's Causeway, and the horse country of county Monaghan where the McCareys hailed from, but he didn't want to hear any of it. I had not only denied his chosen path for me, but his faith as well. I might as well have turned informer. An unforgiving race, indeed.

Still, it was always good to see Maggie and the boys and baby Kerry. And it was good to be cradled for a while in the thick green of the Valley. The boys and I would take long hikes in the woods. I watched as they climbed young saplings and "swung birches" as I had done as a kid. Once, they showed me a nest of copperhead snakes that they'd found. Another time we witnessed the migration of silvery elvers — the improbable journey by tiny eels of more than a thousand miles from the Sargasso Sea in the Atlantic Ocean to our swimming hole in Oscawana Brook. And I could see in their sense of wonder a love of the natural world that would sustain them through the tough times ahead. As it always had for me.

Now and then I would see Jane, strikingly beautiful despite the anarchic spurts of teenage growth — one summer she was all eyes and hair, the next all legs and breasts. She was a quiet girl and when I told her a sea story, I never knew if she was impressed or bored. No matter. I rambled on anyway.

The lads and I still gathered in the cabin nestled in the woods. Rippy, now an aspiring biologist, wanted to hear everything about the whales I'd seen off the Azores. Guy, who already knew more nautical slang than I, wanted to hear all about hawse pipes and gypsy heads and belaying pins. And Davey wanted to hear about the painted ladies of the Pigalle, the donkey show on the Reeperbahn, and the cathouses that lined Canal Street.

Later, we made the rounds of the sixteen bars and taverns. But this summer, all the talk was of Billy Tompkins. Billy was not the sharpest knife in the drawer, but he was a cheerful kid who wanted nothing more than to work on the town's road crew: plowing snow in the winter, trimming brush in the summer, filling potholes in the spring and fall. He loved to fish, he loved to hunt. And that ultimately was his undoing. He was drafted into the Army, and soon found himself in the highlands of Vietnam. One day, while tramping through the bush and dreaming perhaps of hunting season in the Valley, Billy Tompkins took a pot shot at a bandied-bellied squirrel. He was cut down in a hail of bullets. Killed by friendly fire.

No one knew quite what to make of this war. As country boys we had a healthy sense of patriotism. But as country boys too we were also aware that patriotism is the last refuge of scoundrels.

It was a long gray winter at Maritime. I took courses in meteorology, admiralty war and celestial navigation, among others. I also took a course in naval weapons, an NROTC requirement. I would be a Naval Reserve Officer — Ensign McCarey — on graduation. Studying the variety of big guns, rockets and missiles employed, I was struck by the remote killing aspect of modern naval warfare. No one boarded enemy ships with grappling hooks anymore, nor fought at close quarters with dirks and cutlasses. You never saw the whites of your enemies' eyes. Instead your vessel unleashed fierce firepower on a distant target. Or you yourself were the target. I wondered: What is it like to be on a ship knowing that at any moment you could be blown to bits by an unseen enemy? In the not-too-distant future I would find out.

Our last voyage on the *Empire State* took us to Portugal. As the training ship steamed up the Tagus River past Belém, I could see the monastery of Jerónimos. Centuries ago, monks would gather there to watch the great fleets set sail to bring the Christian faith to the heathens.

Just upriver was the Monument to Discoveries, a massive modern sculpture of a sailing ship, its bow jutting out over the Tagus. It was from Belém that wooden caravels set out more than 500 years earlier to explore the unknown world. The Portuguese were the first to discover the remote islands of the Atlantic: the Azores, the Madeiras, the Cape Verde Islands. They were the first to circumnavigate the globe, and the first Europeans to set foot in places like the Congo, Brazil, the Philippines, Japan. They also established the first truly global empire in history with colonies in Africa, Asia, South America and Oceania.

Portugal's colonial possessions brought fabulous wealth to the mother country. Its merchant ships carried gold from Brazil, spices from India, sugar from the Madeiras and slaves from Africa. In his epic poem, "Os Lusiados," the poet Vas de Camões warned that wealth and power were always precarious. And that empires rise and fall not from the enemies without, but from the enemies within: vanity, indolence and corruption. If only the Portuguese had listened more closely to his words.

The training ship docked not far from a cargo terminal just west of downtown Lisbon. It was evening dusk when I headed down the gangway with Stymie, an Army veteran of French-Canadian descent. Stymie was a feisty, pint-sized cadet full of "piss and vinegar," as Maggie would say — the one man you could count on to watch your back whenever trouble brewed. Curly-haired and caramel skinned, he was notorious for making a bee-line for the ugliest woman in a bar. "All I want to do is make two people very happy tonight," he would say. And while the rest of us would be preening and posturing before the all-too-few beauties, little Stymie would saunter out the door with some giantess on his arm, en route to making two people very happy that night.

We wandered aimlessly along the narrow cobbled streets of the waterfront. The buildings were of red brick and in various states of disrepair. Fishers wheeled wagons piled with netting. Beggars sat in alleyways, enervated, emaciated. Hookers plied their trade in doorways. Yet despite their destitute appearance, the fishers, hookers, even the beggars were a handsome people.

When the gold ran out and prosperous colonies like Brazil won independence, Portugal slipped into an inexorable economic decline. By the time of our visit, only the remnants of empire remained: Angola, Mozambique and Guinea-Bissau in Africa, and East Timor in the Indian Ocean. And in even these impoverished outposts, civil wars were raging. Portugal itself was the second poorest country in Western Europe. Now when a Portuguese vessel returned home it wasn't carrying gold, spices or sugar, but more likely sardines, mullet or horse mackerel.

Lisbon itself was like this dowager princess in a ratty velvet dress that had once sparkled with golden sequins and pearl buttons and richly-embroidered lace. The poet Fiama Hasse Pais Brandão captured the feel of the old city in "Lisbon in the Fog."

In the fog
the drunk city tumbles and falls,
the formless buildings lose
the day and place.

The country was still in the clutches of Antonio Salazar, one of the last of Europe's Fascist dictators. He had ruled Portugal with an iron fist for more than three decades, the longest dictatorial reign in 20th century Europe. His main political rival had been murdered just a few months before our ship's arrival by his secret police — the PIDE. They prowled the waterfront streets like a Morality Brigade, looking for signs of moral turpitude, that is, for hookers and johns. They were not out to bust them, I was told, but rather to assure they got their cut of the action.

We strolled into a bar called *O Gato Preto* — The Black Cat. It was smoky, dark, quiet. There were few bar girls and not many customers. The men didn't look like locals; merchant seamen, perhaps. Stymie was soon chatting up a large heavily rouged woman.

"Hey, Maharrey," he said, "I want you to meet Delphina."

Delphina smiled — and she did sort of look like a dolphin.

"*Encantada,*" she said.

"*Encantado,*" I replied.

"We're gonna take a little walk, Maharrey. You gonna be okay here?"

"I'm sure I'll be fine."

"Okey-dokey."

Then with a little salute, Stymie led his dolphin out the door — en route to making two people very happy.

I sat at the bar a while sipping a *sangría* and listening to the music playing on the radio. It was an intense *fado* — the haunting voice of a woman bemoaning ... who knew what? No matter. You didn't need to know the words to feel her pain. It was strange to hear such plaintive music in a waterfront bar. The usual fare — no matter the country — was upbeat American pop. The word *fado* means "destiny" or "fate." It's usually sung by a woman and accompanied by a solo guitar. The songs evoke resignation and melancholy. The Portuguese call it *saudade* — the longing for something forever lost.

I noticed a young woman sitting alone at a little round table. She wasn't drinking and appeared to be lost in thought. Perhaps something in the music had moved her. She wore a powder blue dress with a white pinafore and puffy half-sleeves. And she had long amber-colored hair that tumbled down her back. She wasn't dressed like a prostitute. She looked more like Alice in Wonderland. She noticed me staring at her, and she returned my gaze, but it wasn't a come-hither look. I went hither anyway.

I asked if I could join her. She nodded yes.

"Can I buy you a drink?" She shook her head no. Still, there was a hint of a smile.

She glanced around, wary of watchful eyes, and said: "I am Ema. You want to go somewhere?" She was a working girl after all.

Before I could respond, a barmaid came up to her and whispered something in her ear. Ema rose quickly — "*Desculpe*" — and went to the bar, where she was handed a phone.

"She has big problema," said the barmaid. "Her mother. Her father. They are here in Lisboa. Ema is very obset. They want to meet *su marido*. Her husband."

"She has a husband?"

The woman shook her head no. "This is the big problema. She has no husband. When she leave her family, she say she have a boyfriend and she going to marry with him. She no tell her *pais* is she working here. You can imagine, if they know this. Poof." Her hands danced in the air. "Every time they come to Lisboa, they ask to meet the husband. She tell them he is *marinheiro*. A sailor. And he is far away. On a ship. But maybe they do not believe her no more." She sighed.

Ema put the phone down. Did she wipe away a tear?

Without so much as an "I do," I found myself riding with Ema in the back seat of an old black-and-green taxi, negotiating a maze of cobbled streets in Old Lisbon. The moon had that Cheshire-cat grin, and it barely illuminated whitewashed houses with Roman-tiled roofs. Some had facades of ornately designed tiles and balconies brimming with flowers. Here and there, I caught a glimpse of a castle watchtower or the glimmering waters of the bay.

Ema reached into her purse and took out a gold band and slipped it on her finger. Then she studied my hand a moment. "Your fingers are small."

"Thank you."

She reached into her purse again and took out a handful of rings and poked through them. "This for you." It was a woman's ring, brass with some kind of harlequin face on it. She slipped it on my finger and turned it face down so only the band was visible. I'm embarrassed to say it fit.

"*Maravilhosa!* It looks good, no?"

"Yes. Marvelous," I said drily.

I took Ema's hand. That's what husbands do, I supposed. And I was rewarded with that wan smile.

"Is there anything I need to know," I said. "I mean like: where we met. How long we've been married."

"My mother, my father, they speak no English. So you just ... smile. And this." She indicated my holding her hand. "This is good."

Then she turned back to the driver. *Circo*, she kept insisting. The driver nodded impatiently: I know, I know. Circle? I wondered. Was she taking me around in circles?

Soon we were on a two-lane road that followed a broad greenway. The greenway bordered a lushly-forested hill that jutted up improbably from a neighborhood of weathered urban dwellings.

"Where are you from?" I asked her.

"Here and there," she said. Then she added: "I am sorry. I forget your name."

"It's not good to forget your husband's name."

We turned onto an unlit graveled road and I suddenly wondered if I was about to be rolled. The road led to an open area adjacent to what appeared to be a small stadium, perhaps for soccer matches or even bullfights. We pulled into an empty lot overgrown with grass. In the adjacent lot were trailers, large and small, parked everywhere. I paid the taxi driver, and Ema asked him to come back for us in an hour.

The first thing I noticed was the rank smell of animal dung. The next thing I noticed was an elephant. He was small and wrinkled with both hind legs chained to a truck. A worn-out pair of donkeys were hobbled nearby. In a cage in the back of the truck, Capuchin monkeys were berating the three of them. The truck itself was painted with images of fire-eaters, acrobats, sword-swallowers and clowns. And "CIRCO" in big red letters. That explained it. *Circo.* Circus.

As we walked among the trailers, a pair of midgets shouted "Esmeralda! Esmeralda!" Ah, Esmeralda. Her real name. And now we were surrounded by other circus performers. Though none were in costume — they were dressed more like field peasants — it was easy to see who was the strong man, the fat lady, and the giant, and who — by their posture and demeanor — were the acrobats, jugglers and clowns. Esmeralda introduced her new husband to all of them, and they seemed quite pleased with her choice.

Then a shy young man emerged from the crowd. He was fair-haired like Esmeralda, and small and slender like her as well.

"Daví!" she said and embraced him warmly.

"*Mi irmão,*" she said to me. "My brother." He shook my hand and nodded happily — all without saying a word. I wondered if he was mute. We made our way to her parents' trailer. She took a deep breath then knocked on the door. "*Entra!*" came a shout from within.

Moments later — the awkward introductions made — I was sitting on a gaily-striped ottoman sipping an *aguardente* that was so strong I was getting a buzz just inhaling the fumes. There was a surprising formality to her parents' dress and demeanor. The father — *Papai* — a small man, wore a white suit and sat bolt upright as if at a funeral. Esmeralda chatted mostly with her mother — *Mamãe* — a petite but intense woman who tossed suspicious glances my way. Her father merely nodded perfunctorily, twisting his handlebar mustache and scrutinizing the stranger in their midst. Who was this scrawny young americano anyway? A couple of sips of good *aguardente,* and he already looks tipsy.

Avoiding his penetrating gaze, I studied the black-and-white photos on the wall. The family, it seemed, had a variety of skills. They were aerialists and acrobats and trampoline artists. One photo showed her father on a high wire with her mother on his shoulders. They were both young and attractive. In another photo, Daví and Esmeralda — aged ten and twelve, perhaps — bounced high on a trampoline. She looked exhilarated. In a family photo, *Papai* stood on a narrow balance board with Daví on his shoulders, *Mamãe* on Daví's shoulders and Esmeralda on *Mamãe's* shoulders. There was such joy in Esmeralda's expression that I wondered why she had ever left the circus.

Daví sat by himself in a corner and amused himself with this ring-shaped hat made of black felt. First he shaped it into a Napoleonic bicorn, and — thrusting a hand into his shirt for emphasis — gave me this mock-imperious look. Then he reshaped it into a jockey's cap, and cropped an imaginary horse. Now it was a pirate hat and he lunged at me with an invisible sword. I imagined all this was part of a chapeaugraph routine for the circus. Either that or the man was simply nuts.

"*Senhor!*" The mother was calling for my attention. "*Bebé!*" she said. "*Bebé!*" Was she calling me a baby? I shrugged. "*Eu não entendo.*" I said I don't understand.

Then she rubbed Esmeralda's belly. "*Bebé.* Make *bebé.*"

Esmeralda shoved her hand away in embarrassment. Her mother laughed with a cackle, and I could see she was missing a few teeth. I assumed she was encouraging us to have children. This would be problematic, of course, since I doubted the marriage would ever be consummated.

Then her father spoke up at last. Esmeralda translated: "*Papai* want to know where your ship is coming from."

"We've just come from Morocco," I said. "But soon we will be heading to Antwerp and Gothenburg and Hamburg."

I have been to all those places, he said in Portuguese. But I never have to set foot on a ship.

Chuckles all around. Then her mother asked me something and Esmeralda translated.

"*Mamãe* want to know will you come to the show tomorrow."

Before I could say a word, Esmeralda answered for me. She said my ship was sailing early in the morning. They nodded in disappointment. I realized Esmeralda wanted to spare me another awkward encounter. Still, part of me would have loved to see them perform. I love the circus: the aerialists and contortionists and especially the fire-eaters. I think they appeal to the pyromaniac in every little boy. I was never much for the animal acts however. The great beasts seem so downtrodden and defeated.

So when do you come back to Lisboa? asked her mother. It sounded less like a question and more like an accusation. Both her question and her prosecutorial look caught me off-guard. What should I say? A month from now? A year? Never?

Again Esmeralda answered for me. She said something along the lines of: they never tell him these things. Ships come and go where and when they will. But her response didn't sit well with her parents. I don't know why but I felt the need to blurt out something. I'm a sailor, I said. Sailors go to sea. It was a rather inane observation and certainly didn't help matters.

Papai's posture grew even more rigid than before. *Mamãe* rose up in the chair like a Valkyrie about to take flight. And I thought: oh what tangled webs we weave, when we set out to deceive.

Now everyone was shouting at once — the father stabbing a finger at me — the mother flipping her hand in my direction as if shooing away a fly. In the flurry of Portuguese verbiage I picked up only a few stray words like *magro* and *moco* — which I'd later learn meant "skinny" and "twerp" — and *indolente* and *vagabundo*, whose meanings were obvious.

I was starting to take umbrage at it all. Indolent? A vagabond?! I could take care of my wife quite well, thank you. Besides we were in love, and when you're in love, the whole world is Jewish — or something like that. Anyway I said nothing, of course, but merely nodded as Esmeralda heatedly defended my character, my work-ethic and my size. I picked up words like "*muito generoso*" and "*muito intelligente.*" Delivering the latter with a series of forceful taps to the head. The girl had spunk. And I have to admit I was quite moved by her feisty defense. No one in my life had ever stood up for me quite like that. Daví meanwhile seemed blissfully unaware of the family conflict. He had reshaped the hat into a nun's veil, and was nodding in prayer.

Then, there was a knock at the door and a momentary lull in the squabble. They quickly assumed their formal composures and *Papai* nodded to Daví to open the door. A midget poked his head in and announced that our taxi had returned. *Papai* thanked him. The midget remained at the door, curious, I imagine, about the fuss he'd heard. *Papai* thanked him again, but in a tone that said: you can bug off now. The midget nodded and left. An awkward silence followed. Esmeralda then nodded to me, indicating it was time to go. As we rose, she defiantly thrust her arm in mine.

Papai and *Mamãe* nodded — there was no arguing with this girl. *Mamãe* kissed her daughter on both cheeks. *Papai* indicated I should finish my drink in a single swig — like a cowboy downing a shot of whiskey. I did so, knowing I might never walk again. Then we shook hands. *Mamãe* patted my groin. "*Bebé.* Make *bebé.*"

As the taxi pulled out of the lot, the denizens of the circus waved goodbye. Daví was there. But her parents were nowhere to be seen.

"That went well," I said dutifully.

"*Sinto muito,*" she said. Sorry.

"No worries."

Esmeralda kissed the back of my hand. "*Obrigado.*"

"You're very welcome."

We drove in silence for a while. And I thought: You always hear of people wanting to run away to join the circus, but she was the first person I'd ever met who wanted to run away from the circus. I wondered why she thought life as a prostitute — with its diseases, pimps, occasional violence — was a better choice. I wanted to ask her, but I didn't want to seem judgmental. Besides, here in the rag-tag kingdom of Portugal, a woman seeking freedom and independence would have few other options. That is, unless she found a man. But where was the freedom and independence in that?

"I know it's none of my business," I said at last, "but why don't you want to go back to the circus?"

She shook her head. "The *circo* is not a good place. Not a good life. We make the people happy, but we are not happy. They are good people, *sí*, but you feel like ... like a monkey in a cage."

The road now followed the Tagus River. The waters were as dark as the sky, the moon having set a few hours ago. The city too was dark, the darkest I'd ever seen a city at night.

"What will you tell them when the circus comes back to Lisboa, and your mother and father want to see me again?"

She shrugged. "Maybe that you left me for someone else."

Ouch. She saw my look, then rubbed my arm affectionately.

"No. I know that you would never do that."

"Never. Not this man."

"I will tell them ... you fell off the ship. And drowned."

"Much better. Last seen swimming with sharks."

"Oh, I don't think I like that either."

We drove past the warehouses, whorehouses and bars of the waterfront. Esmeralda insisted that I be dropped off first. I wondered where the taxi would take her next. To wherever she now called home? Or back to the Gato Preto and another night's "work." I didn't ask. I didn't want to know.

The taxi pulled up to the gangway. We sat in silence for a long moment. Her hand still in mine. And watched the ship rise and fall in the wake of a passing vessel.

Two runaways.

9

PALMA!

*I didn't mind seeing in reality, for once,
what I had only seen in dreams.*
                    - George Sand, *A Winter in Mallorca*

alma de Majorca at last! It seemed fitting that we would visit Majorca on our last cruise. I saw it as our reward for enduring the years of discipline and duress at Maritime.

We entered Bahia de Palma under a cloudless sky. The bay is shaped like a scallop, the Egyptian-blue waters turning turquoise in the shallows. To the west are stark rugged cliffs that shelter coves that were crowded with yachts. To the east are sandy beaches crowded with sunbathers. The city is dominated by a massive gothic cathedral flanked by a splendid Moorish palace. An ancient hilltop castle stands watch over all.

The narrow streets along the waterfront were filled with tourists, mostly blonde blue-eyed Northern Europeans with skin so fair it was defenseless against the blistering Mediterranean sun. Soon the Nordic and Aryan gods and goddesses were joined by countless Maritime cadets in tropical whites crowding the outdoor cafes and turista shops.

Mallorca as a popular resort destination is a rather recent phenomena, dating only from the 1950s. In the 1960s, it was still not quite the tourist Mecca it would later become when literally millions would crowd the island in the summer. Still, upscale boutiques and chi-chi restaurants and glitzy clubs had already formed a beachhead along the palm-lined waterfront. They still seemed tacky in a place with such a rich and vibrant history.

Its original settlers, the Balearics, were fierce mercenaries noted for their prowess with the ballo or sling. The Balearic islands — Mallorca, Minorca and Ibiza — were coveted by both Carthage and Rome in their conflicts for dominance in the Mediterranean. Some twenty years after the fall of Carthage, Rome finally conquered the islands. With their civic engineering mindset, the Romans founded the port of Palma. But with the fall of Rome, Mallorca endured a series of invasions by the Vandals, the Goths, the Vikings, the Byzantines and the Normans.

In 902 AD, the Muslims seized control of Mallorca. Palma — then called Madina Mayurqa — became a bustling trading center for Muslim, Christian and Jewish merchants. Churches, temples and mosques were built. Cultural and artistic life thrived. As did the artisanal tradition that I was most interested in: cartography, the art of mapmaking.

I grew up in a house full of maps. They were my sacred mandalas. Not so much road maps; they were surprisingly few in Casa McCarey ... No, I was enamored of the maps in books of exploration and discovery. I also loved those that arrived neatly folded in *National Geographic Magazine.* They instilled in me a yearning to see the places they described: to walk the ancient ruins of Baalbek and Machu Picchu, paddle canoes in the Amazon, dogsled across frozen Lake Superior, ride camels in Lebanon and drive Land Rovers across the Kalahari desert. And one day I would do all those things and more, thanks to a burning desire to see the world — inspired in no small part by maps.

But one map in our household held a special place in my heart. It was a topographic map published by the U.S. Geological Survey: Putnam Valley and its Environs. It described and delineated where I, a skinny country boy, walked the earth. This was the map that showed my place in the world. The main color was fern green, fitting for the Valley. Lakes were powder blue, creeks and marshes aquamarine, hills demarcated by brown contour lines. Paved roads were indicated by red and white striped lines. When they turned to dirt, like Sunken Mine Road, they were stripped of color. Trails were indicated by dashed lines. I would trace with a finger the Appalachian Trail where it skirted Candlewood Mountain — elevation 936 feet the map said — then follow it past Mud Lake and Clear Lake and Stillwater Pond. And having walked that stretch of the trail so many times I could almost see the cattails stirring, hear the cawing of crows and feel the bites of the deerflies.

The map was dotted with black squares representing buildings. I could easily pinpoint the schoolhouse, the firehouse, the Indian Church, the IGA grocery store, Oregon Hardware and every one of the sixteen bars and taverns. And I could see the houses of my friends scattered here and there along country roads. And there was our little bungalow on the squiggly blue line that was Oscawana Creek. I could identify the potato fields, the sheep stables, even the chicken houses of the Feuding Brothers. It was like viewing my whole world from space, long before one could actually do so from one's computer.

At Maritime, I was introduced to another type of map: the nautical chart. The sea is plain white, except in the shallows where it turns light blue. The land is the kind of grayish beige you might expect in a hospital room. The only bright colors on the chart, red and green, are reserved for navigation aids. They feature buoys, lighthouses and towers; spits, cliffs and bays; reefs, rocks and shoals. The chart is dotted with numbers, each representing the water's depth in feet or fathoms. To the landlubber, the chart must seem a rather prosaic thing — a testament to form-follows-function. And when I first encountered them in Navigation 101, I saw them that way as well. Oh for a sketch of a mermaid or sea monster! But once out at sea, I began to see the nautical chart in a new light — less the work of desk-bound bureaucrats and more that of seasoned mariners. It is a compendium of their collective observations made at different points in time. The nautical chart is an ephemeral "snapshot" of an ever-changing seascape. Sand bars are constantly shifting. Buoys are carried away with the tides. Lighthouses are abandoned. Things fall apart. And yet every sea-going vessel is utterly dependent on those charts, as are the lives of those who sail them. Charts — our feeble attempts to portray a restless sea — are by their very nature unreliable.

And knowing that, the pulse quickens just a bit every time you, the navigator, pencil in the ship's position and hope it is as far away from that reef as the chart says it is.

The earliest known maps date back some 4,000 years to the time of the Babylonians. They were inscribed on clay tablets, and one can imagine the dismay of the ancient mariner who dropped a tablet while sailing through the treacherous Straits of Hormuz. The Greeks knew the earth was round and their early maps reflected this: the earth splayed out like half an orange peel. The most enduring map of ancient times was that created by Ptolemy (about 85-165AD), a Greco-Roman citizen of Egypt. Ptolemy was a mathematician, astronomer, astrologer and poet. His *Geographica* is a thick compendium of everything that was known about world's geography in his time. It encompassed the Old World from Spain in the west to China in the east, from Ethiopia in the south to the Arctic in the north. Ptolemy's map was drawn and redrawn by countless mapmakers through the centuries, right up to the time of Columbus. One version, drawn in 1590 by an unknown Flemish mapmaker, is known as the Fool's Cap Map of the World. Imagine the world projected on the face of a court jester. Below the map is inscribed "The number of fools is infinite."

During medieval times, the Ptolemic map was reconfigured by Christian cartographers. The known landmass of the earth was presented as a circle surrounded by water with Jerusalem in its center, and east towards the top. They were more ecclesiastic than cartographic, incorporating religious themes and references. One such map, the Beatus, was used to illustrate the missions of the apostles of Jesus Christ. Another featured religious symbols such as the Tree of Life. The *mappae mundi*, as they were called, were not very helpful when it came to finding one's way in the world — except perhaps in a spiritual sense. The sizes and shapes of the continents were not rendered for accuracy, nor were the cardinal directions. These were maps for believers not travelers.

And yet during that same period, extraordinary advances in cartography were being made just south of continental Europe — on a little island called Mallorca or Majorca. It was here in the crossroads of the western Mediterranean Sea where the most extraordinary maps of the time were created. The 14th century was a golden age for what is known as the Majorcan Cartographic School. Drawing on the knowledge of traders, mariners and astronomers, the Marjorcan cartographers developed their own techniques in crafting what were known as "portolan" charts — they emphasized ports and harbors. Drawn on durable sheepskin or goatskin, these were highly functional nautical charts. Crisscrossed with countless lines that radiated from exquisitely designed compass roses, they featured precisely detailed harbors, river mouths, rocks, shallows — even currents. But unlike the ecclesiastical maps of the time, there were few inland features, and the interiors of whole continents were left blank. Oriented towards the north, these were charts for mariners. For the first time sea captains had something they could use for intercoastal navigation and for making landfall along the coasts of the Mediterranean and Black Seas and the waters of Northern Europe.

The cartographers were mostly Jews. Haym ibn Risch. Mecia de Viladestes. Jacomé de Majorca. The most famed of the Majorcan mapmakers was Abraham Cresques, known as Cresques the

Jew. He and his son Jehuda created the most extraordinary map of the age, the much-coveted Catalan Atlas of 1375.

On our first day in Palma, I found myself, map in hand, wandering about in Mr. Cresques neighborhood. The streets of Old Palma have not changed much in the seven centuries since Abraham and Jehuda walked them. Sandstone walls of ochre and beige. Balconies of wood or stone. Narrow walkways and alleys. The Jews of Cresques' time lived in "calls," ghettoes that dated back to the Roman era. Though segregated, they prospered in medieval Palma as traders and merchants, astronomers and cartographers, map and instrument makers.

Carrer Sol — Sun Street — was once the heart of the Jewish community. I was struck by how quiet, almost sedate, it was. The neighborhood was now mostly residential. More cats prowled the street than people. It was hard to imagine it crowded with women in shawls and long black dresses, and bearded men in kippahs and flowing robes. Where were the Catalan captains and Arab traders and Saracen pirates? Where were the shops of the map and instrument makers? Where were the Majorcan Jews selling astrolabes and kamals and that amazing new navigational wonder, the floating compass? And where I wondered was the workshop of Abraham and Jehuda Cresques? I had hoped there might be a plaque or something indicating where cartographic history had been made.

Like Ptolemy's map, the *Catalan Atlas* encompassed most of the known world, with the exception of the far north and sub-Saharan Africa which was considered a no-man's land. But unlike other portolan charts, the Atlas featured details of inland cities and rivers, lakes and mountains.

The *Atlas* was not constrained by the rules imposed by Christian clerics, and so the Cresques were free to display the symbols and sacred sites of other known cultures and religions of the era. There was Jerusalem, yes, but also Mecca and Medina. The *Atlas* also featured an African soothsayer, a seer with a crystal ball, and a Chinese monk meditating upside down.

Abraham and Jehuda added whimsical touches as well. The mountains in North Africa were represented by a long chicken claw, the Tagus River by a shepherd's crook, Bohemia by a horseshoe. There were rich illustrations of Bedouin tents and longboats and camels and elephants. People in miniature wandered the landscape: European princes, Arab traders, African kings. Traders trek along the Silk Road in Asia and on camels across the Sahara.

There were cameos of notables past and contemporary. Religious figures yes, but also Alexander the Great, the Sultan of Delhi, King Chabeh, ruler of the Kingdom of the Middle Horde and even Satan himself described as "Lord and Ruler Over Gog and Magog."

The *Atlas* was richly annotated with snippets of local history and lore, customs and travel advice, much of it derived from the travel literature of the time, notably *The Book of Marvels* and the *Travels by Marco Polo*, *The Voyage of Sir John Mandeville* and the narratives of the Moroccan explorer Ibn Battuta. Much of the writing in those works was mere invention including, scholars believe, the very existence of a John Mandeville himself. Still, they contained much new information about Africa and the Orient which the Cresques eagerly incorporated in their *Atlas*. We are informed that there are 7,548 islands in the Indian Ocean, and they are rich in gold, silver, spices, and precious metals. But we are also warned that one island has people "of great size ... like giants, with very dark skins and no intelligence. They eat white men and strangers, if they catch them." In the Kingdom of the Middle Horde, one finds pygmies in constant battle against fighting cranes. "But they are happy and defend themselves valiantly against the cranes which they kill and eat." When riding camelback across the Gobi desert, the traveler must beware of the "voices of devils which are like the voices of his companions and they call him by his name and lead him in all directions through the desert so that he can never find his companions again." Not unlike the bar girls of the Reeperbahn.

The *Catalan Atlas* was prized by Christian kings, and it inspired the same wanderlust in their young princes as the maps in *National Geographic* would inspire in me. Had Abraham Cresques created his *Atlas* some 500 years later, I'm sure it would have appeared neatly folded between the pages of *National Geographic Magazine*. Well, maybe not. The *Atlas* consisted of eight wooden panels which, when laid side by side, made it more than two feet high and twelve feet wide. Today, an original copy is preserved in the Biblioteque Nationale in Paris. It was acquired for posterity in 1381 by King Charles VI of France, known in his time as Charles *le fou*, or "the madman." At least he did one sensible thing.

Carrer Sol leads to a plaza that would one day feature statues of both Abraham and Jehuda Cresques. But when I visited, its most notable feature was a building known as the Castle of the Temple. In ancient times it was a fort, and one could still see the Moorish influence in its arched windows and turreted towers. Later, in the Christian era, it served as a castle for the Knights Templar. And later still, it was used as a prison by the Inquisition. Not long after the conquest of Mallorca by the Spanish kings, the Jews fell on hard times. Most were expelled, unless they converted to Christianity. Those who did convert were called *chuetos*, Catalan slang for the pieces of pork they were forced to eat to prove their conversion was genuine. Among them, was a *converso* named Jaume Riba — the Christian name adopted by Jehuda Cresques, son of Abraham. Still many Jews observed their faith in secret. They were called crypto-Jews or *marranos*. Who knows if Jehuda was among them?

I headed back west from Temple Plaza and walked along the narrow Carrer San Francesc. Sandstone buildings lined a slate-blue street. Iron balconies. Arched doorways. The door to one large building was simply marked Number 7. There was no plaque to mark its place in history. For it was here where the Grand Inquisitor, Canon Arnau Alberti lived in the early 16th century. He was not a pleasant man. Countless Jews fled Majorca rather than face his cruel interrogations. In their absence, the Inquisitor had them burned in effigy. Now where Jews once endured horrific tortures, schoolboys bounced a soccer ball against the bare walls.

Carrer San Francesc ends at a plaza dominated by the Santa Eulalia Church. The church dates from the time of the Spanish conquest in 1229. It was named after a young girl who, as a Christian, was tortured and decapitated by the Romans. What goes around comes around, I guess. The church had a towering gothic spire, an elegant rose window and a carving of St Eulalia above the entrance. And who should come down the front steps but my good friend and shipmate Filario. Filario was a deeply religious person who visited a church in every port. He was also the most amiable of travel companions.

We settled into an outdoor cafe for a *café-con-leche*. Filario had already visited another church in Palma — it had been a busy morning — but this one, he said, was more beautiful by far. I mentioned that there was a place outside of Palma that I had really wanted to see but since I spoke no Spanish, I worried about wandering lost among the cannibals.

"You only go t'rough life once," said Filario in his thick Brooklyn accent. He'd be happy to accompany me. And no worries about the Spanish, he added. He was fluent — having studied the language in high school "wit' Sister Mary Ant'ony who was a real bawl breaker."

And so we set out for Valldemossa.

In anticipation of our visit to the island, I had brought along a little book entitled *A Winter in Mallorca*. It was written by the French novelist George Sand, whose real name was Armandine Aurore Lucie Dupin. She had spent the winter of 1838 in Mallorca with her two children and her lover (scandal!) the composer Frederic Chopin. They were advised the Majorcan weather would be salubrious for Chopin who suffered from tuberculosis. Alas, it was not a pleasant stay. "As the winter advanced," she wrote, "the gloom froze all my attempts at gaiety and calm." Traveling around the island was like plodding through a gauntlet of "rain, torrents, swamps, quickset hedges, ditches." The locals were "monkeys." The homes — even the streets, she claimed — stank of rank olive oil. And even worse for *la francaise* the food was an abomination — every dish "seasoned with so much garlic, pepper, pimiento and corrosive spices of every sort, that one risks one's life with every bite."

When it came to travel, George Sand was somewhat luckless. Once, on a visit to a beach in Italy she was harassed by "enormous lizards that come out by the thousands from under your feet and seem to be following you, with their number always increasing, like a bad dream."

She didn't fare much better in Mallorca. After moving from one inn to another in search of a bed mattress "a little softer and more yielding than slate," they found lodging of a sort in the monastery at Valldemossa. The monastery had been shut down in 1834 during a period when Spain was trying to ameliorate the power of its clerics. A single abbot was left in charge of what became, in 1838, a rather austere guesthouse for visitors. When George Sand and Chopin arrived there was only one other guest: a ditzy Majorcan woman who pilfered their bread and pastries. And worse, the locals shunned them: Sand because she wore men's clothes and smoked, and Chopin because they feared his illness was contagious.

Still, George Sand found a modicum of pleasure at last in the spectacular view from the monastery. She described a mountain vista "which resembled nowhere else." Where Nature "flourishes under the kisses of a blazing sky."

"In Mallorca," she wrote, "I saw the sea at last as I had dreamed of it, as clear and blue as the sky, gently undulating like a sapphire plain ... and framed by dark green forests."

And that was what I wanted to see.

According to my tourist map, the village was about sixteen kilometers northwest of Palma. But oh those sixteen kilometers! If only the map had been drawn by the Cresques, we might have been warned of the steep tortuous road that hugged a mountain-side high above the Mediterranean Sea. On one stretch of road we were accompanied by a pack of stray dogs, and Filario tossed them the cheese and sausages we'd packed for lunch. Dey look a lot hungrier den us, Maharrey. Thank God, the dogs weren't thirstier or he would have offered them our bodas of wine as well. We drank our *vino tinto* — cheap Spanish wine, the tannins strong enough to stain your teeth for life — as we hiked past ter-raced gardens, windmills, stone walls and lush groves of orange, fig and olive trees.

A small farm truck pulled over in front of us and a swarthy man in bristly beard and tweed cap jerked a thumb towards the flat bed: get in. We climbed aboard and sat amongst burlap bags full of almonds. The truck groaned up the twisting potted road past olive and almond orchards and fragrant stands of pine. Now and then we caught glimpses of the sea through the narrow cleaves of the mountains. The wind blew fiercely through these valleys and a gust tore the map of Mallorca from my hands and out of the truck and I watched it flutter away on the wind.

George Sand too was as unlucky with maps as she was with lodgings. During their stay in Mallorca, she was invited to the pal-ace of the Count of Montenegro, "a sad, somber home if ever there was one ruled over by a somber priest." She and Frederic Chopin were given a tour of the library and its remarkable collec-tion of medieval and Renaissance art and artifacts. There were an-cient manuscripts, ornate coats of arms, colorful flags of Spanish and French nobles, a priceless collection of Greek, Roman and Moorish medals. Then they were shown the *piece de resistance*: a magnificent nautical chart drawn by the Majorcan cartographer Valesqua in 1439. It was once owned by Amerigo Vespucci him-self, though it predated the discovery of the continents that would be named after him.

To the delight of their guests, the chaplain unrolled this rare and precious treasure revealing a work of art in calligraphy and topographical drawing. To keep the chart from rolling up on itself, servants placed objects on each corner. One such object was a full bottle of black ink. With no stopper. Bad idea. "Pushed perhaps by some evil spirit," wrote Sand, the bottle tipped over and emptied onto the chart. There was a general cry of horror. "Alas!" she wrote. "The Chart had been flooded, and the pretty little kings painted in miniature were literally floating on a sea, blacker than the Black Sea."

Everyone lost his head. "I think the chaplain fainted," she added. Servants tried to clean the chart "with great swoops of the sponge and the scrubbing brush, haphazardly sweeping away kings, seas, islands and continents." George Sand and Frederic Chopin fled the scene. "But I am certain that we will take the blame," she wrote. And the accident "would be attributed to the French."

"Damn!" I said as I watched my own map floating on air over a grove of almond trees towards a golden plain to the east. "No worries, Maharrey," said Filario. "We'll find the place." The man had no need for maps. Every journey to Filario was like a trip to Never Land where the only directions needed were "second star to the right and straight on 'til morning." And that can be a good thing, I suppose. Perhaps, I considered, I'd grown too dependent on maps.

After a good couple of kilometers the truck pulled into a dirt driveway that led to a stone farmhouse. The farmer gave us a wave — our cue to hop off. "*Gracias por todo,*" said Filario in a Castilian Spanish spoken with a thick Brooklyn accent (Grwaw-seeus paw toto). The man looked at him quizzically.

"Thank you!" I quickly added in English.

"*Ah! Seva benvingudaI*" he replied in Catalan. You're welcome!

We continued walking up the road, past groves of twisted and gnarled olive trees with trunks so thick they must have been centuries old. Crude stone walls seemed to start anywhere and end nowhere. The air was filled with the scent of pines, then with the scent of lavender. A kestrel soared against a cobalt sky. The afternoon sun was utterly merciless. Wiser travelers would have filled their bodas with water instead of wine. The thought crossed my mind that we could suffer sunstroke out there in the middle of nowhere. And without our map!

And then, just around the next bend in the road, Valldemossa suddenly appeared. It was like a fairyland village nestled in the steep slopes of the Sierra de Tramuntana. The belfry tower of the monastery overlooked the village and a sparkling sea beyond. We walked along smooth slate streets lined with mottled brick buildings. Tiled roofs, arched doorways, bright green window shutters.

We made our way up stone steps to the Plaza de la Cartuja, Monastery Plaza. And it was surprisingly empty of people. The monastery itself was an imposing, if prosaic presence. Only the belfry tower possessed any flair. It was a bright apothecary blue and richly filigreed. We stood before a large arched entrance-way with a faded rose window above it. The main entrance to the monastery was a small doorway off to one side. There a sign dangled from a rusted hook: *Cerrado.* Closed.

"Well, this isn't good," I said.

"No worries, Maharrey, "said Filario. "They're taking their siesta. They gotta wake up sooner or later."

A man in a baker's hat passed by, and Filario in his fractured Spanish asked what time the museum would reopen. The man strained to understand him, then shrugged and tapped his lips as if to say I'm sorry I don't speak Eskimo. Filario repeated the question more slowly, but what came out of his mouth was simply a drawn out version of the previously incomprehensible. Again the man strained to understand him. Then shrugged. "*Lo siento. No comprendo.*" He smiled, tipped his cap and continued on.

I called after him. "Señor?!" The man turned.

"Could you tell us what time the museum opens?"

"Ah!" said the man. "*El museo. Mañana.* Open *mañana.*"

Mañana. Not what we wanted to hear.

Somewhat disappointed, we settled into a couple of chairs in the outdoor cafe in the plaza. The cafe was closed too.

"Maybe it is just as well," I said at last. "George Sand was convinced the place was cursed. I just wish we could have gotten in to see the garden," I said. "It's supposed to be really beautiful. Lemon trees, fig trees, bougainvilleas. And their rooms, you know. We would have seen their rooms just as they left them. Even Chopin's piano. The one on which he composed 'Raindrop Prelude.' You know ..." I hummed a few bars.

"Nice tune, Maharrey."

"And there's an art gallery somewhere in there too. I think they have Goya, Picasso, Miró. You know, the biggees."

"Picasso. Yeah, I heard of him."

"And we would have seen the old apothecary. It still has all the jars of stuff that Chopin took for his cough. Julep syrup, couchgrass tea, marshmallows. I mean it's all still there. Right on a shelf. And they have all these old photos —"

"— Maharrey," Filario interrupted. "We didn't come here to see some old piano or fig trees or friggin' jars of marshmallows, did we?"

"No, we didn't."

"Up there, Maharrey." He pointed to a ridge above the monastery. "That's why we came here."

And so we hiked up to the ridge, following a narrow path through groves of olive and almond trees until we could see the blue tiled belfry of the monastery well below us and the tiled roof tops of the village angled against each other like in a Cubist painting and beyond that the sea, glittering in the afternoon sun. And all of it — sea — valley — village — monastery — framed by the massive limbs of an ancient olive tree that surely stood there in George Sand's time and much earlier — some 600 years ago when the first stones were laid in place for what would become the monastery.

"It is one of those views that completely overwhelms one, for it leaves nothing to be desired and nothing to the imagination," wrote Armandine Aurore Lucie Dupin. "All that a poet or a painter might dream of Nature has created here."

And we both felt strangely content, Filario and I. Simply sitting there in silence. Sipping our wine. Savoring the view. Bells rang out in the village church just downhill from the monastery. The call to an afternoon novena, perhaps.

"Dear God," wrote Madame Dupin, "blessed art Thou for giving me good eyes."

There were other memorable moments in Mallorca. There were sultry nights in dance clubs throbbing with music. There were fine meals of *arros brut* -- saffron rice cooked with chicken, pork and vegetables and *tumbet* — a rich stew of potatoes, peppers and eggplant, and *pa amb oli* — Majorcan bread rubbed with sliced tomato, drizzled with olive oil and topped with anchovies and serrano ham, and *ensaimada* — a sinfully sweet pastry. And there were beaches graced with sinfully sweet Dutch girls and French girls and Swedish girls in bikinis.

But there is one other place that I needed to see. Las Cuevas del Drach — the Caves of the Dragon. The caves are a popular tourist destination, and at first I had no inclination to go there. But an English girl I met in a café told me the overwhelming magnificence of the caves was worth enduring the presence of numerous turistas.

We took a bus this time, Filario and I, to Porto Cristo on the eastern coast of the island. The bus dropped us off in a picture postcard village on a quiet cove. But where were the caves? "*Cueva?*" Filario asked a flower vendor. But it came out more like *corva*, Spanish for "tendon." Had he pulled a tendon? Whatever. Eventually we were directed to follow a steep cobbled road up to a park-like setting that overlooked the sea. The entrance to the caves was marked by what appeared to be the fossilized spinal bone of some prehistoric creature.

The caves were first explored and mapped in 1896, by the geologist Édouard-Alfred Martel. Martel was a pioneer in speleology, the study of caves. He explored thousands of caves in his native France and abroad, including the Marble Arch Caves in Ireland, the Gaping Gill in England and even Mammoth Cave in Kentucky. He would measure and map them and calculate their depths with a barometer. Though he would explore some 1,500 caves in his time he never lost his sense of wonder or the thrill of discovery. "No man has gone before us to these depths," he wrote. "No one knows where we go nor what we see."

We joined a small group of German tourists at the mouth of the cave and were led by a talkative Majorcan guide down a steep pathway with a thin iron railing and into the caves. I'd always known the Germans to be a rather fun-loving people, but this group played to the stereotype: stern and officious. One of them was counting out loud as he descended the path. "*Ein, zwei, drei, vier ...*"

"Why is he counting?" I whispered to his well-fed fraulein.

"He counts the steps."

"... *fünf, sechs, sieben ...*"

"But why?"

"He always counts the steps."

"Oh."

"... acht, neun, zehn ..." and so on, down through a series of cool, damp chambers: Cueva Negra, Cueva Blanca, Cueva Luis Salvatore. The guide jabbered on in not-so fluent German and English — we had no idea what he was saying. So we fell back from him and the counting Germans so we could experience the caves as Martel might have: without a crowd. And it was an extraordinary sight. Imagine thousands of massive stalactites — like huge white icicles — hanging down from the cavern roof and stalagmites jutting up from its floor. It truly was like venturing into the mouth of a dragon. In some places the limestone had formed thick knotted columns; elsewhere there were grotesquely shaped sculptures that might be part of a dreamscape by Dalí. And it was all artfully, if eerily, lit. Cavern walls basked in gold and vermillion; grottos were lit as though aflame; pools of water shimmered in every shade of blue and green.

After a long walk through the caverns, we reached a kind of amphitheater. It overlooked one of the largest subterranean lakes in the world: Lake Martel. The guide indicated for us to sit on the narrow benches that faced the lake. Lights were dimmed. The German stopped counting. Then, we heard the plaintive strains of a violin. And out of nowhere it seemed, a small boat appeared, its gunnels ringed with light. There were small lanterns on the bow and stern, and they illuminated a single oarsman rowing the boat and a violinist standing on the bow. The violinist was a dark Marjorcan woman in a long black dress. She played a melancholy nocturne that resounded off the cavern walls. It was so haunting, so moving that it was all I could do to hold back tears. Filario was not as restrained. I noticed him wiping away a tear.

"Nothing so strangely beautiful was ever presented to us," wrote Édouard-Alfred Martel, "and we ask each other the same question: are we not dreaming?"

At last, the little boat turned and disappeared back into the netherworld. It was one of those moments that would be forever etched in my memory. The concert over, the guide told us that for a small fee we could ride across the lake in one of the boats. We could see oarsmen sitting in a couple of them off to one side. Or we could simply continue walking along the path that skirted the lake, he said, and exit that way. The Germans rose in unison from the benches and walked on, taking the free route. But Filario was not so inclined.

"We gotta do the boat, Maharrey."

"Or we could spend the last of our pesetas on lunch."

"We gotta do the boat."

I knew what was coming next. Especially when he took a few deep breaths — an actor prepares — then turned to face the boatman, a short, swarthy Majorcan with a cherubic smile. Filario gave him the Look. Imagine the sorrowful face of the sinner in Goya's

"Mournful Foreboding of What is to Come." Or the sorrowful eyes of a basset hound that's been denied a bone. Or the expression on the face of a hungry boy. "You Can Feed This Child or You Can Turn the Page." That was the Look. Something Filario had perfected in countless churches and whorehouses. Only the most heartless fiend could ignore the Look.

"*Venga venga*," the boatman said. Come come. He was beckoning us to step into the boat.

Again: the Look.

"No pay," the boatman added sheepishly.

"*Muchas gracias, señor, por eso*," said Filario. And the man smiled and shrugged — he didn't speak Eskimo either — and we climbed into the boat. Another boatman shoved us off, and now our own Ferryman was rowing us across the River Styx — to eternal life, one hoped. The creak of rowlocks, the splash of water echoed with every stroke. Here in the Underworld, dark stalactites hung so low we could almost reach up and touch them. The boatman began to hum to himself.

Filario dipped his fingers into the cool crystal waters and blessed himself. Holy water. The Majorcan stopped humming. And we crossed the lake in silence.

I studied my good friend. His sunny disposition belied a difficult past. His father had been a leader in the longshoreman's union. He had fought long and hard to rid the union of elements of organized crime. A little too hard. He was murdered by the mob when Filario was just a young boy. He was raised by his mother — a large, big-hearted woman — in a household of sisters. No one in his family wanted him to have anything to do with ships or the sea. But the call of running tide, as the poet John Masefield wrote, is a wild call and a clear call that may not be denied.

The boat nudged against a limestone shore. We bid the boatman farewell and walked up a steep stone stairway and into the light of day. We were greeted by the sight of peacocks foraging in a bed of flowers and a glimmering sea beyond.

Ah, Mallorca. You were all that was promised and more. But our last day there was somewhat bittersweet. We were in a boat drifting aimlessly: Stymie and Rays, Wishbone and the Troll, Filario and I. Drifting in Bahia de Palma. We'd lowered one of the ship's lifeboats, hoisted the canvas mainsail and jib, and lashed down the tiller, so that the boat turned in a great lazy circle. The Troll passed a leather boda bag. He sang:

Three six nine
The goose drank wine
The monkey chewed tobacco on the streetcar line.
The line broke, the monkey got choked
And they all went to heaven in a little row boat.

The T.S. *Empire State IV* dipped in and out of view as the boat rocked in a rogue swell. It wouldn't be long before we'd be making our last ocean crossing on her — heading home. "You live on a ship long enough and cuss her enough and all of a sudden you wake up and discover you're in love." So wrote Ernest K. Gann in *Sirens of the Sea.*

Someone brought up the war. Ghost Ships were being taken out of mothballs at an accelerating rate. All bound for Vietnam. There were rumors that we would be graduated early to meet the burgeoning demand for officers to man them. The Rogues, deeply suspicious of Authority, had mixed feelings about the war. Red Menace. Domino Theory. Escalation. Some things just didn't ring true.

Light airs nudged us through all points of sail. Now luffing, now tacking, now reaching, now running. It hardly felt like the boat was moving. Instead it seemed like Palma de Majorca was circling around us. The medieval cathedral, the ancient castle, the battlement towers, the royal palace.

We drank in silence. This was the last time that we would sail together. The Fall would be spent studying for the grueling Coast Guard exams for a third mate's license. Come Spring, licenses in hand, we would go our separate ways riding tankers and freighters to God-knows-where.

"A gone shipmate, like any other man, is gone forever," wrote Conrad. "Goodbye brothers! You were a good crowd."

Now the wind had utterly died. The sea was flat as a mirror. Countless shearwaters sat motionless on the surface of the water. Yet they, like we, were being carried along ever so slowly by an unseen, unfelt current.

PART TWO:

DAT OLE DAVIL SEA

10

THE
SS *FREE AMERICA*

Congratulations!
Today is your day.
You're off to great places!
You're off and away!
                    - Dr. Seuss, *Oh, the Places You'll Go*

The union hall for masters, mates and pilots was on Washington Street in lower Manhattan. It was thick with the rank odors of cigarette smoke, stale coffee and the exhalations of distilled spirits, and had the ambience of an illicit craps parlor. Still, for all its air of decadence, the union hall was living proof that seamen could bargain for the same rights as workers everywhere. That bargaining power was a long time coming.

In 1834, taking a break from his studies at Harvard, Richard Henry Dana Jr. joined the brig *Pilgrim* in Boston Harbor. He looked forward to "a long absence from books, with plenty of hard work, plain food and open air." Dana also had hopes of recovering his eyesight, impaired by a bout with measles. The voyage took him around Cape Horn to the coast of Alta California. There, the ship traded New England wares for cattle hides. Dana found simple joys in "a trick at the wheel, a lookout on the forecastle, a nap on a coil of rigging, a yarn spun by the windlass end, or, as was generally my way, a solitary walk fore and aft." And life at sea did indeed improve his vision.

But a seaman's lot was not always a happy one. Dana noted the long hours of work, the meager provisions and the capriciousness and brutality of the ship's officers. Flogging was the most common form of punishment. It was meted out with the "cat-o'-nine-tails," designed for the purpose. It consisted of nine knotted cords attached to a handle. Every lash by the cat would tear the victim's skin causing excruciating pain, and sometimes unconsciousness — even death.

The flogging aboard the *Pilgrim* was meted out by a sadistic captain who said: "If you want to know why I flog, it's because I like to do it. I like to do it! That's why I flog."

Two Years Before the Mast was published in 1840. The book was influential for its depiction of the miseries endured by merchant seamen. It was also a source of inspiration for Melville's great novel, *Moby Dick*. Richard Dana Jr. — who would go on to become an admiralty lawyer — wrote a handbook called *The Seaman's Friend* which explained to merchant mariners their rights and duties. It inspired them to fight for improved working conditions aboard American merchant ships. In 1850, the U.S. was the first country in the world to ban flogging aboard ships. It wasn't banned in Britain until almost a hundred years later.

The formation of maritime unions gave further impetus to passing regulations for the safety and security of merchant mariners. One of the earliest was the Seamen's Friendly Union and Protective Society which may have been the first maritime union in the world. It was short-lived but at least it demonstrated that, yes, it was possible to organize men on a countless variety of ships in far-flung U.S. ports. The International Seamen's Union (ISU) was founded in 1892 to provide a strong single voice to speak for the sailor in the halls of Congress. The ISU was instrumental in passing The Seaman's Act of 1915. This bill ended imprisonment for seamen who deserted their ships, and required that all U.S. vessels carry (heavens forbid!) lifeboats. It mandated eight-hour instead of twelve-hour watches and dictated the size of the living space for men in the fo'c's'le — their quarters. Sailors often slept in three-tiered bunks in cabins described as "too large for a coffin, too small for a grave." The Seaman's Act was called the emancipation proclamation for seamen of the world.

But the struggle for decent working conditions didn't end there. It took a series of crippling labor strikes in the 1930s to finally guarantee fair wages and working conditions. The strikes were extensive and tumultuous. Union picketers were shot by police and scores were injured.

Some of the labor leaders seemed right out of central casting. There was the pugnacious, cigar-chomping Paul Hall whose arms and legs bore knife scars from waterfront battles. He had sailed as an engine room wiper before helping to found the Seafarers International Union.

"Big Joe" Curran was an Irish-American from the Lower East Side of Manhattan. Curran had a nose that had met one fist too many. He sailed as an able seaman and boatswain aboard the SS *California*, and led a sit-down strike to protest working overtime without pay. The seamen refused to leave the ship until they were compensated. But the strikers were not only blacklisted, they were charged with mutiny — a federal offense. It took the intervention of Secretary of Labor Francis Perkins for the charges to be dropped. And out of that struggle the National Maritime Union was born, with Big Joe Curran as its president.

From its inception, the union was racially integrated. Its secretary-treasurer was a black Jamaican named Ferdinand Smith who had worked as a ship's steward. Like many labor leaders in the 1930s, Smith was a Communist sympathizer. It came back to haunt him during the Red Scare after World War II. He was labeled an "Alien Red," briefly jailed and eventually deported from the U.S. in 1951.

The unions squabbled among themselves as fiercely as they fought the shipping companies. Yet there's no doubt that good came out it all. American merchant seamen won the same basic rights as laborers "on the beach," as sailors say. And in return they willingly risked their lives during World War II, when more than 1,500 ships were sunk by Nazi U-boats — often with all hands lost at sea.

The roots of my own union, the International Organization of Masters, Mates and Pilots or MMP, went back to 1887. It was a time when pilots were held accountable for marine casualties but had no say in marine safety requirements. A group of New York harbor pilots banded together and formed the American Brotherhood of Steamship Pilots. Soon the union expanded to encompass all merchant deck officers serving on U.S. flag vessels. While the MMP took part in the labor strikes of the 1930s, it was relatively free from the intra-union strife that plagued the other maritime unions.

Now, along with a handful of older deck officers — my new-found "brothers" — I studied a big chalk board that listed the ships with job openings. And I thought: Wow! This is it. This is where the adventure truly all begins. After four long years of spit-and-polish bullshit. Rome! Rangoon! Rio! Here I come!

But almost all the ships listed were tramps with the same destination: FAR EAST. They were Ghost Ships heading for Vietnam. With no seniority, I was assured the worst of the lot. The dispatcher called out the jobs one by one. No one bid on the SS *Free America*, a freighter now docked in San Francisco.

The next day, I found myself standing at the foot of a gangway ladder staring up at a weathered old cargo ship. Black hull streaked with rust. Paint on the housing peeled away. Smoke stack covered with soot. She had a port list and was leaning away from the dock. Should the mooring lines part, she would have capsized. A wake rolled in from a passing freighter, and the ship surged a bit, the gangway ladder rolling creakily towards me, beckoning.

"So this is your first ship," said Captain Allnutt. He pronounced it "fuhst ship" — a New Englander.

"Yes, sir."

"Well, it may be your lahst." I liked a man with a sense of humor. Only he wasn't smiling. I signed on, taking note of the last line in the Ship's Articles: "No grog or dangerous weapons allowed and none to be brought aboard by crew."

"The very foundation of the British Navy," wrote Winston Churchill, "was rum, sodomy and the lash." Apparently the tradition lived on.

The SS *Free America* was a C-2 freighter built during World War II. 470 feet from bow to stern, 66 feet across the beam. She was called a "stick ship" for the cargo booms that loomed over the five hatches. C-2s and Victory ships were the aged beasts of burden of the Vietnam War. Many had been rushed to sea with minimal inspection. Winches and wires, shackles and swivels snapped, crackled and popped. Hull plating cracked, hatch covers leaked and propellers fell off.

I checked in with the chief mate, Mr. Wussler, who was supervising the loading of cargo. Gimlet-eyed and rum-nosed, the Mate put an arm on my shoulder and pointed to a pallet of Old Iron City beer. "We put the delicate cargo amidships," he said, "where it won't take such a pounding." Besides the beer, the "delicate cargo" would include crates of Wild Turkey bourbon, Gordon's gin, Seagram's 7 whiskey, Red Mountain wine and Champale — all to be safely tucked away deep down in the No. 3 hold.

Then the longshoremen loaded the cargo that would take a pounding: a thousand tons of ammo packed in wooden crates. The pallets were winched aboard at the Navy Ammo Depot in Suisun Bay on the Sacramento River. It was here in 1944 that a massive explosion destroyed two freighters, the Liberty ship *E.A. Bryan* and the *Quinalt Victory*, both fully loaded with small caliber bullets, fragmentation devices, depth charges and aerial bombs. The explosion was heard 200 miles away. All crew members aboard both ships died instantly.

Days later, with a full load of bullets and booze, we steamed downriver, crossed San Francisco Bay, then sailed under the Golden Gate Bridge and out into the Pacific Ocean. The ship slowed just off Point Bonita to drop the pilot off, the sexagenarian taking an acrobatic leap from a dangling ladder to the deck of the pilot boat. Then, like Winken, Blinken and Nod, we were off on a river of crystal light, into a sea of dew.

The captain set a great circle course for Manila in the Philippines, 7,000 miles across the open ocean. Manila was the staging area for cargo operations in Vietnam. At fifteen knots, our rated speed, it should have been about a three week crossing. But we would never do fifteen knots, even in the best of weather. None of the creaking hulls I sailed on would ever approach their rated speed.

I was assigned to the eight-to-twelve watch, mornings and nights — the better for the captain to keep an eye on a green third mate. My watch mates were two able-bodied seamen and an ordinary seaman. Each took a ninety-minute stint at the helm. When not steering the ship, they stood lookout on the bow or worked with the bosun or lounged in the crew mess. On the first half hour of the watch, the lookout would strike the ship's bell once, adding a strike every ensuing half hour until eight bells were rung, marking the end of the watch. Also on the half-hour, the lookouts would report to the bridge via intra-ship telephone: "All lights burning bright. No ships in sight."

With his scuffed-tweed cap and deeply-lined face, the able seaman on my watch looked like he'd stepped out of a depression era photo. But Philly was a savvy hand, having sailed on merchant ships since he was sixteen. During World War II, he was on the North Atlantic run, carrying supplies to the Allies on the treacherous passage to Mermansk in Russia. One of his jobs was chipping ice off the masts so the ship wouldn't capsize from the weight of it. One day, high up on a mast, he could see all the other ships in the convoy, including one that had been struck by torpedoes. The sinking ship was surrounded by lifeboats bobbing in the gray seas, the seamen desperately trying to pull their shipmates from the icy waters.

The other AB on my watch was King Sing from Shanghai, an ageless Chinese with the demeanor of a Happy Buddha. On the crew list it said he was sixty-four years old, but he looked twenty years younger. When he came up to the wheelhouse, he would bring me a cup of jasmine tea from his own private reserve. He would watch eagerly as I took the first sip.

"It is delicious, King Sing," I would say. "Thank you."

"Za za!" he'd reply. I had no idea what that meant, nor would I understand much of what he said during the crossing. No matter. King Sing was a soothing presence for a nervous twenty-one-year-old on his first voyage as a deck officer.

Stuckey, the ordinary seaman, was a shy young man who was born with a normal sized torso but stubby arms and legs. Here out at sea he'd found refuge from the gawking stares that followed him everywhere "on the beach." His dream was to become a radio officer, and we passed the time on the bridge speaking to each other in Morse Code.

"Dit-dah. Dit-dah. dit-dah," I would say in greeting.

"Dah," he'd reply.

Fraternization between officers and crew was discouraged on merchant ships. Still, the men on my watch were decent souls and seasoned sailors, and I was lucky to have their company. It was Philly whom I'd come to depend on most. He counseled me on how to navigate the rocky straits between captain and officers, officers and crew, company and union. A task difficult in the best of times, but one made even more so by the war. "Most guys who ship out are okay," he said. "When the going gets rough you can count on 'em, mate. Especially the older hands. But this fucked-up war has brought in the lunatic fringe. The Merch is desperate for men, so the unions take in every nutcase who comes along. Hopheads, mopheads, dickheads. Young guys out of reform school. Older guys that were kicked off ships years ago, and now they're back and crazy as ever. They're the flotsam and jetsam, mate. The flotsam and jetsam."

Every ship, he said, was a Ship of Fools. "And on this one, mate, you better watch out for the gas-hounds." That is, the drunks.

Big John, the other third mate, was a boisterous drunk. He was a giant, bullet-headed man who tapped Morse Code on the diminutive radio officer's skull. "Beep-beep-BEEB-beep. Beep-beep-BEEB–beep. Get my message, Sparky? Fuuuck you. Hah-hah-hah-haaah." Big John reeked of Aqua Velva. Not from splashing it on himself, but from drinking it.

Mr. Nye, the second mate, was a dangerous drunk. Dangerous to himself, that is. A martial arts expert, he once emerged from his cabin with bloodied hands and feet having kicked and pummeled the bunk, desk, chair, and walls. He would tear telephone books in half with his bare hands. No book, in fact, was safe around him.

Mr. Wussler, the chief mate, was a sociable drunk. Unfortunately, I was the one he wanted to socialize with. "Come on, kid. You're not on watch for another hour. How about another Tom Collins. Hey, BR!" — he was calling the Bedroom Steward, a pale Finn who skulked about the ship like the living dead — "bring us some more ice!"

Captain Allnutt was a reclusive drunk. He took all his meals in his cabin, and rarely ventured out on deck or up on the bridge. But he was often heard conversing with unseen and unheard companions.

"Yeah, you gotta watch those gas hounds," said Philly. "You see how much booze we're carrying. A shipload of temptation. Let's see how much of the hooch makes it to port. Let's see how many crates we lose to 'bad weather.'"

Philly was a prescient man as well. Despite days of smooth sailing, the logbook was rife with references to "heavy seas" and "damaged cargo." Underlined for emphasis were references to crates of "leaking combustibles" that had to be "tossed overboard." Not surprisingly, the leaking combustibles consisted of alcoholic beverages. Which had been consumed by the crew, not tossed. Thus the SS *Free America*, my first ship, staggered across the Pacific with an explosive cargo and half-looped crew.

The four hours on watch passed ever so slowly. On the morning shift, I would take a sextant altitude of the sun every hour on the hour. Each sight and its calculations took about five minutes. The remaining time was spent gazing out at the horizon. I would stand out on the bridge wing to avoid the twin temptations of idle chatter with the crew and the comforts of the captain's chair. Both verboten.

On the evening shift, there was little to do but watch for other ships. Still you needed to stay alert. Things go bump in the night. Reading the navigation lights of ships encountered at sea is an acquired skill. The red and green side lights, the white masthead and stern lights all reveal the other ship's heading relative to your own. They tell you whether you're overtaking or meeting a ship, whether it is crossing or has already crossed your path, whether you are the "privileged" or "burdened" vessel. The privileged vessel must maintain course and speed, the burdened vessel must alter course to prevent a collision. These are the Rules of the Road. Other lights indicate if a ship is towing or being towed, at anchor or aground, fishing or sinking. Sinking is what happens if you misread the lights.

In fog or rain, we relied on the radar to determine the course and speed of other ships. Unfortunately, the radar on the SS *Free America* — like the radio direction finder, the loran, the anemometer, the bridge telephone and the toilet in the captain's head — had crapped out. Well, not entirely. The radar screen displayed strange green blotches instead of little blips — as if detecting aliens.

The open ocean is like a vast watery desert. Occasionally we'd see pilot whales swimming along the ship's bow, or spinner dolphins leaping acrobatically into the air, or flying fish bursting from the waves like silvery angels. Or in the skies, a lone frigate bird or albatross. At night, patches of luminescence hinted at tiny life forms below the surface. But mostly there was nothing, as John

Masefield wrote, but "the lonely sea and the sky." Those who go down to the sea in ships soon learn the difference between solitude and loneliness. One's own personal heading could swing like a ship's bow towards either destination.

Often I thought about Jane. She was a young woman now, and I hadn't seen her in a long while. It was springtime in the Valley. And even from out here — on the opposite side of the world — I could smell the wild honeysuckle and hear the chirping of song sparrows.

At last we sighted the coast of Samar in the Philippines. We hadn't seen land in three weeks. Nor had we seen many ships. Except for a few isolated events — Sparks dumping a plate of mashed potatoes on Big John — the engine room wiper seen wearing a dress —the bedroom steward caught sleeping with the second cook — the day man throwing all the board games over the side ("Now let's see you mother-fuckers cheat me!") — Monopoly money, Chinese checkers, rooks and queens, Colonel Plum and Mr. Mustard all left in our wake — it had been an uneventful crossing.

The moon was new and we were heading into the San Bernardino Strait through the southern Philippine Islands. The air was so thick you could taste it. The haze was from the smoke of burning cane fields, and it smelled wonderfully sweet. King Sing was at the helm, chatting away as usual, and, as usual, I didn't understand a word he was saying. Besides I was a bundle of nerves. There were ships everywhere, either heading towards the Strait or emerging from it. Lights flickered on every quarter, and the haze was growing thicker as we neared land.

I saw a set of lights a few miles off the starboard bow. They appeared to belong to a large bulk carrier with a deckhouse forward and another deckhouse aft — both superstructures lit up like Christmas trees. I decided the ship was crossing ahead of us from right to left and had the right of way. I took a bearing with the gyro compass on the bridge wing. If over time the bearing didn't change, it would mean we were on a collision course, and we'd have to turn to starboard. Which I was reluctant to do since there was another ship slowly overtaking us from that quarter.

So I watched and waited. Long minutes passed and I took another compass bearing on the ship and, no, the bearing hadn't changed a lick. I considered waiting just a tad longer before changing course — there was that other ship to starboard after all. But then I remembered the advice I'd read in the *Merchant Marine Officer's Handbook*: "Give plenty of room, and when you give way, do it as soon as possible."

I told King Sing to come right ten degrees rudder.

Now, as we came right, the ship was dead ahead. And it was enormous. I could see the lights on the forward-deckhouse off our port bow — the lights on the after-deckhouse off our starboard bow. The ship now appeared to be much closer than I had thought. In fact: I had WAITED TOO LONG! And FUCK! — we were about to plow right into it — cut the vessel clean in two. "King Sing, hard right!" I shouted. "HARD right! HARDER!"

King Sing shouted back: "IZ-LAHN-SUH! IZ-LAHN-SUH!" What the hell was he saying? A prayer to the Taoist God of Imminent Disaster?

I rang up FULL SPEED ASTERN on the engine telegraph — though I knew it would take four to six ship-lengths to stop a vessel going full speed ahead. That's about a half mile. And the big bulk carrier was just spitting distance ahead of us.

I called down to the captain — his ship's phone didn't work, so I had to blow into the tube that ran from the bridge to his quarters and shout down through 20 feet of brass: "Captain! Can you come to the bridge please! I think we have a problem!" King Sing was still coming hard right — still shouting "Iz-lanh-suh!" But the ship ahead was closer still — I could see the lights of the forward-deckhouse now very far to the left, and the lights of the after-deckhouse very far to the right which meant amidships was dead ahead — though lightless and invisible — like the eternal void we were all about to enter. I blew the ship's whistle — the three short blasts that meant "I am reversing my engines." It was so loud it could wake up the dead — it could even wake up the crew — and it did — and now they were staggering out on deck like zombies, scratching their heads, their hinds and their balls wondering what the fuck was going on.

The captain wondered that too — he was up on the bridge now — still wearing his skivvies, he expressed it to me thusly: "Jesus Mary and fucking Joseph didn't they teach you anything in that fucking boy scout academy — you shit-for-brains pissant — can't even read a fucking light." Et cetera. He threw the engine telegraph lever back to "Full Ahead," and yelled down to the crew to go back to bed.

By now we'd cut the other ship cleanly in two. Only there was no other ship. At least not the huge break-bulk carrier of my imagination. Oh, there was a real ship far off to port — which we'd now safely passed. But the lights off to starboard were not the lights of its after-deckhouse. They were shore lights a dozen miles away. They were the Philippines. Or as King Sing was shouting. "Iz-lahn-suh." It's land, sir.

"Rough night, eh mate?" said Philly when he took his turn at the helm. He tugged his cap and smiled that gapped-tooth smile of his. "Ah, don't worry about it. Could have happened to anyone." And then he told me the story about a young mate who took his ship miles off course to rescue what he thought was a lifeboat adrift — but which turned out to be a foul and fetid whale carcass. I would have taken comfort in this story, except he was referring to what I had done just three days earlier.

Coast Guard regulations required weekly lifeboat drills. But the boats were rarely lowered. The logbook would explain why: "No boats lowered due to inclement weather." But sometimes I fantasized about a disaster at sea. The ship's whistle sounds seven short blasts followed by one long blast. Abandon ship! The SS *Free America* is sinking! Holed by a Japanese mine that's been adrift for decades. And all boats are lowered into the sea. I'm in command of the No. 3 lifeboat. Philly is in my boat, as is King

Sing and Stuckey and feisty little Sparks and Manley, the Jamaican cook who sings *soca* in a rich baritone voice. In heavy seas, we separate from the other boats. And now it is up to me to navigate us — without sextant or chronometer — across thousands of miles of open ocean. The lifeboat supplies — such as they were — soon give out. The canned biscuits, the chocolate tablets, the Charms candy, the cigarettes — all gone. Now we must survive on sharks and sea turtles and sea birds. Sparks goes crazy and, like in an old war movie, I have to smack him around a bit until he comes to his senses.

A few days after my false-emergency debacle, I was on the morning watch navigating our way through the Visayan islands. The islands were charred black by the controlled burns of cane fields. The air smelled like burned sugar. And there was the bosun, a surly cuss, running around on deck, seemingly on fire himself. The chief mate was with him as were a couple of other deck hands.

"Pirates," said Philly as he took the wheel. "They raided the ship some time last night." I later learned that a speed boat must have come up from behind, and then the pirates, using heaving lines and grappling hooks, boarded the stern where the men on watch wouldn't see them. Anything light enough to be carried off and lowered into their boat had been stolen. Winch cables, cargo hooks, blocks and tackles, hawsers, life rings, fire extinguishers — all gone. "Thank God, they didn't get into the No. 3 hold," said Mr. Wussler. That's where the booze was stowed.

We anchored off Subic Bay in the Philippines, home to a U.S. naval base. I took a water taxi ashore, and a land taxi to Olongapo City on the outskirts of the base. Olongapo lay just beyond "Shit River" as the Navy swabs called it. It was a lawless strip of rattan whorehouses, bamboo bars, tin-roofed strip clubs and adobe cockfighting pits. (Where a sign warned: "Leave your weapons at the door.") I was walking down main street, when I saw coming towards me a tall gawky red-head in rumpled khakis. God's teeth! It was Filario!

We bellied up to a bar, and, over piss-warm San Miguel beers, commiserated. Filario was sailing on an old Victory, the SS *Halcyon Tiger.* "I dunno, Maharrey," he said. "It's crazy on dese ships." His stories were scarier than mine: The captain firing his pistol at seabirds, the day-man stabbing the bosun with a marlin spike, the second cook pissing in the oatmeal; the wiper hurling a wrench at the oiler.

I told him about a report I had come across in the ship's office. It was issued by the U.S. Coast Guard about the rampant lawlessness aboard U.S. merchant ships bound for Vietnam:

> Cases investigated by marine inspection officers include assaults, marijuana use, hard narcotics, desertions, gross misconduct, stabbings, drownings, pilfering cargo, sodomy, drunk on duty, incompetence, murder, sabotage. The master of one vessel was relieved for being intoxicated during ammunition handling. A ship's bosun was accused of running a "house of ill repute." One unpopular seaman with a prosthetic leg woke up to find it had been thrown overboard.

The SS *Free America* never made it to Vietnam. Instead we were diverted from Manila to Inchon, Korea, then back to Manila then over to Okinawa then on to Kaohsiung, Taiwan — had anyone a plan for this war? — unloading a few crates of ammo here and there. But the booze — or what was left of it — was not unloaded. At every port, the cargo gear at the No. 3 hold, where the crates of alcoholic beverages were stowed, mysteriously broke down. Cables were found parted, motors burnt out, winch controls missing. Which meant the booze couldn't be discharged. Finally back at Subic Bay, the Navy sent a barge with a crane to unload the last of it. By now there were only a few pallets of Iron City beer left. The crew gathered at the railing to watch it being discharged, as if bidding farewell to a beloved old shipmate.

On the long voyage home the crew went into withdrawals. Big John broke down into a two-day crying jag. Mr. Nye punched a mirror breaking his knuckles. The chief mate stumbled down a ladder requiring daily injections of morphine to "ease the pain."

And the captain disappeared completely. A rumor spread that he'd jumped overboard. But the steward confirmed that plates of food left by his cabin door were later found licked clean. He reappeared the day we sighted land on the horizon: the hills of San Francisco. Captain Allnutt was a shadow of the man he had been only three months before. Gaunt, pale, disheveled, he shielded his eyes from the sun.

Then he turned to me and said: "So. Your last ship?"

11

Pearl Of
The Orient

Whose boat plies the river mists
Offering so many river songs
To move these mountains and rivers, our nation.
- Traditional Vietnamese *Ca Dao*

But it wasn't. I sailed on another and another and yet another. Ghost ships carrying thousands of tons of munitions and meat, tanks and toilet paper, napalm and ice cream to the War Zone. The Beast was growing now and its appetite was insatiable.

Going up the Saigon River was like running a gauntlet thirty-five miles long. Naval Guards would come aboard and help us prepare for the passage. Grenade screens were installed on portholes. Fire fighting gear was broken out. Sandbags were stacked around the bridge. We donned helmets and flak suits. The presence of the river patrol boats offered little comfort. They couldn't protect us from snipers taking potshots at the men on the bridge — a half dozen mariners had been shot already. Nor could they prevent the seeding of the river with mines. The merchant ships *Berea Victory, Margaret Brown, Seatrain Texas,*

Petrarca, American Hawk and *Green Bay* had all been crippled by Vietcong sappers.

On my first trip upriver, we almost ran aground. Bends in the river sucked the ship towards the banks — the prop churned up river bottom — and the ship was drawn now towards Charybdis now towards Scylla. When we reached Saigon, we anchored in the river instead of docking at the pier. All cargo operations had been suspended, the Vietnamese longshoremen refusing to work on Ho Chi Minh's birthday. But wasn't Ho Chi Minh the enemy? Welcome to the riddle, wrapped in a mystery, inside the puzzle that was Vietnam.

I spent the day wandering about the city. There was an elegant decadence to the "Pearl of the Orient." Tree-lined boulevards and splendid colonial buildings and graceful arcades. Ripe with the stench of piss and shit. The streets were crowded with bicycles and rickshaws and pedicabs. Sidewalks teemed with skinny men in shorts and sandals, young women in *ao-dais*, old women in black pajamas. A pedicab zoomed by, crowded with giggling school children. It passed another pedicab, pushing a flatbed stacked high with crude wooden coffins.

At the entrance to an ancient pagoda was a wooden boat, bow and stern swept up in graceful arcs. Through a haze of burning incense, I could see monks chanting. Mythical creatures gazed down upon them from the ceiling — snake-like dragons and winged serpents. The celebrants — women and children mostly — set offerings before a statue of the Buddha. Coins and fruits. Bottles of Coca-cola.

In the open market, toothless old women squatted before baskets filled with tropical flowers or exotic fruits or strange misshapen vegetables. A vendor sold song birds in ornate wooden cages. Another sold huge crickets — fighting crickets, both black and fiery red. A stall offered moon cakes: sticky rice stuffed with peanuts, seeds or in times of insurrection: secret messages. Another was decorated with cellophane lanterns shaped like dragons, toads, carps and unicorns.

"Everything in this world has a hidden meaning," wrote Nikos Kazantzakis. "Men, animals, trees, stars, they are all hieroglyphics; woe to anyone who begins to decipher them and guess what they mean."

I wandered into a small shop bursting at the seams with books, most in French. Sartre was here. As was Camus. Dumas *pere et fils*. Victor Hugo. There were also a handful of books in English, mostly paperback westerns and mysteries. Since going to sea, I'd become a voracious reader. *Magic Mountain. Soul on Ice. Childhood's End. Summerhill. Cat's Cradle. The Lord of the Rings. The Ginger Man. Dharma Bums. One Flew Over the Cuckoo's Nest. Siddhartha. Catch 22. A Clockwork Orange. Trout Fishing in America. The Secret Sea and LSD. Another Roadside Attraction. Been Down So Long it Looks Like Up to Me.* Books that created the *lingua franca* of my generation. I read and reread the classics: anything by Hemingway, Fitzgerald, Conrad, London, Joyce, Dickens, Melville. As well as the eclectic collection found in the ship's library: *The Comedy of Errors. How to Abandon Ship. The Nuts Among the Berries.*

The bookseller saw me browsing the French section, and he bid me "*bonjour*." I returned his *bonjour* with the caveat that I read French much better than I speak it. "*Moi aussi*," he said with a smile. He apologized for the slim selection of books — it had been hard importing them lately — but if I was interested he had just received the complete works of Victor Hugo. I told him I'd just finished reading Hugo's *Ninety-three.*

"*Ah, oui*," he said. "*La revolution francaise. Que triste!*" How sad. What was sad, I said, was the way the peasants seemed to side with the very people — the priests and the nobility — who were oppressing them. Oppression has many faces, said the bookseller. Many faces.

He turned to his daughter, sixteen perhaps, who was re-shelving books. He said something to her in Vietnamese and she nodded and smiled demurely. She was the spitting image of the bookseller, right down to the oversized black rimmed eyeglasses. She wore a pure white *ao-dai* that covered her from chin to toes. The bookseller asked me if I'd like to join him in a cup of tea. "*Oui, merci,*" I said. He guided me through the beaded curtain into the back room, leaving his daughter to mind the store.

We sipped tea at a low table, surrounded by stacks of books like ancient Grecian columns. "*Mes trésors,*" he said, gesturing to the stacks. I asked him why there were so few books in Vietnamese. He said that in the brief period of peace after the last war, there were many works of literature written by Vietnamese. But with the coming of the Americans, people wanted books that entertained. Foreign books. Perhaps when we are our own country, he said, we will create literature again. In truth, he said, Vietnam has an oral not a literate tradition. "*Nous sommes poéts,*" he added with a flourish of his hand. We are poets. Every peasant, he continued, can recite hundreds of *ca daos.* The *ca dao* is a poem sung *a cappella.* Riddles, proverbs, lullabies, histories, legends, love songs. Many are centuries old. They are filled with soldiers and sages, kings and peasants, sun and moon, bamboo and egret. But mostly they speak of love. Of concubines and royal lovers, of doomed marriages and unrequited love. Some are "*tres* sexy," he added with a twinkle. But no matter the subject, the *ca dao* speaks to the illusory nature of the world. The bookseller set down his teacup, cleared his throat. Then he sang a haunting verse in a slight quivering voice. When he was done, I simply said "Beautiful." He smiled then he translated the song into French:

> *A monk sleeps under a banyan tree,*
> *When he awakens, he wonders:*
> *Am I a man dreaming I am a butterfly?*
> *Or a butterfly dreaming I am a man?*

Bells jingled. Someone had entered the bookstore. Suddenly we heard his daughter shouting in urgent tones:
"*Cha! Cha!*" Father! Father!

The bookseller hurried back into the front room. I heard him yell something in Vietnamese. Then I heard mocking laughter in response. Male voices. I parted the beaded curtains and saw two South Korean soldiers in a narrow aisle. They had the daughter trapped between them. A third soldier, thick and squat as Odd Job in *Goldfinger*, guarded the door. They had drawn closed the curtains to the shop window and it was dark in there now.

Korean troops had been stationed in Vietnam since 1965. The U.S. had invited them in and paid for their company. They were our mercenaries. There were now some 40,000 Koreans in three divisions: the Tigers, the White Horses, the Blue Dragons. The ROKs [Republic Of Korea], as they were called, were renowned for their superb fighting skills, for being extraordinarily effective in rooting out and killing Viet Cong. But they were also known for their cruelty, including skinning their enemies alive during interrogations. And they'd committed atrocities towards Vietnamese villagers that were only now being reported.

The bookseller shouted at them again. But the Koreans only grinned in response. Then Odd Job glanced over and saw me in curtainway. He nodded to the other two ROKs. They turned towards me. Eyes as opaque as charcoal.

Odd Job barked an order, and my heart raced. They remained where they were — perhaps sizing up the slight young man before them. But that slight young man was an American in a khaki uniform. And he wore an officer's cap.

Odd Job barked another order. The three Koreans looked to each other then towards me. Then, inexplicably, Odd Job gave me a little bow. His expression seemed almost apologetic. As if to say: this has all been a silly misunderstanding. He nodded to the others and they too bowed. Then he retreated to the door, and together the three of them stepped out onto the busy sidewalk. Another little bow — all in unison. And they were gone.

The bookseller put a consoling arm around his daughter who was shaking. He led her into the back room. I heard exchanges with an older woman — his wife perhaps. Voices were raised. Perhaps she was chastising him for leaving the daughter alone in the store. The bookseller came back into the front room and closed the window curtains even tighter. Then he turned to me. "*Merci beaucoup, monsieur.*"

"*Je n'ai fait rien,*" I said. I didn't do anything. "*Au contraire,*" said the bookseller — to the contrary. The Koreans know who *le patron* is, he said. They know who is the boss. And they never offend the boss. He went to the door and flipped the sign to read "closed" in Vietnamese. I took this as a cue for me to leave. "I do not know why they are in my country," he said, shaking his head.

He could very well have been asking the same of me.

One day, I was sitting in an outdoor café in Saigon, sipping Tiger beer and watching a parade of regal ladies in silken *ao-dais* passing by. They walked in slow measured steps to the accompaniment of a moon lute played by a one-eyed street musician. The lute had silken tassels of red, gold and aquamarine. When the player plucked the strings, the lute evoked a human voice. The women walked as if obeying that voice.

Suddenly there was a loud explosion from somewhere up the street. People shouted and screamed and ran. The patrons in the café dove for cover under tables. But I was too stunned to move. Black, acrid smoke came billowing down the street. The lute player was gone. As were the stately women. A mangy three-legged dog scampered by.

The parade was over.

12

CAM RANH BAY

"Whoever sows wind shall harvest storm."
- Vietnamese proverb

Captain Stanislav Wodka was the first to admit he was not a well man. He was skipper of the SS *Beaver Victory*, a tramp freighter bound for Vietnam carrying tons of munitions and a dozen Patton M-48 tanks on deck. The captain had a thick Polish accent and the perpetual hang-dog expression of a confirmed hypochondriac. The chief mate, Mr. Muttle, a loose-limbed straw man out of *The Wizard of Oz*, had had enough of the captain's imagined ailments, and so he sloughed off the duties of ship's medical officer to me.

There is a radio frequency set aside for medical emergencies on the high seas. Should a seaman get acute appendicitis, say, a ship's officer might have to perform an appendectomy at sea. And he would be guided through the operation by a physician in Honolulu via the radiotelephone. But to Captain Wodka, the emergency frequency was all that stood between him and his

Maker. He woke me up in the middle of the night. "Mr. Mate! Get up! Get up! You must come to radio room now! Please! Tell Sparks to go to emergency frequency. You must tell them captain has medical emergency."

"Sir, what's wrong?"

"Headache! Opset stomach! Fever of ninety-nine degrees! Please! Call them now! Hurry!"

Oh Christ, I thought. Here we go again. I roused Sparks.

"Look, mate," said Sparks, "you got to have him sign one of those forms. You know, so we can perform a mercy killing."

Sparks raised the emergency frequency with Honolulu, and I was on the radio relating the captain's symptoms.

"Is the sick man Captain Wodka? Over." asked Honolulu.

"Yes. Over."

"This isn't the first time we've had a call regarding your captain. Could you remind him please that this frequency is for medical emergencies only? Over."

"Yes, sir. Will do. Over."

"Give him two APC tablets and a tall glass of water. And tell Wodka to lay off the vodka. Ha-ha-ha. Over and out."

The ship itself was in far worse shape than its captain, and its ailments were not imaginary. The canvas life-boat covers were shredded like the overcoat of a homeless man. Most of the wiring was old and brittle. Fans worked intermittently. The bridge-to-engine phone didn't work. And the panel for our navigation lights needed rewiring. The lights would flicker on and off in no discernible pattern. One moment the display of lights would indicate we were fishing at sea; the next moment that we had run aground.

More problematic was the erratic behavior of the radar. We were sailing through the South China Sea at the height of the southwest monsoon season and needed to thread our way through the countless thunderstorms. But the radar continually displayed phantom storms and failed to detect real ones.

The following evening — and still not recovered from his own phantom storms -- Captain Wodka came shuffling onto the bridge wearing slippers and a robe.

"Evening, Captain," I said.

He sniffled loudly in response and settled into his chair. "I vas looking for you before watch and couldn't find you. Where was you?"

"Sometimes when I'm off watch I like to hang out on the stern."

"There is no one on stern but crew. You are officer. You should not be ... be socializing with crew."

"I like to watch the sharks following the ship."

Which was true. I was getting more and more interested in the kind of marine life that did not inhabit the vessels themselves. Now and then, there were intriguing hints of life below the water's surface: A patch of ocean boiling with baitfish. The purple sails of Portuguese man-of-wars drifting on the Gulf Stream or moon jellies pulsing in the South China Sea. Or the occasional glimpse of a shark's fin as it rode the ship's wake awaiting the tossing of garbage.

Once while sailing on a C-2 off the Ryukyu Islands in Japan, the seas exploded with light with every breaking wave. It was a stunning display of bioluminescence.

Later that night, I tossed a bucket over the side to collect some of the seawater. I stirred the bucket with my hand and it glowed like a plastic saint. I poured out some of the water on deck and it splashed with dazzling sparkles. I wondered about the tiny organisms in the water that created the "phosphorescence."

When we arrived in Yokosuka, I bought a cheap microscope. And, back at sea, collected plankton by straining the seawater with cheesecloth. I could see through the microscope the most bizarrely shaped creatures — like aliens from another world. I made sketches to eventually share with Rippy who was now in grad school studying marine biology. When I wasn't sketching plankton I was prowling the decks with binoculars watching for seabirds, whales, dolphins and sharks.

But all this enthusiasm for the natural world was lost on the captain of the SS *Beaver Victory.*

"So. Captain is sick and you are vatching sharks. Ve don't need shark-vatchers on dis ship! Captain had very high fever today. And you vere shark-vatching."

"Feeling better, Captain?"

"No t'anks to you!"

I tried to change the subject. "I see the Navy has rerouted us to Cam Ranh Bay"

"Dot place is notting but dysentery," he sniffed. "And syphilis. And malahria."

"A lot to look forward to, sir."

And so with both an ailing captain and ship we sniffled our way to Cam Ranh Bay. The *Beaver Victory* had already been to the port a number of times and none of the men aboard looked forward to it. They called it Can't Run Away.

About a hundred miles from land we saw U.S. reconnaissance planes flying search patterns overhead. They were part of what was called Operation Market Time intended to cut the flow of men and war materials from North Vietnam to the south. Small junks and sampans, large barges and trawlers would — under cover of darkness — drop off arms, ammunition and enemy soldiers in hidden areas along the coast. Many were Chinese-built coastal freighters that carried tons of arms and ammunition. The search planes — especially the SP-2 Neptunes and P-3 Orions — were armed with Bullpup missiles capable of blowing the gun-runners to smithereens.

One of the more tragic incidents involved the U.S. Coast Guard cutter *Point Welcome.* Incredibly, it was mistaken for a Vietcong supply ship and was fired on by three U.S. Air Force planes. Its commanding officer and a crewman were killed. This happened about a year before our own arrival on the weather-beaten *Beaver Victory.* Thus the sight of U.S. planes soaring overhead was not always a reassuring one.

As we approached the southern tip of the Cam Ranh peninsula we could see about a dozen Swift Boats in a cove. They too were there to intercept suspicious looking vessels. A Navy watch tower guarded the entrance to the bay proper. It was like entering a forbidden kingdom.

The first Americans to visit Cam Ranh Bay arrived in 1964 aboard the USS *Epping Forest*. Mine Division 33 was charged with conducting hydrographic and land surveys to determine the feasibility for establishing military facilities. They were assisted by reconnaissance aircraft, a seaplane tender, a helicopter detachment, surveillance and underwater demolition teams, and a squad of marines — all a microcosm of what was soon to come.

What they found was a secluded tropical paradise with long stretches of white sand beaches on the South China Sea. The bay was sheltered by a narrow peninsula some eighteen miles long. It was mostly uninhabited, with groves of palm trees, rocky outcrops and forested hills, the southernmost high enough to capture the monsoon rains and create a crystal-clear fresh water lake. At its rocky southern tip, were secluded coves, dramatic cliffs and one of the finest deepwater harbors in Southeast Asia, if not the world. The waters of the bay were so clear one could see all the way down to the bottom -- every seashell, stone, and wreck.

The mouth of the bay opened to a long thin waterway lined with lush mangroves. Here and there were small fishing villages and a handful of French colonial mansions in decay. On the northern section of the peninsula was My Ca, a Catholic monastery set on a quiet lagoon. One could hardly imagine a more peaceful, even idyllic place.

But Cam Ranh Bay was no stranger to war. In 1905 during the Russo-Japanese War, a fleet of some fifty Russian warships anchored there. They were part of the Russian Imperial Fleet under the command of Admiral Zinovy "Mad Dog" Rozhestvenski. One can imagine what an impressive sight this huge assembly of battleships, cruisers and destroyers must have been to the local villagers. And they would have been just as stunned by the news of its fate. Sailing through the straits of Tsushima in the Sea of Japan, the Russians were met by the Japanese Combined Fleet under the command of Admiral Heihachiro Togo. Togo's fleet was thoroughly drilled and trained, and fitted with modern firepower. The Japanese decimated the Russian fleet sinking twenty-one vessels and killing more than three thousand men. Even "Mad Dog" himself was captured.

In 1940, the Japanese invaded Vietnam. Rice and rubber were appropriated for their war machine. Cam Ranh Bay was used as a staging area for the invasion of other countries such as Malaya. The War of the Pacific was in full swing. In 1944, American B-29 bombers dropped hundreds of armed mines in the harbor to cripple the Japanese fleet. It was called — with no intended irony — Operation Mad Dog.

The war years were hard on the Vietnamese, more than a million died from disease and famine. To the Vietnamese, all of the war's participants — the French, the Japanese, the Chinese, the Americans — seemed like mad dogs. But World War II also provided an opportunity to throw off the French colonial yoke. With the support of the U.S., the Soviet Union and China, Vietnamese insurgents fought both the Japanese and the Vichy French forces. Among the most effective groups were the Viet Minh, under the leadership of a man from the small village of Huoag Tru named Nguyen Sinh Cung. An avowed Communist, he had once worked as a cook's helper on a merchant ship.

He would later change his name to Ho Chi Minh.

In 1954, Cam Ranh Bay would play another important role in history. It served as the principle evacuation port for the French Army, marking the end of more than a century of colonial rule. But only ten years later, the tides of war would once again come rushing into the bay. Three days after the survey by Mine Division 33 was completed, the first Gulf of Tonkin incident occurred. Cruising off the coast of North Vietnam in international waters, the U.S. destroyer *Maddox* found itself in a brief firefight with three North Vietnamese torpedo boats. Who actually fired first is still the subject of debate. The *Maddox* was hit by a single machine gun bullet causing little damage — but it was the principle of the thing.

Even more dubious was the second Gulf of Tonkin incident — the one that triggered the official U.S. entry into the war. In fact, the engagement may never actually have occurred. During a night of rough weather, heavy seas and low-visibility, the radar and sonar of the destroyers *Maddox* and *Turner Joy* received signals that appeared to indicate an attack by the North Vietnamese Navy. Both destroyers opened fire, and when the signals disappeared from their electronics they reported the enemy vessels had been sunk. Yet no bodies or wreckage were ever found.

The commanding officer of the mission quickly sent a cable to Washington: "Review of action makes many reported contacts and torpedoes fired appear doubtful. Freak weather effects on radar and overeager sonarmen may have accounted for many reports. No actual visual sightings by *Maddox*. Suggest complete evaluation before further actions taken."

Later, it was learned, there were no North Vietnamese ships in the area. The "enemy targets" were most likely storm-induced phantoms on the radar and sonar, not unlike those that often plagued the SS *Beaver Victory*. Still — damn the torpedoes and full speed ahead! — President Johnson and the U.S. Congress would use the Gulf of Tonkin incident to justify American military intervention in Vietnam.

Cam Ranh Bay would soon undergo the most dramatic transformation in its history. Some 51,000 construction personnel were brought in to build a massive U.S. air and naval base. Soon the peninsula was covered with ammo and petroleum depots, warehouses and administrative buildings; barracks, hootches and Quonset huts; mess halls, snack bars and post exchanges. There were hospitals and chapels and a convalescent center that served a thousand patients at any given time. There was a library, an outdoor movie theater and even a miniature golf course. The fresh-water lake would become the Tiger Lake Recreation Area, complete with picnic tables, floating docks, lifeguard stations, a diving tower and a marina where one could go water skiing or sailing. It was the soldiers' and sailors' own private Kokomo.

On the northern end of the peninsula, a large airbase was constructed with two ten-thousand foot runways for Phantom jet fighters and Hercules transport planes, for Huey and Cobra helicopters, for Stratofortress and Aardvark bombers, for Crusader and Voodoo fighter-bombers. All this lethal airpower winged in and out of the airbase in sight of the century-old monastery.

On the southern end of the peninsula were floating piers capable of handling six cargo ships at a time and one deep draft Ammo pier made of thick concrete pilings. There were fuel jetties and pipelines, cargo handling gear and huge maintenance sheds. All these structures were now the dominant presence in what had once been a quiet fishing village.

The new facilities on the peninsula were connected by seventy miles of roads and a float bridge to the mainland. During peak use, Cam Ranh Bay would be home to tens of thousands of military and support personnel. The total construction costs of the Cam Ranh Bay installations were estimated at about 250 million dollars. Or, as one pundit noted, enough money to modernize every school and hospital from Hanoi to Saigon. Still, the military had created what was proudly called "little America" in Vietnam.

The very first U.S. combat troops to be deployed in Vietnam disembarked in Cam Ranh Bay. It soon became the destination for thousands of green troops arriving from the states. President Lyndon Johnson himself visited the airbase, and in a speech to the troops declared "Because of what you men are doing here today you may prevent a wider war, a greater war, a World War III."

Our own contribution to this noble effort, the SS *Beaver Victory*, could not even manage to drop an anchor. The Navy had wanted us located a good ways off from the freighters carrying cement, construction vehicles, food supplies and other nonexplosive cargoes. But when we first dropped the four-ton hook, the brake on the windlass failed and all of the anchor chain — some 4,000 feet of thick-linked metal — came rushing down the hawse pipe with a terrible rumble and a cloud of rust and dust. Somehow the bitter end held or all of the chain would have ended up on the bottom of the bay. Now — as the afternoon winds picked up — we began drifting ever so closely to the other ships. The captain — clutching his chest — called down from the bridge on his walkie-talkie for the chief mate "to do something! Do something! You give me heart attack up here!" But Mr. Muttle was in a quandary. If we hauled in the errant chain we might not be able to bring it up quick enough to keep from plowing into another ship, which, while it would provide Cam Ranh Bay with a spectacular fireworks display, would not look good on the resume. But if we steamed out of harm's way the bitter end might pop free and then we'd have no way of retrieving the anchor chain.

The bosun and the crew anxiously awaited the chief mate's orders. At last, Mr. Muttle stroked his chin and nodded. He had come to a decision. He would have a beer. And so he sat on a capstan, turned off the walkie-talkie and the ranting of his captain, and awaited the delivery of his brew. Meanwhile the wind shifted, and the ship was pushed away from the other freighters and towards where we had first dropped anchor. Slowly but surely the intrepid crew of the SS *Beaver Victory* hauled up the anchor chain. Proving once again, that in the American Merchant Marine two wrongs do make a right.

We were told it would be a day or two before we could berth at the ammo pier. And we were all a bit antsy to go ashore. A Navy liberty boat pulled up alongside to shuttle us to a boat dock near the cargo piers. But before we could board the boat we were asked to show our health cards to the boat captain. He said it was to assure our inoculations were up-to-date. Apparently there had been an outbreak of plague in Cam Ranh Bay — which seemed to confirm our captain's assessment of the place as a pestilential hell-hole. "Hah! You see? Did I warn you? Captain is not so crazy, is he?"

Undaunted by the prospect of plague, a dozen of us scrambled into the liberty boat. We passed picket boats and skimmers of the Harbor Patrol. They were conducting random sweeps of the harbor, looking for the tell-tale bubbles of enemy divers. Now and then, they would drop a grenade in the water in the hopes of bringing up to the surface a Viet Cong diver. Instead the bay was littered with dead fish.

The waters of Cam Ranh Bay — once crystal clear — were now murky with the run-off from construction sites. The bay was also infested with jellies. I saw a few dolphins being fed by a sailors on a Boston Whaler. The sailors were part of the Navy's Inshore Underwater Demolition Unit. In the not-too-distant future, the Navy would release a specially trained pod of dolphins into Cam Ranh Bay called the MK 6 — trained to locate enemy divers and skewer them with a lance attached to the beak. Even Flipper would be drafted into this war.

We walked down the long sandy road to the village. Palm trees loomed overhead. Up on the beach were long slender sampans with their upswept bows and sterns. The bow of one was painted with the face of a sea dragon. We were soon joined by stray dogs and stray kids. The kids were mostly boys and all were barefoot. A few had cigarettes dangling from their lips.

"Hello mistuh. Want fuckee my sistah?"

"Mistuh mistuh! Want get high?" Little outstretched hands offered joints and pills.

There was no town or village on this side of the harbor, only a makeshift strip of bars slapped together with old boards and corrugated tin. The string of shacks on stilts sat over the gently lapping waters of the bay. Colorful bed sheets hung in the doorways to keep the flies out. The first had a sign that said simply BAR. An older woman — the mamasan no doubt — stood in the doorway and beckoned to us. She was fat and missing a few teeth and had a beehive hairdo. She shouted "Come in! Come in! Number one girls inside!" And the crew of the *Beaver Victory* — in no mood to shop around — eagerly rushed past her and into the bar. I thought — oh boy — Praise the Lord and pass the penicillin.

The venereal disease rate in Cam Ranh Bay was notoriously high, and there was little the military was doing about it. They were afraid that any effort to screen the girls for VD would be met with opprobrium stateside from both Congress and the pulpit. The military would be accused of aiding and abetting prostitution.

And so this festering health problem was ignored. At some point, however, they would at least attempt to address security problems through what was called the "guest system" by the brass and the "meat market" by the GIs. Village girls looking for GIs would enter a compound surrounded by a chain link fence. It was open from 9 A.M. to 11 P.M. GIs would peer through the fencing and pick out a "girlfriend." The girls would be searched for drugs and contraband, then be allowed to accompany the GIs to the beach, clubs or mess halls. The rest of the base was off-limits — especially the barracks. This did nothing to combat the rampant STDs (Sexually Transmitted Diseases), but it gave the military the satisfaction of implementing yet another SNAFU, that is, Situation Normal, All Fucked Up.

Leaving my shipmates in the care of Mamasan, I continued on down the beach. A gangplank led to the last bar on the water. NUMBER ONE was painted in huge letters over the entrance. I entered by pushing aside a drab red blanket hanging in the doorway. GIs in green fatigues sat drinking with Vietnamese bar girls. The women were so petite, they looked like marionettes on the soldiers' laps. A mamasan guided a six-foot GI and a "boom-boom girl" wearing a leopard-skin miniskirt into a curtained room for a quickie.

The place smelled of rotting fish and marijuana and coconut massage oil. The music did little to enliven the place. The Beach Boys' "In My Room" blared from a portable radio. Call it the Joyless Luck Club. I stuck around just long enough to down a piss-warm San Miguel.

I hitched a ride to the Base Exchange to buy some film for my camera. A couple of GIs in a jeep picked me up. They looked like high school kids — skinny, pimply, wide-eyed. Their shiny fatigues and new boots gave them away as new arrivals. Of the more than half a million troops in Vietnam only about 80,000 were combat troops. The rest languished in the massive military facilities in Saigon, Da Nang, and Cam Ranh Bay as support troops. They were restless, bored and homesick. The combat troops derisively called them "pogues." Or People Of Good Use Elsewhere. The boys had been in Cam Ranh about six months and were already chewing at the bits to get out "into the field" and see some action.

"The thing that gets you here is the sand. It's everywhere. When the wind picks up the sand gets in your boots, your clothes, your eyes."

"You get sand in your hair. Your food. Your teeth."

"In your crotch. Up your ass."

"At least out in the bush it's green, you know."

"I'm from Wisconsin, man. I miss green."

"And there's nothing to fucking do, here."

"You go to the beach and it's all guys. Yeah you can bring a local girl and they're really nice but it's not the same."

"Not enough 'round eyes.' Not enough Dollies." The Dollies were Donut Dollies, as the female Red Cross workers were called. There were never more than a hundred or so on any given base. But they provided what one T-shirt proclaimed:

A touch of home
in a combat zone
A smiling face
at a bleak fire base
The illusion of calm
in Vietnam

We drove past a shed not much larger than an outhouse with a crude sign over the window that read "RE-UP." It was where one signed up to reenlist. There was no one waiting in line.

Just up ahead, however, was a very long line that led to the new base exchange. Inside, the spacious aisles were crowded with servicemen. There were also a few Donut Dollies clutching cans of hair spray and other female ablutions. White uniform dresses, bouffant hairdos, perky expressions. The men gazed upon them as if they were movie goddesses.

The Base Exchange was like a vast shopping emporium — the Walmart of Vietnam. There were the usual items available in most small post exchanges — beer, cigarettes and the ubiquitous Zippo lighters on which the GIs would engrave with things like: "If you found this on my dead body, FUCK YOU." But there were also refrigerators, electric fans, hot plates, toasters, coffee percolators. There were high-end cameras, watches and jewelry. And an entertainment section with televisions, movie and slide projectors, portable radios, reel-to-reel tape decks and stereo record players. Little America, for sure.

Village women manned the cash registers, and one can only imagine their astonishment at the vast selection of consumer items available to the average American soldier. Their own troops, the ARVN, were lucky to get dog-meat rations and boots that fit.

I browsed through a long rack of record albums. Most were innocuous fare — Percy Faith, Eddy Arnold, Mitch Miller and the "Bing Crosby Christmas Album." But there were also the bad-ass albums of The Animals, The Rolling Stones and The Doors — background music to the war itself.

There was also a section with souvenirs from Vietnam. Embroidered shirts and blouses, silk scarves, lacquered pieces inlaid with mother-of-pearl. There were little conical straw hats with village scenes painted on them. Buddhist prayer bells, bamboo flutes. Wood carvings of camphor and cinnamon portraying water buffaloes, turtles and tigers. Almost everything had "Vietnam" written on it. Even the items made in the Philippines and Thailand.

And it struck me that for the majority of American troops these souvenirs — and the boom-boom girls, of course — might be the closest they would ever get to Vietnamese culture — a rich civilization a thousand years in the making. They would never hear the haunting melody of a *hát ru* lullaby. Or a *ca dao* poem sung *a cappella*. Or savor black frogs sautéed in garlic, fish sauce and shallots or freshwater eels wrapped in sugar and grilled over charcoal. Or witness a game of chess played with human figures. Or the elegant theater of water puppets. Or even a simple fan dance.

I wondered how much of that traditional culture could still be found in Cam Ranh village. Camera in hand, I took the long walk down to the village. The wind had kicked up, harbinger of a monsoon storm perhaps, and with it blasts of sand. I pulled my t-shirt collar up to my eyes.

The village was set on a quiet cove dotted with palm trees. It was hemmed in by barbed wire. I entered through an MP guard station. The MPs were there to check the IDs of locals entering and leaving the village. But they were less officious than one would expect and were often gracious in their interactions with the villagers. A few months earlier, two MPs had delivered the baby of a village girl in the guard station.

There were countless shacks crowded together on streets of sand. They were made of corrugated tin, plywood and whatever other scrap material was available — including Coca-cola signs. I took a photo of a girl of seven or eight drawing water from a well. The tin bucket was square and dented. In fact, every bucket and barrel, pot and bowl that I saw in the village was dimpled, dented or half-crushed. I took another photo of an old man with a wispy gray beard playing checkers with one of the few young men I saw in the village. Most of his friends, I presumed, were off fighting the war. A circle of women squatted on a crude wood platform, sharing bowls of shrimp and rice. These are people who spend much of their lives on their haunches. They ate quickly and in silence. An ancient crone stared at me, her mouth dripping with the dark red juice of betel nuts. Rats scurried among bags of rice. Rats were the culprits in the recent outbreak of plague that had infected dozens of villagers.

There was a pervasive atmosphere of listlessness in the village. An elderly women wearing shiny black pants and a rose-colored blouse lay sleeping in a street of sand. Alongside her were large straw baskets filled with *sapodillas*, custard apples and strange-looking fruits as spiky as puffer fish. The strange fruits, I would later learn, are called *sai rieng*. "One's own sorrows."

But ah the children! A dozen or so had gathered around two little girls, one playing a lute, the other a small banjo. I have no idea what the girls were singing but all the kids seemed to enjoy it and clapped along with them. An older boy — twelve perhaps and wearing a GI cap — sat on a battered trunk, smoking a cigarette and listening to them. In another time, he might have joined in, but during war, kids grow up too fast.

The next day the SS *Beaver Victory* weighed anchor and moved to the ammo pier. I stood the twelve-hour day watch, 8 A.M. to 8 P.M., to give the other mates some time ashore. At the ammo pier, the GIs worked the ships. Most of the men looked pretty green, and it took a while for them to get into the swing of things — much to the frustration of the Army stevedores — sergeants mostly — who spent the day screaming things like "You got to screw the fucking pin in the fucking shackle! Get it?! Screw fucking pin in fucking shackle!" You'd think that given the highly explosive nature of the cargo the Army would have assigned a more experienced crew to work the ship. But then it wouldn't have been SNAFU.

The GIs unloaded the deck cargo first: trucks, jeeps and tanks. One of the hoisting cradles on a tank came undone, and I cringed at the sight of it dangling over the pier, suspended only by a single cradle, its main gun pointing down. It looked like an elephant hanging from its tail and swinging this way and that. Later, the longshoremen opened the hatches to discharge the M9 flamethrowers, Claymore mines and grenade launchers. I couldn't bring myself to watch them unloading the crates of ammo, so I took my coffee up to the bridge wing and watched the sampans go by. One was rowed by a young woman in a white blouse and black pants and wearing the classic conical straw hat. Another young woman, dressed the same, trailed a leisurely hand in the water. It was a scene out of a French Impressionist painting.

Later that afternoon heavy monsoon showers rolled in, and cargo operations were halted. Hatches were closed and canvas tarps drawn over them. The GIs filed off the ship in the rains.

The wind and rain intensified, the ship rocked at the pier. I went aft to check the mooring lines. There, sitting under the sheltered fantail, were three GIs who had not left the ship with the others. They were quietly smoking dope and watching the rains. The men sported boonie hats and handlebar mustaches and had the lean and hungry looks of men just in from the field or "the bush," as the war zone was called. I asked them why they had stayed aboard. A rail-thin Indianan with a nasal twang shrugged and said they'd rather hang out by the water than back in the "fucking hootch."

The tallest of the three was a square-jawed guy with leading man good looks. But his face was drawn, and the fire had gone out in his eyes. He introduced himself as Jefferson.

"Are we cool?" he asked.

"Sure," I said.

"You want a hit?" asked the Hoosier. "It's good Buddha, man." Buddha was a marijuana joint laced with opium.

"I'm on watch."

"What are you watching for?" asked Jefferson.

"He's watching us, man," said Indiana. "He's watching us."

The Hoosier did this weird thing where he put imaginary binoculars to his eyes and pretended to be focusing on me. And the third guy — shirtless and wearing love beads and bracelets — let out this maniacal laugh. It was all a bit unsettling.

The Hoosier flipped open a P-38 — a small metal can opener — and began cutting into the tops of three cans of Iron City.

"The crew gave us some beers," said Jefferson.

"They do that," I said.

"You could kill a man with one of these," said the Hoosier holding up the can opener so I could see the razor-sharp blade shaped liked a shark's fin. "Creep up behind him. Slit the jugular."

"Out in the bush," said Jefferson. "That's what you do."

"Fucking A!" said Shirtless.

We chatted a bit, and I was surprised to hear how much they missed being in combat. "No one likes being a pogue," said Jefferson.

"Too fucking mellow back here," said the Hoosier. "Out in the bush, it's happening. You get the best dope, clean pussy."

"It's like being on a hunting trip with your buddies," said Jefferson.

"Hunting dinks," said the Hoosier.

"Pow-pow! Hunting dinks!" said Shirtless.

One downside to life in the field, they said — other than getting killed, one assumed — was the prospect of stepping on a punji stick. "The VC hide these sharp stakes in the grass."

"They smear their own shit on 'em."

"You step on one and you're fucked. Can't walk. And you get sick as a fucking dog."

The conversation was peppered with references to "dinks" and "gooks," "slopes" and "slants," "zits" and "zipperheads." Vietnamese women were "moose" or "du-mommies." "Du" meaning "fuck" in Vietnamese. Scorched with napalm, they were all "crispy critters."

I left the trio to check on the bow lines. As I eased out the forward spring, I could hear mortar fire coming from somewhere ashore. The Naval Patrol was shooting flares that illuminated the surface waters of the bay.

I went back to the fantail and the three GIs were still there. The flares cast a ghastly yellow light on their faces.

"They're looking for sappers," said Jefferson. "The VC slip into the bay using the rains for cover. Then they go to work. Sticking mines on the freighters."

"They'd love to blow up this boat," said the Hoosier. "Can you imagine, man? With all the explosive shit you're carrying?"

"I can imagine," I said.

"Fucking boat is old as hell too, right? It's falling apart. It's like this floating fucking turd."

"No offense, mate," said Jefferson.

"None taken."

"I couldn't do what you do," said Jefferson. "It's like sailing around on a Claymore mine. At least we get to shoot back. All you can do is hope they don't blow you to fucking kingdom come."

"Any second now. Ka-boom!"

"Ka-FUCKING-boom!" said Shirtless.

"Just sitting on this boat can freak you out," said the Hoosier. "Freaks me the fuck out."

And I wondered why — if they found being on an ammo ship so nerve wracking — they had remained on board. The answer came soon enough.

Jefferson lit another joint. Took a drag, passed it to Shirtless who certainly didn't need another hit. "So, mate. Would you be interested in buying some weed? It's excellent stuff."

"Ex-uh-fucking-lent-ay," said the Hoosier.

"Home grown," said Jefferson. "Which in Nam means pretty fucking good."

"From the fields of glory, man," said the Hoosier.

"The fields of fucking glory!" said Shirtless.

"We can give you a good deal," said Jefferson.

"The shit's worth big bucks back home, man. Big big big fucking bucks," said the Hoosier, grabbing his crotch for emphasis.

"You pay up front, and we bring you the dope when we come back for the day shift."

I put a Lucky Strike to my lips.

"I take it that's a maybe," said Jefferson.

"It's a 'no thanks.'"

"Suit yourself," said Jefferson clearly disappointed. "Suit yourself." He handed me his Zippo and I lit my cigarette.

"Check out the engraving, mate."

I read it by the flame of the Zippo.

We the Unwilling
Led by the Unqualified
To Kill the Unfortunate
Die for the Ungrateful.

"That's us, man," said Jefferson. "That's us."

I made my rounds again, and when I came back to the fantail the three were gone. Later that night, they were seen skulking around the crew quarters mooching beers and dealing dope — "Excellent weed, man — bad-ass shit — real cheap — we'll bring it by tomorrow" — until the bosun roused Mr. Muttle who promptly threw them off the ship.

We spent more than a week in Cam Ranh Bay as the twin demons of bad weather and military bumbling conspired to bring cargo operations to a slow crawl. But I never saw the three again. Nor did the crewmen who gave them hundreds of dollars on the promise they would deliver some excellent dope from the fields of glory. And I thought about the young GIs who had given me the lift to the PX. How long before they too were twisted, spent and jaded?

The last of our cargo would be unloaded in Da Nang, a port city further up the coast. We anchored in the explosives zone in Da Nang harbor and awaited the barges mounted with cranes that would do the unloading. The Navy Guard came aboard to watch for Viet Cong sappers. One of them told me that Bob Hope was in town for his Christmas show. It was being held on the outskirts of the city at the US military base at Freedom Hill. He was disappointed he had to stand watch and wouldn't be able to see the show. But he encouraged me to do so. "I mean they got like Raquel Welch, man. Ever see the knockers on her? Jesus!"

So I took a liberty boat ashore. Then hitched a ride to Freedom Hill in an army truck, sitting in the back with half dozen other GIs. It was great fun, laughing and drinking beer. Until the boys got a little too rowdy, tossing empty cans of beer at "dinks" walking along the road.

When I got to Freedom Hill, it was already crowded, a sea of green fatigues. I found a spot up on the hill, far, very far, from the stage. But I'd brought the ship's binoculars. There was a great roar from the crowd — Les Brown struck up the band — and I could see Miss World from Peru and Raquel Welch, and they were bumping and grinding to the Twist. And now the man himself, Bob Hope came on stage dressed in Army fatigues. Mugging and grinning, he took the mike and began his trademark deadpan patter. The speakers up here on the hill were too distorted, and I couldn't make out a word.

But after a few initial chuckles no one seemed to be laughing at Bob Hope's jokes. The silence was deafening. Though not for long. It started with a few jeers, a few catcalls. And now they were booing him. Something he said must have ticked off the grunts and swabbies and jarheads. And they were booing him. I couldn't believe it. They were booing Bob Hope. And so was I. I was booing him too. I turned to the marine next to me. "Why are we booing Bob Hope?"

"I dunno. He's an asshole." Bob Hope? I thought we loved Bob Hope. Loved the Christmas show.

On the ride back to Da Nang, everyone was quiet as sin — we'd just killed a joint — and I asked the GIs what Bob Hope had said to piss everyone off. No one seemed to know. "He's just a smug fuck," said one. "Fucking war-monger," chimed in another. "Fuck Bob Hope, you know. Fuck him and his fucking Christmas show."

On the return trip from Vietnam, the SS *Beaver Victory* carried what the military called "retrograde equipment" — broken-down tanks and helicopters, jeeps and trucks — to be repaired back in the States. Halfway home, heavy seas unleashed a half-dozen jeeps that had been lashed down on the weather deck. They wheeled around the deck as if driven by mad spirits, and smashed into each other again and again with every roll of the ship. It was like a phantom demolition derby.

The men returning from Vietnam were also retrograde equipment. But no one knew this yet.

13

THE RUIN OF MANY
A POOR BOY

There's a moon over Bourbon Street tonight
I see faces as they pass beneath the pale lamplight
I've no choice but to follow that call
The bright lights, the people, the moon and all.
　　　　　　　　　- Sting, "Moon Over Bourbon Street"

W hen we arrived in San Francisco we learned the SS *Beaver Victory* was to be laid up for repairs. No worries. I'd had it with the assortment of crazies who seemed drawn to the ammo ships like moths to a flame. And I'd had it with the ships themselves: rusty derelicts that were little more than floating mines. And so when I went down to the union hall in Frisco I was delighted to see an opening for a third mate on a ship bound for South America. I'd never been south of the equator and just pronouncing "Buenos Aires" was a thrill. This was why I had gone to sea in the first place. To explore the Buenos Aires of the world — not to make endless voyages to the same disheartening destination. Buenos Aires, *sí!*

My heart sank though when a mate with more shore time than I bid on it. "Shit!" I said, a little too loudly.

The old-timer studied me for a long moment. But his glare slowly softened into a look of sympathy. Perhaps he saw the glazed look in my own eyes — the thousand-yard stare one gets from riding too many ghost ships to the war zone. He asked me if I had a cigarette. "Sure."

I offered him a Lucky, and his hand shook as he took it. He had the DTs of a gas hound and could barely hold the match flame to the cigarette.

"What was your last ship?" he asked.

"An old Victory. Carried tanks and ammo to the usual shit-holes."

He nodded.

"You want that ship, kid?"

"Yes. I'd like it. Be good to go somewhere else for a change."

"It's yours."

"Thanks, mate."

"Thanks for the cigarette."

The SS *Crescent City* was berthed in the Crescent City itself: New Orleans. I grabbed the first available flight and after a pleasant flight — first class, no less — arrived in the Big Easy that same night. The taxi driver I hailed at the airport was a smooth-talking man with a Creole accent as thick as Mississippi mud.

"So you be wantin' duh port." I had to think about that. It was about 10 P.M. and I was pretty hungry. I asked him what time the restaurants closed.

"Close? Dey don't never close, mon. Dis is Nu-Awlins. Yes-suh. You wan' de Nu-Awlins gumbo. Crawdaddies, shrimps, fat-back crab, tomaters, awn-yons, pinch of feel-ay. Youse put it all in two fingers of waw-tuh. Yessuh. Aw-kra. Yessuh. Sweet sawsage. Yessuh. Hot sawsage. Yessuh!"

That settled it. I'd check in with the ship first; dump my sea-bag, see what time they were setting sail, then head down to the French Quarter and grab a bite to eat and a well deserved drink.

We drove down streets with names like Napoleon and Cal-
liope and Tchoupitoulas until we reached the port area. The Port
of New Orleans is like something out of Fritz Lang's *Metropolis*.
Warehouses, silos, towers, tanks and cranes crowd the landscape.
Countless railroad tracks crisscross the yards. Big lumbering semis
and tankers rumble about. At night the whole scene is illuminated
by a colorful array of lights — red, amber, blue, white, yellow.

The port boasts the longest wharf in the world — almost two
miles long. It can serve fifteen ships at once. The freighters bring
in sugar, steel, coffee, rubber, and gypsum. They carry out corn,
wheat, soybeans, cars and manufactured goods. Chiquita Banana,
meet King Corn. The Port of New Orleans is an integral part of
the world's digestive system. As we wove our way through Metropolis, the taxi driver talked on about the drinks I should sam-
ple while in town. Creole Mary, Mint Julep, Sazerac.

"And you gots to have de Hurricane. Yessuh de Hurricane.
One part light rum. One part dahk rum. A splash of Grenadine.
Lime juice, orange juice. And juice of de passion fruit. Yessuh.
De passion fruit. The wimmens like dat passion fruit. Hee-hee.
And we got some wimmens here in Nu-Awlins. Yessuh! Ever
color you want. Black wimmen, white wimmen, brown wimmen,
yaller wimmen. Me, I like every color. Ever color wimmen. Long
as she gots some meat on de bone."

I asked if there was any place he recommended.

"I likes to heah de music. Maison Bourbon. Yessuh! Nu-Awlins jazz. Yessuh yessuh yessuh!" He be-bopped a little number.

Wow, I thought. Wine, women and song. Sounding better all
the time. But first: find the damn ship.

She was slated to be docked at Pier 7 in the Henry Clay terminal — the world's longest wharf. Dodging heavy cargo traffic we
managed to find Pier 7. But no *Crescent City*. Instead there was
a banana boat flying a Panamanian flag. I checked in at a security
trailer, where we were informed there was no *Crescent City* at
the Henry Clay terminal. He suggested we try the adjacent Milan
Street terminal.

And so we drove on, looking for a ship. There was no sign of her at the Milan Street Terminal, nor the Nashville Avenue Wharves nor the Jourdan Road Terminal. It was now close to midnight. I was very hungry and dying for a drink, but where was the damn ship?

She's at the France Road Terminal, a dispatcher said. They had moved her there just today. The taxi driver scratched his head. He'd never heard of the France Road Terminal. It's not on the river, the dispatcher said. It's on the Industrial Canal. In Desire. Desire is where the eponymous streetcar made its last stop.

En route, the driver took me through the French Quarter. And there it was: the Vieux Carre, with its gaslights and the bold colors of the tropics and lacey iron balconies festooned with hanging ferns and bougainvilleas. Music poured out of every doorway. Signs beckoned: Jazz Night! Get Down in the Bayou! Creole Marys two for one! And there they were: Black wimmen, white wimmen, brown wimmen, yaller wimmen. Yessuh! Ever color you want. It was a sweltering New Orleans night and they were all in mini-skirts and micro-minis. Legs gleamed with sweat.

At first I thought: Hell, why not dash in for a quick bite and a drink or two. But no. This was not a QuickStop. This was a place to be savored at a leisurely pace. Besides, I needed to drop off my damn sea bag and sextant on the ship.

As we left Bourbon Street in our wake, the neighborhoods quickly changed. They seemed to deteriorate with every block, and none were as rundown as Desire. No wonder the streetcar went no further. I didn't want to either. It was not so much the poverty, as the sullen intimidating looks of its inhabitants. Black men huddled on street corners, liquor bottles in hand. Glaring at everything that passed by, especially the white boy in the taxi. Even the driver seemed a little spooked by the place. "We calls it de Dirty D," he said. "You wants to get robbed, you come to de Dirty D."

At last we found the France Road Terminal. There was no one at the guard station. We drove in anyway. And there was the

Crescent City, docked at a lonely pier. There was no sign of life anywhere and very few lights. The ship itself was streaked with rust. The mooring lines badly frayed. A rat scampered down one of them.

I asked the driver to wait for me, and he said fine, but he needed to be paid for this trip first. "Yessuh, you gots to pay me fuhst. De sailor disappear. Not dat you would, suh, but de sailor disappear. Yessuh. Dey disappear on de ship widdout paying."

"Okay," I said as I paid him, "but you'll wait right here, okay?"

He looked around nervously. "Yessuh. I be heah."

I grabbed my seabag and sextant and made my way up the accommodation ladder. The rail was loose and the ladder was missing a few steps. A cargo light trained on it was flickering and spitting as if the bulb were about to blow. And the ship was awfully quiet.

An old black man in a guard's uniform appeared.

"Can I help you, suh?"

"I'm the new third mate."

"T'ird mate?" He studied me with eyes glazed over with cataracts.

"The third officer, eight-to-twelve watch. Where's the crew?"

"Ain't no crew."

"What about the captain?"

"Ain't no captain."

"This is the *Crescent City*."

"Yessuh."

"Bound for Buenos Aires."

"No suh. She ain't bound for nowhere."

"No, I have the papers right here." I flashed them before his opaque eyes. "SS *Crescent City*. New Orleans to Belém. Buenos Aires. Montevideo."

"She ain't bound for nowhere. 'Cepting maybe de scrap yawd."

"The scrap yard."

"Yessuh. You lookin' at a whole lot of metal heah. Gots to be woith somet'in."

I heard the taxi take off. "Hey hey!" I shouted. I stumbled halfway down the gangway after him. Too late. The taxi disappeared into the New Orleans night.

"He gwine home, dat mon. Nobody stay here. Dey too scared."

"Of what?"

"You don't wanna be knowin', suh. You don't wanna be knowing."

"Jesus."

"You welcome to stay aboard. Ain't nobody bother you on de ship."

"No, I'll find a hotel. Maybe downtown somewhere."

"How you gwine to gets dere? Ain't no taxis round heah."

"I'll walk til I find one."

"You gwine to walk in de Desire. At night. All by yo' lonesome? You got de Lawd wit' you, suh? Cause you gonna need de Lawd wit' you, if'n you be walkin' in de Dirty D all by yo' lonesome at night. Yessuh. And a white boy, too. You gwine to need de Lawd."

I have had the Lord with me in many a rough port. And I've also had a kind of sixth sense for trouble and enough street savvy to avoid it: wallet in front pocket — avoid dark areas — keep to middle of street — walk quickly with the bearing of a gladiator. The closest I came to a dangerous encounter was one night in Amsterdam. I was with Stymie, the pint-sized French-Canadian, and we were three-sheets-to-the-wind looking for a tattoo parlor. We'd been told there was one somewhere near Canal Street but somehow ended up in a dark alleyway. There we encountered a gang of Elvis look-a-likes. They were Rockers. Many young people in Europe had fallen into two camps: Mods and Rockers. Mods wore their hair in moptops and dressed like and listened to the Beatles. The Rockers wore their hair in pompadours, dressed like Elvis and listened to the Stones. The only thing they had in common was their disdain for Americans in uniform.

I asked one of the Rockers — not only the biggest but the one who sported the most enormous pompadour — if there was a tattoo parlor nearby. He looked to his gang, then to me. Then snapped open a switchblade.

"I give you tattoo," he said in a thick Dutch accent.

Well, he didn't know who he was fucking with. No, not me. I was quaking in my shoes. But Stymie. Stymie had that short man thing going for him. "Short people have no reason to live?" I don't think so, Randy Newman. They have a feistiness that can be downright intimidating. Plus a fight with the small man is a lose-lose situation. You look bad if you beat him, and worse if you don't. Short people know this. Stymie knew this. He stepped between me and the Rocker.

"Put the fucking blade away."

The Rocker looked back at his friends — ooh, check out the little guy — but closed the knife.

"Funny little man," he said.

"You want to see how funny?"

"Oooh," he said again in mock fear. But he and his gang moved on, taunting us with Dutch epithets like *hondenluls.* Dog dicks. We would be mugged verbally instead. Which was fine by me.

But back in New Orleans I was not up for another walk on the wild side. Especially without Stymie. I wandered around the ship instead. A dark and abandoned one at that. The guard had lent me his flashlight, and I had to keep whacking it to maintain a beam. The officers' quarters were on the boat deck and I entered a small cabin with a chair, desk and rack. I threw my sea bag on the chair, set my sextant down on the desk and stripped the bedding off the rack. The mattress was mottled with stains that I dared not identify. I saw a pair of worn loafers on the deck; the previous occupant must have been in a hurry to leave. I went into the head and saw in the open medicine chest: a shaving brush, denture cleanser (how old was this guy?), and a bottle of Aqua Velva.

I made my way up to the bridge and sat in the captain's chair. And I thought what a strange profession this is. How many people show up at a new job only to learn their workplace is about to be converted into a pile of razor blades?

Still, it was a perfectly fine night. Warm, sultry even. I had two or three little bags of peanuts from the plane to ease the hunger pangs. Oh, and look: a bag of pretzels! I shook the bottle of Aqua Velva. There was certainly enough left for a gentle buzz at least. And yes, there would be music too. The flickering of the cargo light created a kind of dance club ambience. And so I sang to an audience of one:

There is a house in New Orleans
They call the Rising Sun
And it's been the ruin of many a poor boy
And God I know I'm one.

14

THE HUNGRY SEA

*A singular disadvantage of the sea lies in the fact that
after successfully surmounting one wave you discover
that there is another behind it just as important.*
- Stephen Crane "The Open Boat"

The SS *Potomac* rode up and down the steep swells — sea
and sky roiling in a dozen shades of gray — prop spinning idly, engine shot. Flying from the halyard were two
black balls signaling VESSEL NOT UNDER COMMAND, that
is, helplessly adrift. And all anyone talked about was the Rock.
Rumors circulate like cheap dope and liquor on a merchant ship,
and word had it that somewhere in the North Atlantic was an
uncharted islet about the size of a large boulder. "'Tis like a fist
of stone," said Peeper, the Irish seaman on my watch. "A fist
of stone thrust up from the ocean floor. Many a ship has been
hurled against the Rock in seas like these, Mate. And neither ship
nor men were ever heard from again."

"That's why we have radar," I said.

"Radar? Hah! Good luck with that. The Rock, you see, is
covered with a sheen of moss. A sheen of moss. Which makes it
completely invisible to radar."

"That's why we keep a lookout."

"Lookout? I can see you don't know much about the Rock, sir. You see the sheen is such that it perfectly reflects the color of the surrounding waters. Which makes it completely invisible to the eye as well. That's why 'tis never been charted. No one knows where 'tis. Oh, but you'll see it all right. And when you do, t'will be the last piece of land you'll ever see."

Peeper hailed from the village of Knockalough, and was as pale, spooky and twitchy as a white rabbit. He had the disconcerting habit of peeking into the portholes of officer's staterooms. Particularly those of young men like me. Hence the nickname "Peeper." He was also given to Cassandrian warnings, dour admonitions about everything from the ship's food ("I hope you didn't eat that pork tonight. People die from trichinosis.") to the ship's bedding ("'Tis rife with microscopic mites! And those mites love human flesh, Mate. Especially ... the testicles.")

Still, even if one shrugged off the rants of a ditzy seaman, our present situation was grim. We were lost and adrift in a raging North Atlantic storm on an aging relic from World War II, a converted T-2 tanker carrying 25,000 tons of coal. But Captain Fen Knudsvig seemed uncharacteristically quiet about our present situation. Also known as "The Man Who Knew Too Much," the captain loved sharing his encyclopedic knowledge with the captive audience that was his subordinate officers. At every meal, he would give lengthy dissertations on subjects as diverse as "The Origins of Limburger Cheese" or "Why the Sky Appears Blue."

But Knudsvig had no answer to our most pressing question: Where the hell were we? We were out of range of LORAN and RDF signals, and had to rely on celestial navigation. Unfortunately we were drifting under a swirling mass of clouds. Sun, stars and moon had not been visible for days. Should the ship begin to take on water — should we need to radio for assistance, we could not give the rescuers our position. We were, as the Brits say, stuffed.

I had signed on the SS *Potomac* in Philadelphia. After that long lonely night aboard the *Crescent City* in New Orleans, I went to the union hall the next day. There I worked myself up into a royal rant over the bungled job call, cursing the union, the shipping company and the merch itself. Yadda yadda yadda. The dispatcher looked at me dispassionately. "What ship you want?" he said.

"What?"

He pointed to the job board. "What ship you want?"

"Really?"

I looked up at the job board. There were several third mate jobs, but all but one were bound for Vietnam. There was however one temp job on a ship in Philadelphia. She was bound for ports in Northern Europe. Which meant fine stout and stout women.

"I'll take that one," I said. "The *Potomac*."

"She's a coal ship bound for Rotterdam. Sails tomorrow. You'll need to catch a flight out today if you want her."

By the time I arrived at the coal dock in Philadelphia, the ship was already battened down and ready to go. I had no sooner signed the ship's articles when the mooring lines were cast off. There was this sense of urgency. They were worried about a tropical storm that was brewing just off the Carolinas and heading north.

"Does anyone know the first officially named hurricane?" asked Captain Fen Knudsvig in the officers' mess. The chief engineer rolled his eyes: here we go again. The chief mate — rigorously sawing an overcooked pork chop with his butter knife — simply ignored him. Babilée, the second mate, a Frenchman from Marseilles, cocked his head to one side with an insipid smile that said: "Do you zink that I even give a sheet?" The captain turned to me.

"Do you know the first officially named hurricane?"

"No sir, I don't."

The captain smiled. This was the correct answer. Every question posed by the captain was rhetorical. The tradition of naming tropical storms, he informed us, began in 1953 with Hurricane Alice. Before then, only the most severe storms were named such as the Galveston Hurricane of 1900. "Which I'm sure you are too young to remember," he added. The captain was a witty man as well.

I did remember Hurricane Diane. It came hard on the heels of Hurricane Connie and pounded the Hudson Valley in August of 1955. Diane was less known for its wind damage and more for its heavy rains and catastrophic flooding. We were living in a small flat-roofed cottage in Vancortlandtville on the Westchester-Putnam border. Across the road was a small stream fed by the murky lake that was our swimming hole. Then along came Diane and its torrential rains. In just a few hours the lake overflowed its banks flooding the surrounding roads. Our little stream was now a raging river. Rain slashed against our window panes, and rat-a-tat-tatted against our door like woodpeckers. We were kids — boys — and it was exciting. We ventured outside in our swimsuits to play in the liquid maelstrom. Surprisingly, my father the Artist — in his pork pie hat, trench coat and galoshes — joined us. He warned us away from the roaring brook, but the front lawn — now a pond — was all ours. We splashed around and kicked the water at each other joyfully.

And that's when I saw them. Giant reptiles coming down the rain-slicked road like a division of army tanks.

"Hey, look!" I shouted. "Snapping turtles!"

"They must have come from the lake," said the Artist. And he was clearly unnerved by the sight of them. He turned to the little ones, Garrett and Brian. "Back inside!"

"But I want to see the turtles," said Garrett.

"I said: back inside!" He quickly herded both boys into the house, but for some reason — a privilege of primogeniture perhaps — left me outside to witness the march of the turtles. There were at least a dozen of them. I could see their thick necks and fierce jaws. They were each maybe two feet long, and weighed 30 or 40 pounds. They hissed and stank. I was thrilled. The boy in me loved the turtles. And loved the storm that brought them into our world.

But a hurricane on the high seas would not be child's play. And the SS *Potomac* was making an ocean crossing at the height of the season. This was the first year in which the National Hurricane Center was in operation. While June, July and August were reported as unusually calm, the Center warned that the prospects of a quiet September were slim. As the old tanker cruised down the Delaware River on that fine September morning, there were tropical waves forming everywhere in the mid-Atlantic.

In fact, one was stirring to life somewhere west of the Cape Verde Islands. Within days it would become a fast moving tropical storm heading northwest across the mid-Atlantic. The soon-to-be-named Hurricane Arlene was on a collision course with the *Potomac*. But no one — not even our most erudite captain — knew this yet. Instead, we were determined to outrun a weak tropical depression off Cape Hatteras.

The Delaware is a broad, sluggish, heavily-trafficked river. Where it flows into Delaware Bay, it's bordered by salt marshes of Spartina grass. Crabbers and flounder fishermen work the shallows, while a parade of tankers and freighters follow the ship channels dredged in the bay. At its mouth, two capes form a kind of pincer. Cape Henlopen to the south is a state park with swimming beaches on both the bay side and the ocean side. Cape May to the north is a classic seaside resort. Its waterfront is lined with Victorian homes called "painted ladies" for the dainty colors on their gingerbread trim, their gables and turrets. Standing watch over all is a classic lighthouse: a tall, white tower.

In his book *The Atlantic*, Simon Winchester described the Flemish paintings of the 16th century. "Invariably there is the hungry sea, its waves translucent green and white-capped, the troughs between them deep and dangerous and all providing a savage contrast to the distant comforts of cow-grazed meadows and church steeples."

And I wondered for how many sailors lost at sea the storybook village of Cape May — the quintessence of hearth and home — was the last sight of a world they would leave behind forever.

As we left Cape May on our port quarter, the sea was calm as a duck pond. The ship glided through an endless series of long lazy swells. The sky was clear — exceptionally so — and bright blue. The air was thick and warm.

"I don't like it," said Peeper. "'Tis a harbinger of worse to come. You can rest assured of that, mate."

For once, he was right. They were the signs of an impending tropical storm. By evening there was a sheen of cirrus haze in the skies, growing thicker. And the barometer, at first oscillating as if in denial, began its inexorable plunge downward.

We were en route to a rendezvous with Arlene.

Before the advent of weather satellites, ships on the high seas were mostly dependent on observations made aboard ship. Watch officers would routinely note barometric pressure and temperature, wind speed and direction, sea and swells, cloud forms and precipitation.

For estimating wind speeds, one relied mostly on the Beaufort scale. It was devised in 1805 by Royal Irish Navy officer Francis Beaufort, and it's still a useful guide today. One gauges the wind by reading the surface of the sea. Ripples and wavelets whose crests have a glassy appearance indicate a light breeze with winds of four to six knots. When the sea heaps up and foam from the breaking waves is blown in streaks, it is a near gale with winds of 28 to 33 knots. And when there are huge waves, "the sea completely white with foam and the air filled with driving spray" you're in a hurricane with winds blowing more than 73 knots.

But reading the sea in the open ocean is not as simple or straightforward as the Beaufort scale would lead you to believe. "It's a confusing pattern that the waves make in the open sea," wrote Rachel Carson in *The Sea Around Us*, "a mixture of countless different wave trains, intermingling, overtaking, passing or sometimes engulfing one another ... some doomed never to reach any shore, others destined to roll across half an ocean before they dissolve in thunder on a distant beach."

Mariners also seek clues to imminent weather conditions in cloud formations. A parade of white fluffy cumulous clouds means fair weather ahead. Wispy cirrus clouds called "mares' tails" are the first signs of an approaching system. The ripples of altocumulus that form a mackerel sky mean the storm is now closer.

Sky colors too are important. "A dark, gloomy blue sky is windy," notes the *Merchant Marine Deck Officers' Handbook.* "But a light, bright blue sky indicates fine weather ... and by the preponderance of red, yellow or gray tints the coming weather can be foretold very nearly — indeed if aided by instruments, almost accurately." One rule of thumb dates back some 2,000 years. "Red sky at night, sailors delight. Red sky in morning, sailors take warning." Sailors love their rhymes, especially when it comes to the weather.

"Mackerel sky, mackerel sky: never long wet, never long dry."

"Rainbow to windward, foul fall the day; rainbow to leeward, rain runs away."

"Beware the bolts from north or west; in south or east the bolts be best."

"A backing wind says storms are nigh, veering winds will clear the sky."

Mariners also foretell the weather from the appearance of haloes and coronas around the sun or moon. The halo is a rainbow-colored ring with the red band nearest the celestial body. It's a harbinger of fair weather. A corona has narrower rings with blue as inner band. If the corona grows smaller in size, a storm is approaching.

Moon dogs and sun dogs, moon bows and fog bows, glories and auroras. Crepuscular rays and St. Elmo's fire and *Fata Morgana.* All are celestial wonders that for millennia have presaged the coming weather.

With the advent of radio transmissions in the 1930s, shipboard observations were routinely radioed in to the U.S. Weather Bureau. There they were compiled and retransmitted in code back out to the ships at sea. Every ship in radio contact had access to this information where it could be used to create a synoptic chart of the weather.

On the SS *Potomac*, that task fell to me. Always the weather maven, I looked forward to it. We were about two hundred miles east northeast of Cape May, when I drew the first one. I laid a sheet of tracing paper over a small scale chart — that is, a chart that covered the North Atlantic Ocean — then penciled in symbols for wind direction and speed as well as barometric readings. Where a clear pattern was seen I drew isobars to identify centers of highs and lows.

I sketched in a low pressure area off Greenland. Another off the coast of Ireland. But I had little information south of our position. Most of the data came from vessels sailing in well-traveled shipping lanes. Outside of these highways in the sea, there was a paucity of observations, especially in the lower latitudes, birthplace of tropical storms. Until the advent of weather satellites, hurricanes like Arlene could swirl across the high seas with little indication of where they were headed. A smaller system might even go unnoticed.

The only clues to Arlene's imminent arrival lie in our own shipboard observations. The barometer was falling steadily now, and there was that tell-tale veil of cirrus clouds on the southeastern horizon. With my back to the wind, my left hand pointed to the center of the low: southeast of us. If it followed the normal trajectory for storms in the North Atlantic, it was headed our way.

To Captain Fen Knudsvig, there was still no cause for alarm. We held our course: great circle for Lands End, England. His thinking, one assumed, was that it would take us far enough north of whatever was brewing southeast of us. But we were not privy to his reasoning. For that night, as the ship steamed through ever-steeper swells and the wind whistled in the rigging, he expounded on the origin of the tin can. The first ones were so thick, he informed us, they had to be pounded open with a hammer.

Unlike, say, the tin can that was the SS *Potomac*. T-2s had hulls that consisted of "dirty steel" plates that had been hastily welded together in the rush of the war effort. Now decades later, the tankers were breaking apart like eggshells — especially under the stress of storms like this one. Five ships had sunk in the space of four months; two tankers went down in the same storm, in the same place, on the same day. One lost its battle with forty-foot waves when its forward hatches crumbled. The hold filled with water and she quickly sank, drowning all but three of her crew. Another split apart at the bow, taking the officers and crew to the bottom.

Come morning, the sky was a sheet of metal. I was on the eight-to-twelve watch, out on the bridge wing gauging how to dodge the approaching squalls. I could see on the horizon, great streaks of lightning illuminating the boiling seas.

The chief mate, bosun and a few other deckhands were making their way forward, checking and retightening the metal fasteners or "dogs" on each of the five hatch covers. Some dogs were missing, some frozen. On other hatches the coaming itself — the raised barrier designed to keep water out of the holds — was almost rusted through in places. This was not good. Many a freighter has gone down because of seawater in the holds.

Out on the bridge wing, the wind was so stiff — maybe 45 knots and gusting higher — that I could barely stand. I was drenched from the spray that flew skyward with every pitch of the ship into the heaving swells. And we were still not in the heart of the tempest. I had no business being out on the bridge wing, of course. But this was my first great storm at sea. And the boy in me wanted to savor every moment of it. It was like something out of Jack London.

Jack London was just seventeen years old when he signed on a three-masted schooner bound for the Far East. Somewhere off the coast of Japan, the ship encountered a typhoon. He described his experience in *The Cruise of the Snark*. "The wind snatched the whitecaps from their summits filling the air so thick with driving spray that it was impossible to see more than two waves at a time." Despite his youth, he was called to take the wheel, thus putting in his grasp "the wildly careening schooner and the lives of twenty-two men." A huge wave came over the stern. "I saw it coming, and, half drowned, with tons of water crushing me, I checked the schooner's rush to broach to." To "broach to" is to capsize. That the schooner didn't was a defining moment in Jack London's life. "My delight was that I had done it ... Life that lives is life successful."

Well we were certainly living life on the *Potomac*. The seas were now a cauldron of white foam. The wind was howling in the rigging. One rogue wave hit us straight on sending the bow lurching skyward and me stumbling backward where a random gust would have sent me over the rail and into the hungry sea. Time for the boy to come inside. I had the AB — an old Greek named Homer of all things — take the ship off autopilot and steer by hand on the big wheel of wood and brass.

The captain soon joined me on the bridge. He was wearing his customary uniform of sweat pants, sweat shirt and sneakers. His parrot — yes, his parrot — was on his shoulder where it shat at will.

"The bird doesn't like this weather," said Captain Knudsvig.

"And we're in for it too, sir."

The bird squawked in anxiety.

"Does it have a name?" I asked.

"It's a bird for god sakes. Why would it have a name?"

Both bird and captain were uncharacteristically quiet as I showed Knudsvig my latest synoptic chart. The storm had moved into the shipping lanes, and a flurry of weather observations had been forwarded to us by the Weather Service. It now had a name: Arlene. A hurricane is divided into four quadrants; the most dangerous is the right front quadrant where the speed of the wind is added to the movement of the storm itself. We were now on the outer edge of that quadrant.

The plotted lows showed Arlene was moving at about thirteen knots heading due north. In general, a hurricane will turn to the northeast as it approaches the higher latitudes. That was same direction the SS *Potomac* was sailing. If we continued on our current course we could be traveling with the storm for days.

Whereas if we simply hove to — that is, if we cut our engine speed and simply rode out the storm — we would soon fall safely behind it. It would outrun us. Provided it did indeed turn northeast. If it continued on its current path — hove to or not — we would be in for some rough sailing.

Captain and bird stared at the rain now slashing against the bridge windows. It was like being in a car wash.

"Half ahead on the engines," he said at last.

"Half ahead, sir." I rang the engine telegraph. And the brass pointer rang half ahead in response.

"What's your heading?" he asked Homer at the wheel.

"Maybe oh-thirty degrees, sir. She's swinging all over the place."

"Where's the wind, mate?"

"From the east, Captain."

"Let's keep on this heading for a while and see what she does." The parrot squawked in agreement.

At noon, I was relieved by the other third mate, an affable man named Billy Farrell who had the disconcerting habit of forgetting to shower or shave. He'd show up on the bridge with bed hair, day old facial stubble and sleep in his eyes, his khakis all wrinkled as if he'd slept in them — which he might have for all I knew. But he was a good hearted soul with nary an ill word for anyone.

He stepped into the rolling wheelhouse and went slip-sliding across the deck, like Chaplin in that tottering cabin in *The Gold Rush.*

"Are those slippers, you're wearing?" said the captain.

"Oh. Yeah. Guess I need my shoes, eh?"

The parrot squawked in agreement.

"Does it have a name, sir?" asked Farrell.

"It's a bird for god sakes. Why would it have a name?"

I went down to my cabin thinking my life was now in the hands of a disheveled space cadet, a book worm for a skipper and a snarly parrot. Someone had puked in the passageway outside my cabin, and the smell of it made me nauseous as well. My cabin too was a mess. Books and stuff thrown all over the place. Despite cutting the engine speed, we were still taking a brutal pounding from the incoming waves.

That evening I skipped dinner — couldn't eat anyway — and headed back up to the bridge to relieve Monsieur Babilée who stood the four-to-eight watch. The captain and the chief engineer were in the chartroom having a heated argument. The captain had insisted that we continue heading into the seas, the engine driving us into the waves. The chief strongly disagreed.

"This floating piece of shit cannot take a pounding," he said. "She was not made to take a pounding." He wanted to allow the ship to fall off the wind and take her own position relative to sea direction. Even if it meant wallowing in the troughs of the swells.

"She's too deeply laden," said the captain. "She'll ship too much water."

"We can run her at half speed, so she won't take on so much."

The ship rose up over a massive wave and slammed down into the trough with a boom! Then rose up again shaking like a wet mutt.

"You feel that?! We're gonna pop every fucking weld on the ship!" The chief engineer had good reason to be concerned. The SS *Potomac* was originally about 500 feet long, but a few years before our voyage, another 75 feet was added to her length. The segment of a hull of another WW II vintage T2 had been welded in amidships. The chief didn't trust the welds or the "dirty steel" of the hull itself.

"Brownie, you do your job. I'll do mine," said the Man Who Knew Too Much. And that was that. End of discussion. The Chief stormed out of the chart room.

For the next twelve hours green seas rolled across the length of the ship. They pounded the masts and superstructure. The waves had huge white overhanging crests that evoked the classic woodprint "The Great Wave" by Okusai.

One danger on a bulk cargo ship in heavy seas is that it will nose down so deeply into an incoming swell that it will simply never come up again — like a harpoon thrown into the sea. Or should the ship lie perfectly poised on the crest of the wave, the prop can spin in the air like a child's pinwheel causing a burnout.

And that's what happened to the SS *Potomac.*

"The thrust bearing is shot," said Chief Brown glaring at the captain. "Are you happy now?" The thrust from the propeller is transmitted to the hull via the thrust bearing. No bearing, no thrust. No thrust, no movement. The ship was dead in the water. And we might soon be too.

We hoisted the two black balls that indicated "Vessel not under command," that is, without power. We next had to fix our position which led to another confrontation with the captain, this time from Ruggles, the chief mate. Ruggles was a small, boney, gray-haired man in his fifties. He was quiet and competent.

"I wouldn't trust that fix, captain. No stars. No horizon. Ship rolling like hell. Can't see how he got it. It's too fucking perfect." He was talking about the navigation fix taken by Babilée, the Frenchman. Babilée, as second mate, was our navigator. He took morning and evening star sights. In celestial navigation, star sights are the most accurate because they give you the most lines of position — one for each star. Should they all intersect at the same point — like an asterisk — then you can be fairly sure of your position.

On our first day out on the open sea, I had joined Babilée to take evening stars, just to keep my skills up. Every star sight I took kissed the horizon perfectly in my sextant mirror. Still, after going through the calculations, my plotted lines intersected in a kind of trapezoid. But Babilée's fix was exquisite. Every line intersected at the same point. A perfect asterisk. An indisputable navigational fix. When I complimented him, he gave me that classic Gallic shrug and said "Eet comes only with eggs-pair-ee-awnse." Experience.

But days later, with an overcast sky melded into a gray horizon, the ship rocking and rolling in choppy seas, and not a star in sight, Babilée still produced an absolutely perfect star fix. When I asked him how he was able to do so, he gave me a Maurice Chevalier wink and said again, "Eggs-pair-ee-awnse." Who was I to doubt him? What did I know? Besides, why would he knowingly plot a false position?

"Because they are like that!" said the chief mate when the captain posed the same question. "It's a French thing. Everything has to be *tres* fucking elegant. He thinks he's a fucking artist with his perfect fucking star fixes. He thinks he's Monet."

"What's done is done," said the Man Who Knew Too Much. There was no sense confronting the second mate. There was no way to prove his navigation fix was bogus. On the other hand, the captain couldn't radio it in as our Last Known Position. We had no Last Known Position.

And that's when the rumors of the mysterious uncharted island began to circulate among the crew. Instigated by Peeper, of course. "Aye, the Rock," said Peeper who now wore his lifejacket 24/7, a lifeboat whistle hanging from his neck like a St Christopher medal. "'Twas sighted by St. Brendan — you know, the Irish monk who first discovered America. Not that the fooking dagos would ever admit it. But he did indeed, a t'ousand years before Columbus. 'Tis all in Brendan's account of his crossing. He sailed from Ireland in a curragh with fourteen monks. All witnesses, mind you, to what he discovered. An island paradise of birds, another full of grapes ... And then there was the Rock. It was cold and wet and barren and in the middle of the sea. And you know who lived on that Rock, mate?"

"I have no idea."

"Judas Iscariot himself. Banished there by the Lord. And haunted there by demons from Hell. Many a lost ship has met her end on that Rock, Mate." And for emphasis: "Many a ship as lost as we are."

By now the storm had definitely turned northeast, following our original track. It would outrun us, yes, but leave in its wake an expanse of steep swells that extended for hundreds of miles. With no power, all we could do was ride them out. Slip-sliding up and down steep walls of water. Up on the bridge, I was mesmerized by the clinometer. We rolled thirty degrees this way, thirty degrees that way. Oops! there's a roll of thirty-five. With every roll I held onto whatever was handy: the radar housing, a compass binnacle, the captain's chair. The human body is not made to scamper uphill and downhill every minute of every hour of every merciless day. To walk along the passageway was to slam violently against one puke-splattered wall, take a few steps, then slam violently against the other. Then there were the rogue swells that tilted the ship almost 45 degrees and spilled you out of your bunk or your chair or off your feet and onto the deck and sent a frisson of fear up your spine. Oh, Jesus this is the one! We're going over! – oh man! Oh God! Oh fuck!

Looking through the porthole of my cabin, I could see nothing but gray skies one moment, gray seas the next. Seated in my desk chair was like riding in a roller coaster car sitting sideways. I slept – well not slept actually – I rolled around in my bunk for hour after hour. I thought about putting my lifejacket on. But what would be the point? Should the ship capsize I would no doubt be trapped in my cabin and go down with her. It was frustrating knowing that my fate was completely out of my hands. It was all up to this mindless, meteorological meta-system that would never take into account my worth as a human being, such as it was.

And all this went on for five long days. Five long days of rocking and rolling in enormous swells. The officer's mess lived up to its name. There was kitchenware scattered everywhere: plates, cups, utensils, serving trays. The mess men were green as aliens. They sat on the deck, backs against the wall, rocking side to side in unison like Buddhist monks in prayer. Hoping that no one would show up to be served. Not to worry. No one did. We survived on Saltines and Ginger Snaps.

And throughout it all, there was no sign of our captain. I imagined him in his mahogany chair, absorbed in a thick volume of the *Encyclopedia Britannica* reading about Emperor penguins. The Bird peering over his shoulder and squawking obscenities.

Meanwhile, deep in the bowels of the ship, the black gang worked on as if Man Could Make a Difference. I thought it might assuage my gnawing fear to see them at work. I pulled up the lever on the heavy metal door that led to the engine room, and the heaving ship swung the door towards me with such force it almost knocked me down. I quickly stepped onto the grated landing, and the door slammed shut behind me. It was jungle-hot in the engine room, and it smelled like metal and oil and sweat. And it was loud: the rumbling of the steam engine in concert with the roar of the hurricane. The scene below the landing evoked Chaplin's *Modern Times*. There were massive boilers and condensers, and myriad pipes and tubing of all sizes — nickel and copper colored and asbestos white. Some ran parallel to each other; others elbowed off to feed various gizmos. There were countless steam and water gauges, white letters on black face, black letters on white face. And two large brass wheels, one with the spokes painted red, another with the spokes painted green. The main circulator pump squatted in a command position like a giant R2D2. A sign warned: ALWAYS USE TORCH WHEN LIGHTING OFF BURNER.

I carefully descended the narrow steps, leaning this way and that with every roll of the ship, hands gripping thin metal railings that were hot to the touch.

And there was the black gang: gathered around the massive drive shaft. The engine crew is called the black gang because in the days when ships were fueled by coal, men shoveled the nuggets into boiler ovens, and were soon all in blackface from the coal dust. Now they were covered with grease and grunge and sweat. I was always amazed that anyone would want to be an engineer or oiler or wiper. Why would you choose to spend eight hours a day in a sweltering, stinking, roaring inferno? This was where they sent you after you've lived a life of sin. But there they were, working away on the thrust bearing. And in a raging storm to boot. The rolling ship tossed men and tools about like playthings. Loud curses would break through the incessant din. But they'd pick themselves up and resume whatever they were doing with their wrenches and hammers and blow torches. I saw the chief engineer — gulping down what must have been a quart of water. Then he saw me. He pointed to the water bottle and without so much as a hello simply mouthed "more ... water."

I found the ship's steward — a big burly Jamaican — in his office. He was slowly rocking in his chair, hands gripping the armrests tightly, a pained and fearful expression on his face. He might have been in the electric chair.

"The men in the engine room need water," I said.

He looked up at me with an expression that seemed to say: "Please don't pull the switch."

"Find ... Agapito," he said. "He bring ... da water." Agapito was the Filipino messman. The last time I saw him he was kneeling on the pantry deck praying for mercy to Bakunawa, the Tagalog sea serpent god.

I enlisted Peeper to give Agapito a hand carrying the Igloo down into the engine room. "The Union's not going to like this," said Peeper. "Nowhere in the ship's articles does it say Declan O'Gorman, water boy."

"Suit yourself. But if we don't bring them water, they'll get dehydrated. They get dehydrated, they'll go stark raving mad. Is that what you want? A ship full of crazy oilers and wipers? Then who'll fix the friggin' engine? You want to drift around like this forever? Drift around until we hit ... well, you know."

His head twitched.

"Yes, the Rock," I said.

"I can help him with that, sir."

On the fifth day, the sun broke out on the morning watch. At Local Apparent Noon, I took a sun sight and calculated our latitude. Incredibly it was not that far off from Babilée's last known position.

And even better, the heavy sideways roll of the ship became a gentle forward pitch. We were heading into the seas again, making way. The black gang had succeeded in a temporary fix of the thrust bearing.

That evening, I ventured up to the bridge to take stars with Babilée. There was still a long low gentle swell, the skies were clear and the stars we use for navigation glittered like sparklers. To the east was Deneb in Cyrus the swan. And overhead Vega in the lyre of Orpheus. To the north was Polaris in the Great Bear and to the west, Arcturus in the Plowman. Antares, the bright red heart of the scorpion, glittered on the southern horizon. In my sextant, each star kissed the horizon like a chaste lover. The lines I drew on the chart formed a near perfect asterisk. Except for one — Altair, the eye of the eagle. It was oh-so-tempting to nudge that line just wee bit closer to the others. But no. I'd leave that sort of thing to Babilée. He was the artist. The chart was his canvas.

The following morning at breakfast, the captain announced that we would be heading to a shipyard in Rotterdam for repairs. This was followed by a lengthy discourse on the history, culture and cuisine of the Low Countries. "Brussel sprouts, you know, really did originate in Brussels," said the Man Who Knew Too Much.

"Is that so?" said the chief engineer, his voice quivering with barely suppressed rage. The man had not had a wink of sleep in days. "Brussel sprouts. So I guess they invented flatulence too. Is that right, Captain? The fart? The Walloons invented the fart?"

It was going to be a long voyage home.

15

NEVER LAND

The moment you doubt whether you can fly, you cease forever to be able to do it.
 - J.M. Barrie, *Peter Pan*

It was early February. The trees were bare. The sunlight pale and niggling. The house I came home to was not the little cottage I was raised in. Maggie and the boys had been evicted by the Feuding Brothers. But she had found another place, a big two-story house on a duck pond. It sat conveniently across from the Spruce Hill Tavern.

The Artist had abandoned ship. The details of the split emerged: the rumored infidelities, Father chasing Mother around the house firing at her with a .22 rifle. "See the bullet holes?" chirped the wee ones pointing to the walls. The whole fiasco ending when Garrett, now seventeen, dragged the Artist's sorry Irish ass out into the snows and pummeled him until he swore to leave and never come back. He now lived in the River Town in a tiny apartment that smelled of wet newspapers and old man.

Maggie too was seldom seen. She tended bar at the Spruce Hill Inn and was drinking up the meager profits. She would come stumbling in late at night, curl up with the hounds on the couch and pass out. Every night, it seemed, was a three-dog night.

The Green House, as the boys called it, was like Never Land. Lost Boys and Girls from all over the Valley hung out and often slept there. It was a house without parents and thus a house without rules. The three older boys, Garrett, Brian and Neal, were essentially raising themselves, as well as sister Kerry, now five, and Patrick, who'd just turned three. The boys were lean and sinewy with long hair worn in pony tails tied with colorful bandanas. They would have made very fine pirates.

Here in my home port, I did what seamen everywhere do: spent my swag as quickly as possible. For the Green House, I bought a new washing machine and dryer and refrigerator and television. For the kids: shoes and clothes and baseball gloves and ice skates and record albums. For Maggie: cartons of Kent cigarettes, Irish sweepstakes tickets and liters of cheap vodka.

The family was on welfare, and Maggie asked if I wouldn't mind making a pick-up at the Methodist Church where Good Samaritans doled out government food. Neal the prankster, now ten, came with me. I drove the dented station wagon — the seats covered in dog hairs and loaded down to the marks with assorted crap — to the Tompkins Corners Methodist Church, a classic white country church. There in the basement, canned goods marked USDA were stacked high on folding tables. We fell in line behind Mrs. Ebenezer Smith. The Smiths were the gangly, liver-spotted descendants of the early settlers in the Valley, English stock that displaced the Dutch in the 17th century. For two hundred years their forebears had eked out a hard living from the rocky soil. Apple and pear orchards, horse and dairy farms. Their family names marked the Valley's intersections: Adams Corners, Croft Corners, Tompkins Corners, Gilbert Corners. But now their only legacy was the myriad stone walls — rife with briars and copperhead snakes — that encompassed overgrown fields and anemic woods. For the Adams, the Crofts, the Tompkins, and the Gilberts, the gene pool had clearly run out.

I picked up a can labeled: MEAT USDA. I'd seen similar cans in the pantry back at the house. They contained a flesh-colored luncheon meat mottled with black-and-blue bruises and encased in a gelatinous ooze. The meat was de-canned by opening both ends and pushing it through and out. Somehow the meat maintained the ring indentations of the can. Another can was labeled: TURKEY USDA. This too kept the shape of the can, but it had a lighter more festive coloration, bright as snow and mottled with yellow stains as if a dog had pissed on it.

There were also stacks and stacks of canned cranberry sauce. You could take all you want. There'd been a health scare recently concerning cranberries. It had been in all the newspapers. Something to do with cancer and pesticides, and cranberry sales had plummeted. But industry spokesmen argued one would have to consume trainloads of cranberries to get the cancer. And what better way to prove it than by providing the poor with a plentiful supply of canned cranberries to eat. They wouldn't complain. The Great Unwashed — families like the McCareys — probably don't read the papers anyway — if they can read at all.

No less depressing than the canned goods were the expressions on the familiar faces of those doling them out. They radiated good-will-towards-men. These were people I knew. The school bus driver. The wife of the hardware store owner. The captain of the Valley Volunteer Fire Department. It was humiliating. But I suppose that's the way it should be. What if everyone had had my mother's attitude: For free - take, for buy - look. The whole free enterprise system would collapse. Better to dish out a healthy dose of humiliation along with the gelatinous meat.

But I had my limits. When my social studies teacher showed up just oozing empathy, I grabbed Neal by the collar and fled the scene. We drove to the River Town and the First National Supermarket where I had once worked as a bagger with Guy and Rippy. We bought steaks and chops and roasts. Cheerios and

Captain Crunch. And real dog food for the scroungy mutts that were always underfoot. We bought a huge turkey that was actually shaped like a turkey.

Later, as we unloaded the bounty from the car, Maggie told me that Jane had called. My heart skipped a beat. I'd been trying to get up the nerve to call Jane. Though I hadn't seen her in a year or so, she had never been far from my thoughts. Especially when out on the lonely sea. I would remember our times together. Rowing across Oscawana Lake, the autumn leaves floating on the water like paper boats. And in winter, racing our sleds down the twisty path that skirted spruce trees and granite boulders. And in summer, hiking up to the potato field to pick the gnarled pears from the twisted old tree that stood like an aging sentinel. Then savoring what she used to call the "sweetest, ugliest fruit in the world."

In my fantasies we would meet up once again, and our eyes would reveal a mutual surrender to destiny. I would ask her to come away with me. To some enchanted isle. To Majorca, perhaps. Yes, to Majorca. The steep cobbled streets, the balconies festooned with bougainvilleas, the outdoor cafés overlooking a green-blue bay out of Monet. Come away with me, Jane. Come away.

We met in the River Town. In a seedy tavern just across from the linoleum-sided row-house she was living in, and just down the street from the Dunkin' Donuts where she worked. When she came through the door I hardly recognized her. Her hair, once flowing long and silky down to the small of her back, was now swept up into a beehive as tall as a bishop's miter. Her eyes, once shimmering pools of dark waters, were ringed with heavy mascara, giving her the appearance of a raccoon with big hair.

But still ... it was Jane. Jane. Jane! A young woman now — and a pleasantly filled-out woman at that. We hugged, took a table near the dart board. The bar was empty. The beers came — two Schaefers on tap — and we clinked our glasses in a toast — the first time we'd ever had a drink together — and she downed the beer in a series of loud swallows — wiped the foam from her lips then turned to me and smiled.

It was then I noticed that her two front teeth seemed to glow. Yes, they were glowing. With that muted yellow-green cast of lightning bugs or glow worms or moss on rotting logs.

"Do you like my new teeth?" she asked. I was taken aback. Surely she was not referring to the fact that they glowed in the dark.

"They look lovely," I said.

"They're new," she said. A few months ago, she had been in a car accident, she explained. She had been alone behind the wheel when the car went off the road and rammed into a stone wall, and she had smacked her face against the steering wheel, loosening her two front teeth.

"I was really weested," she said. Weested? Ah, wasted. But no one in the Valley said "weested." That's how they spoke in the river towns. Along with the Eeyeah roy-ite for the "yeah, right" that punctuated every exchange. She went on and on — and for a woman who was once such a quiet young girl — she went on quite a bit. She said that the first set of replacement choppers had been oversized. The dentist "dint like 'em neither." He said a pretty girl like her deserved a pretty smile, and so he replaced them free of charge. And she was glee-ud - glad - that things had worked out because her new teeth looked as good if not better than the originals.

I agreed. They were a fine looking pair of teeth. With the additional feature, I might have added — but didn't — that they could be admired in the dark as well. But then who was I to criticize someone's teeth? My own mouth contained more cavities than ivories. And yet there was something unsettling about the woman who sat before me. She seemed nothing like the girl who had inspired my own first feeble attempts at poetry:

Night and stardust in her eyes
Impish smiles caress her face

Nature's gift perfumed in pine
Every drop bathed in her grace.

My Fair Lady had been transformed into a Cockney street moll. Was there some perverse Henry Higgins behind all this? The answer came shortly. She had been seeing a guy named Vinnie Dagioso, and he was from the Point. Of all the vile river towns, the Point was the vilest. If you take the dregs of Italian-American society and let them intermarry with the dregs of Irish-American society, you get a race of people who can neither cook nor hold their drink. Who can neither carry a tune nor tell a good story.

And she was pregnant by him. "Prob'ly on the same noy-ite as my other accident." She'd been thinking about moving in with Vinnie but he had gotten another girl pregnant, and the "skank" moved in first. But it didn't really matter, she said, because Vinnie was about to get drafted. "Prob'ly knock up some Vee-namese girl while he's over there."

There was a long silence. I could see her life stretched out ahead of her — she'd have three more kids — all by different men — all raised on a steady diet of MEAT USDA.

"Do you have enough to get by, Jane?"

"Yeah. But thanks anyway. The thing with Dunkin' Donuts is that there's no tips. I want a job where they tip you."

"Look Jane if you ever need anything."

"I know," she said. "You've always been like a brother to me." If she only had only known. As Hank Williams knew:

I've waited all through the years love,
To give you a heart true and real ...

The truth was, Jane had been no more real to me than Cinnamon from Zanzibar was to my father. What a burden you place on someone when you love them that way. They can never simply be loved for themselves.

I asked her if she remembered the pear tree in the potato field. And the taste of sweetest ugliest fruit in the world. Her eyes glazed over and she nodded, but I know she didn't.

"There's a lot of trees in the Valley," she said. "All kina trees." More small talk — she had heard all about my travels — where was I headed next?

"Anywhere, I hope, but back to Vietnam," I said.

She smiled — the teeth glowed — and she said "I wouldn't want to go no place where they don't speak English." We finished our beers.

"It's been good to see you, Jane."

"Will you send me a postcard?"

"Sure I'll send you a postcard."

"Ee-yeah royite."

We kissed goodbye. The chaste kiss of siblings. The first and last time we ever kissed.

16

Bad From Mornin'

Disturb us, Lord, to dare more boldly
To venture on wider seas
Where storms will show your mastery;
Where losing sight of land,
We shall find the stars.
                    - Sir Francis Drake, 1577

Broke and somewhat disheartened, I was soon back in the union hall on Washington Street looking for a ship. I bid on a freighter out of New Orleans that — like all the others on the job board — was bound for Viet Nam. The ship had already left port so I would meet her in Panama. I would take a flight out from JFK in the morning.

That night I stayed with my Uncle Joe and Aunt Georgiana in their apartment on East 65th Street. Joe Agnello was a proud Sicilian with wavy salt-and-pepper hair, a classic Roman nose and a regal bearing. He looked like the *maitre d'* of an elegant restaurant. In fact, he was a taxicab driver or "hack" as he called himself.

Georgiana, my mother's older sister, was a skinny, hard-drinking chain-smoking sprite of a woman. And scrappy as a tenement dog.

They shared a love of dancing. And Joe's cooking. Joe was an excellent cook, and now he was making my favorite dish, *spiedinis* — beef rolls stuffed with breadcrumbs, parsley and grated cheese. Georgiana, already soused after two or three highballs, sat in the easy chair alternating the cigarette in her mouth with the one in the ashtray.

It was a small apartment: a narrow kitchen with a connecting bath; a living room with couch, easy chair and TV stand. A bedroom that faced the street two stories below. And a room the size of a walk-in closet where I would be sleeping. The apartment had photos of long-lost relatives — including Nanny Bridget — as well as kitschy knick-knacks I had brought them from my travels: a fan from Spain, a Celtic cross from Ireland, a lacquered plate from Vietnam featuring a water buffalo.

Georgie and Joe had married late in life because Joe — as the eldest Agnello — was taking care of his parents. They had lived in this same apartment since the 1920s. The neighborhood had gone dramatically upscale since the days when it harbored Irish and Italian immigrant families, but the apartment was rent-controlled and, like any New Yorker, Joe would rather self-immolate than give the place up.

He looked up from the beef he was hammering with a mallet. (*The tougher the beef the more flavorful. Some people use sirloin. Sirloin for spiedinis. Jesus.*)

"You know, Kev, you've been all over the world, haven't you? I mean for a kid your age, that's something."

Sprinkles olive oil on the beef.

"I was born in this apartment. In 1918. And I never moved out. I took care of my mother and father, God bless them, until they passed away. I was the oldest. That's what you did when you were the oldest. You took care of *i genitori.*"

Now he's grating the Romano. (*Has to be Romano. Some people use Parmigiano. What the fuck do they know?*)

I thought he would now launch into what was now a familiar refrain to me from those less-traveled than I. Wish I could have done the same, life got in the way, stuck on the same rut, etc. But no, this was Uncle Joe.

"Fifty-three years, I've lived in this apartment. Fifty-three years. Never lived anywhere else. Never been anywhere else. But why would I want to, you know? I don't have to go anywhere else. The whole world comes here. I had a guy in my cab the other day. He was from Yemen. Ever heard of Yemen? He was dressed in white like a sheik or something and he smelled like, like mint. Really. My whole cab smelled like mint. I took him to a girly club on 2nd Avenue. He was very excited. Very happy. Kept saying '*shok-run shok-run*'. I think that means 'thank you' in Yemen. Left me a twenty dollar tip. On a three dollar fare. *Shok-run*, I said. *Shok-run*. I don't know, maybe it means 'fuck off' in Yemenese."

He's crushing stale bread crumbs. The bread is semolina that must only be purchased in one place: Astoria, Queens. (*Some people buy their bread in Little Italy. Fuck do they know?*)

"The thing is, Kev, I got a nice place here and ..."

"And a gorgeous wife," slurred Georgiana.

"And a gorgeous wife. And I got the OTB right down the street for when I play the horses. Which is every day. And I get good reception on the TV. Which is great because I am a couch potato. And I know where to buy my cheese, my bread, my wine. And every day I get in my cab and I pick up people from all over the world. From all over the world, Kev. I don't have to go anywhere. You see what I'm saying?"

Fresh parsley. Italian parsley. Chop-chop-chop. And garlic too. Chop chop chop.

"I know you're still a young kid, and it's good you're getting to travel some. But at some point, Kev, you've got to stop and smell the roses, you know what I mean? Get yourself a nice girl, settle down wherever feels right for you — and smell the roses." Then in *sotto voce*: "Or the pussy. Heh-heh-heh."

"I have ears, you know!" said Georgiana.

"I'm just giving your nephew a little advice."

"You're giving him a load of BS."

Mix parsley, bread crumbs, cheese in a bowl; put globs onto strips of beef. Roll beef, stick toothpicks in to hold in place; separate with slivers of bay leaves; drizzle with Sicilian (only!) olive oil. Pop into oven.

"Okay, that's my speech for today, Kev. Remember: a rolling stone gathers no moss."

"Isn't that supposed to be a good thing?" I said.

"I don't know. I think a little moss is good for you."

Very early the next morning, we walked to the corner of 65th St. and First Avenue, and Uncle Joe hailed a cab for me. To Joe, I was still the ten-year-old hick from the sticks who needed to be protected from the sharks of the city. "Look, I'm a hack," he said to the cabbie, evoking what I assumed was a code among New York City taxi drivers. "And this is my nephew. Okay? He's going to JFK. You take care of him, alright? You take good care of him." The cabbie nodded, "I'll take good care of him." Joe paid the man an undisclosed amount of cash, put my seabag in the trunk and gave me a Sicilian kiss on the cheek. And I was off. Shedding what little moss I had gathered.

I took a Pan Am flight to Panama City on the Pacific side of the isthmus. From there I would catch a train to Colón on the Caribbean side where the ship would be anchored while awaiting passage through the Canal. That night, the ship's agent brought me to a compound in the American sector — that is — the U.S. Canal Zone. For some reason, I couldn't go into Panama City proper — something about not having signed on the ship yet and therefore being an illegal alien. I was to stay in a cabin — one of a dozen or so set on the edge of a rainforest. All the other cabins were empty; I was the only "guest." I spent a long night in an Army cot, the ceiling fan whump-whumping away but having little cooling effect on air as hot and thick as oatmeal. The thin walls did little to damper the eerie shrieks, cries and howls of the Panama jungle. I closed my eyes and thought of Uncle Joe's *spiedinis*.

The Panama Railway was completed in 1855. It was built by American investors seeking a short cut for bringing California Gold east. More than 12,000 people died in the building of the railroad. Disposing of the dead was such a problem, that the Railroad company started "pickling" the corpses in barrels and selling them to medical schools. Ah, that Yankeee ingenuity!

But it was one lovely ride. Because of the shape of the Isthmus of Panama, one travels — illogically — in a northwest direction going from the Pacific to the Atlantic side. The track followed the Canal for much of its journey, though now and then it veered off into lush green mansions. It passed through the infamous Gaillard Cut which took untold lives in its construction, then rumbled over the narrow causeways of Gatun Lake to Colón.

Colón was a strange city. The land crabs were making their annual migration, and they were everywhere scuttling across streets and sidewalks. Vultures picked at countless crab carcasses crushed by passing vehicles or underfoot by gleeful street boys.

A water taxi took me out to the SS *Green Wave*. She was anchored offshore awaiting her turn to enter the Canal locks. The *Green Wave* was a C-4 freighter some 530 feet long. Clean looking, newly painted — fresh from the shipyard and a major overhaul. But she looked odd. Instead of the two deckhouses of ships of her class, she had one incredibly tall superstructure aft. And she was enveloped in a dark shimmering cloud. As the water taxi drew closer, I could see it was a cloud of butterflies, black butterflies.

Captain Ragnar Dunderborg brushed butterfly carcasses off his desk. "Gol-damn dings are everyvere," he said. The captain was a Norwegian with the long, dour face of a minister in an Ingmar Bergman film. "Vy dey haf to be black?" he asked. "Souls of da dead." He signed me on, but with a caveat. "This is a dry ship," he said, "no booze is allowed on board. You bring any liquor aboard and I vill kick your rumpeballe off dis ship." I think he meant "ass." I told him I looked forward to sailing on a dry ship.

The chief mate, Mr. Toner, was on his hands and knees in his cabin picking dead butterflies off the floor. "Damndest things I've ever seen." The chief mate was a young guy out of the U. S. Merchant Marine Academy at Kings Point. He was like an excitable hound, always sniffing the air and wagging his tongue and grabbing at his crotch.

He shook dead butterflies off a sheet of paper in his hand – it was the cargo list – then reviewed the stowage plan with me and Mr. Foster, the other third mate, a round little Hobbit from the Cayman Islands. Foster had the most expressive eyes I've ever seen. They mostly expressed fear.

And with good reason. The SS *Green Wave* was loaded down to the Plimsoll marks with some 2,000 tons of warheads, nose rockets, mortars, depth charges, torpedoes, missiles and 500 pound napalm bombs.

"Dis ship is bad from mornin', mate," said Carroll Flowers. "She bad from mornin'." Flowers, the able-bodied seaman on my watch, was a wiry black Honduran from the island of Roatán. He was toothless which made him look much older than his sixty-four years, the result of a severe bout of *ciguatera* poisoning. It is a disease of the nervous system caused by eating poisonous fish – in his case, a grilled barracuda. He spent weeks in the hospital with headaches, diarrhea and gut-wrenching nausea. His skin itched for months and was soon covered with sores from scratching. Then, to add insult to injury, all his teeth fell out. "Well, Flowers," I said. "I guess that was the last barracuda you ever ate."

"Oh no suh," said he. "I still eats da barra." He saw me looking at him like he was crazy. "Cause it is da sweetest fish in da sea."

Bronzino, the other AB on the eight-to-twelve watch, was a former acrobat. A short stocky Italian, he did back flips on the bridge, cartwheels on the bow and handstands on the boom.

"Dot mon could fly if he had da mine to. Yessuh!" So said the ordinary, Wilbert Ebanks, a big man from Cayman Brac. It was Wilbert's booming laughter that drove the poor captain to his Bible for solace.

The SS *Green Wave* wended its way through the canal locks and Gatun Lake. Howler monkeys and colorful parrots screeched at us from the lush green rainforest. The black butterflies fluttered about the ship, following us like tiny Furies. But they bid us farewell when we steamed out of Panama Bay and into the open waters of the Pacific. Perhaps they knew something. Soon we were bucking huge waves generated by a low off western Mexico. I was up on the sky-high bridge watching the bow rise then fall with a horrific boom! The vibrations from the impact traveled the length of the ship, then worked their way up the superstructure to the bridge deck — and then up from the soles of my feet to the top of my head. With every pounding wave, my insides jiggled like Jello.

The ship originally had two deckhouses: one forward, one aft. But the Military Sea Transportation Service — the supply arm of the Beast — deemed it necessary to increase the ship's cargo carrying capacity. To free up space for another hatch, they set the forward deckhouse on top of the after deckhouse. This created one incredibly tall superstructure — the bridge was seven stories high and overlooked a long span of cargo hatches. What was not foreseen was that with every whack from a wave the upper decks would vibrate like the tines of a tuning fork.

Everything on the bridge was vibrating. The gyro and magnetic compasses, the ship's wheels, the engine telegraph. The radar screen displayed nothing but luminous squiggles. Everyday tasks — like holding a sextant steady or drawing a line on a chart or steering a straight course — were near impossible challenges.

Even in my cabin, reading or writing was difficult. Sentences danced on the page. Sleep came in fits and starts. It was like trying to nod off in a blender. Nor was there any respite lower down in the officer's saloon and crew's mess. Pots and pans rattled on hooks. Chess pieces moved of their own accord. Even casual conversation was a challenge as one's voice took on the tremulous tone of someone on the verge of a nervous breakdown. Which was now the state of mind of every Jack-Tar one of us.

Breakfast in the officer's saloon. Eggs jiggled on plates. Sausages skittered off forks. Coffee spilled out of cups. The chief engineer said we really needed to run at half-speed for a while to cut down on the vibrations. He was worried about valves coming open, steam pipes bursting, things like that. But Captain Ragnar Dunderborg would hear none of it. Picking at his cheese, liver paste, cabbage and herring — the captain's every meal — the herring quivering on his plate as if it was alive — he reminded us that Suffering is the Human Condition. And we'd all be the Stronger for it. Besides, he had a schedule to keep and — by golly — he meant to keep it. Chief mate Toner — lap dog that he was — concurred.

Beyond the collective descent into madness, there was another adverse effect of the constant vibrating: the effect on the ship's explosive cargo. The wind had kicked up to Force 8 — about forty knots. A fresh gale. The crests of waves broke into spindrift and foam was blown in feathery streaks. The SS *Green Wave* shook and rattled like never before. Up on the bridge, I could feel the fillings in my teeth loosening. It had been a long, long watch, when at last the ship's clock rang eight bells and it was time to turn the bridge over to Mr. Foster. I couldn't wait to go below — way below this time, perhaps all the way down to the engine room — just to settle my innards. And here came Foster now — carrying half a cup of coffee — the other half having spilled out on the long shaky climb up to the bridge, scalding his hand and soaking the cuff of his khaki shirt.

Then, as I was giving him our course and speed and position, we suddenly heard a resounding BONGGGG! And then another. BONGGGG! It was the sound of metal colliding against metal. And it seemed to be coming from a cargo hold somewhere amidships. This was where we had stowed the 500-lb fuel-air explosive defoliation and anti-personnel bombs. Tacked over the chart table is Naval Directive 10-11-1966: "Ammunition is sensitive to friction, shocks, sparks, or heat. Immediate action must be taken to secure explosives, or cargo stored with explosives, that shifts or goes adrift while in transit."

"Oh my, oh my," said Foster — sweat bursting from his pores — his huge squirrel eyes darting about. "Oh my, oh my."

On Christmas Day 1969, some 1500 miles northwest of Hawaii, a weather-beaten ghost ship was riding out a similar gale, and the winds and waves shook her to her ribs. She was the SS *Badger State* en route to Da Nang in Vietnam carrying more than 8,900 bombs and rockets — equal to about 2,000 tons of TNT.

The munitions had been loaded at the Naval Depot at Bangor, Washington. It was a rush job — the Beast impatient for its needs — and the captain registered his concerns. The ship's holds were only half full — always a concern for stability — and worse the pallets holding the bombs seemed flimsy. But the authorities turned a deaf ear.

The captain sent a radiogram to Naval Headquarters asking to be rerouted to calmer seas. Fleet Weather Central redirected the ship further north where the synoptic charts showed good weather. In fact, the seas up there were even rougher. Suddenly the men heard the haunting sound of metal striking metal. There was a bomb loose in the No. 3 hatch. The deck crew worked quickly to build a new cradle and maneuver the 500-pound bomb into it. But just when they had finished, other bombs sprang loose from their cradles, the metal holding-strips snapping like rubber bands. Day and night all hands worked feverishly to secure the explosive cargo. They'd secure one batch, and another would spring free.

Then in the No. 5 hatch the 2,000-pound bombs came loose. There was no way the crew could wrangle those monsters back into cradles. So they threw wood, mattresses, blankets, hatch covers even sides of beef down into the hold to slow the rolling of the bombs. All to no avail.

The captain sent off an SOS, and the distress signal was picked up by a Greek freighter, the SS *Khian Star*. The ship reversed course and steamed towards the *Badger*. Just as the *Star* appeared on the horizon, there was an incredible explosion aboard the *Badger State*. A 2,000-pound bomb blew an eight-by-sixteen foot hole in the hull just above the water line. The impact of the explosion sprung other one-ton bombs from their shoring, and soon they too were rolling around, knocking into each other like pin balls and exploding. The stern of the *Badger State* was quickly engulfed in flames.

The captain ordered most of the crew into the No. 1 lifeboat, the only one functional. Pounding waves had loosened the No. 2 from its cradle and it now dangled helplessly over the side. Five men remained with the captain to help him lower the lifeboat. Once they saw the lifeboat bobbing safely in the seas they turned to their own survival. It would be too dangerous to leap into the water on the weather side where the lifeboat was launched. Instead — wearing life vests and clutching life rings — they jumped from the lee side where the water was somewhat calmer. In the icy seas, they swam desperately for the *Khian Star* — now visible a few miles off. Three men disappeared in the frothing waves. Three men — including the captain — succeeded in swimming to the rescue ship.

Meanwhile, as the lifeboat drifted towards the stern of the *Badger State*, wind and waves kept it pressed against the ship. When the boat passed the No. 5 hatch, the men on the lifeboat could see into the hole in the hull. Everything within was aflame and there was the stench of burning wood and mattresses and meat. Suddenly a loose bomb shot out of the hole and landed in the lifeboat, capsizing it. Those who weren't instantly killed were treading water in 20-foot seas looking for something, anything to cling to.

Only fourteen crewmen were saved by the *Khian Star*. Heavy rains, high winds and thick clouds impeded the search for the others by rescue planes. They found no signs of twenty-six missing men, some of whom were last seen clinging to life rafts and fending off giant albatrosses that swooped down and pecked at their eyes and flesh.

Now on the SS *Green Wave*, chief mate Toner divided us into search parties to find the source of the banging noise. Flowers, Bronzino and I were assigned the No. 2 hold. The deck cadet, Larry Fosdick, joined us. Fosdick, like Mr. Toner, was from the U. S. Merchant Marine Academy at Kings Point. There is no training ship at Kings Point. Instead the cadets spend a year on a merchant ship getting hands-on training. They are exposed to life in the real merchant marine. Which might explain their high drop-out rate.

Fosdick was raised on the shores of Lake Superior in Wisconsin. He was a tall gawky kid, very shy and very nervous about finding a loose bomb.

"What do we do with the thing?" he asked.

"I have no idea," I said.

"You got to t'row a mattress on it," said Carroll Flowers.

"Will that work?" asked Fosdick anxiously.

"Debbil if I know."

BONGGGG! The sound resonated throughout the ship as we descended the narrow metal ladder into the darkness of the No. 2 hold below. "Yessuh," said Flowers. "Dis ship is bad from mornin'." The sound was louder now as it reverberated off the inner wall of the hull. It was like we were in this giant bell. But where was the gong? Sounds carry strangely on a ship and locating the source wouldn't be easy.

The ship heaved and rolled, making it difficult to climb down the ladder. The hold smelled of bilge water, Bunker C oil and fresh-cut lumber — sickly sweet — the odors melding together into a rank stew. I flashed a light over the cargo in the upper tween deck and could see row upon row of silvery bombs cradled in wooden pallets. Each bomb had two rings around it — like the rings of Saturn — that kept the bombs from rubbing against each other. I left it to the acrobat Bronzino to search this area — a dense forest of bracing material. He wriggled his way through the latticework of pallets and disappeared. The rest of us continued on down to the lower tween deck where countless canisters of napalm were stowed.

"What dey do with all dis shit, mate?" asked Flowers.

"They sear the flesh off human beings. That's what they do with it."

"Lawdie Lawdie. What a crack inna head! Don't nobody read da Bible no more?"

Flowers searched the lower tween deck while Fosdick and I continued down the ladder to the lower hold. I opened the well cover and could see it was full of big rockets and missiles braced by heavy timbers, like the flying buttresses of a cathedral. These were the big guys destined to be dropped on North Vietnam. That is, if they didn't detonate first aboard the SS *Green Wave.* Lawdie, Lawdie. Crack inna head. Don't nobody read da Bible no more?

The ship's crew searched the cargo holds for hours, trying to find the source of that elusive BONGGGG. But without success. Now the seas were kicking up, and the clanging of metal against metal grew louder, more insistent. No one asked for whom the bell tolls.

Over a dinner of cheese, herring, liver paste and cabbage, Captain Ragnar Dunderborg told us that he'd made a decision. The synoptic chart compiled by Fleet Weather Central showed light airs and calm seas down by the equator. He sent a radiogram to the Navy asking that they reroute us. "Maybe we can sail in peace down dere. God willing."

After a long run south, we were in the thick of the doldrums heading west. Pewter skies, still waters, not a whisper of life. Yet — incredibly — even the slightest ripple in the seas produced a muted *bongggg.* It was just loud enough and insistent enough to remind us that Suffering is the Human Condition.

As we steamed along the equator, the crew on my watch opened up a bit more about themselves. Bronzino told me about life in the circus and his love affairs with bearded ladies and fat ladies and midgets ("Nose to nose your toes were in it. Toes to toes your nose is in it.").

Big Wilbert Ebanks dreamed of being a *soca* singer, and he reveled in the naughty lyrics of the Mighty Sparrow.

Saltfish - some men gets drunk to taste it
Saltfish - some does go and hide to face it
Saltfish... It was sweeter den meat
When you want to eat all saltfish sweet.

Carroll Flowers, the toothless Honduran, confided in me about a problem that was "vexing" him. Two problems actually — his wife and his mistress. At sixty-four years old, he was on the cusp of the retirement age mandated by the union. But where would he spend his golden years? With his wife of fifty years in their cottage in Roatan? Or with his mistress of forty years in their apartment in New Orleans?

"It is a debbil of a t'ing," he said. For he loved them both dearly. He shook his head — what to do what to do. "It is a debbil of a t'ing to break a heart," said Carroll Flowers. "But one of dem gwine to be broken."

One day, after a long miserable week on the hot, humid equator, the clanging completely ceased. At first we were relieved, but then came the realization that the bomb had simply wedged itself between god-knows-what god-knows-where. If we couldn't hear it, we'd never find it. One rogue wave could jar it loose and blow us all to kingdom come. The captain cut our speed to five knots to stay on the safe side. At this rate it would take forty-four days to reach Saigon.

Cadet Fosdick was disheartened by our new ETA, our estimated time of arrival. He doubted the voyage would ever end. "It's like crawling across the ocean," he moaned.

I tried to pick up his spirits. "Oh come on, Fosdick. It's not that bad. It's more like walking than crawling. Really. Five knots is practically a jog. We'll be in Saigon before you know it. Get all this shit unloaded. Then hurry on home."

The chief mate had been badgering Fosdick lately over petty things. Scolding him for wrinkles in his uniform and scuffed shoes and not sitting up straight at meals. "Fosdick, I see some spinach between your teeth." The constant nitpicking was wearing on the lad. We met secretly in the bosun's locker, among the blocks and tackles, the heaving lines and monkey fists. The bosun's locker also served as the ship's brig, an irony that was not lost on us as we smoked dope and plotted Mr. Toner's murder. We'd throw him down the anchor chain locker. Or shove him into the engine boiler — a superheated 500 degrees and boil him like a lobster. Or simply toss him to the sharks that constantly followed the ship awaiting a free meal. Our fellow conspirator was the engineering apprentice, a portly young man with the nom de whorehouse of Beaucoup Love. He told us it was what the Vietnamese girls gushed as they rubbed his belly: "Beaucoup love! Beaucoup love!" Beaucoup Love was an affable soul and good company. Besides he was the one who'd brought the weed.

At last the broad expanse of the Mekong Delta appeared on the horizon. Soon the pilot and Naval Guard were aboard, and we were steaming up the Saigon River. The Lieutenant said we'd be accompanied by river patrol boats on the passage. The Navy was taking extra precautions because of what had happened to the SS *Baton Rouge Victory* just a few weeks earlier. The *Baton Rouge* was heading upriver carrying a load of trucks and construction gear. About twenty-two miles from Saigon, she was rocked by an explosion. A Viet Cong diver had placed a limpet mine against the ship's hull. It was detonated by a sapper crouching on the river bank. The explosion blew a hole in the hull and seven men in the engine room were killed.

"Good thing she wasn't carrying explosives," said the Lieutenant. "Whole damn ship would have blown up." Unlike, say, the

SS *Green Wave* that was carrying more than 2,000 tons of it.

As we steamed upriver, the pilot was all business. "Left 10 degrees rudder. Half ahead, mate. Half ahead." There was no casual conversation. No wheelhouse chatter. The Land of the Blue Dragon was an idyllic landscape, lush with mangroves and melaleuca, flocks of spoonbills and herons. A peasant girl in a straw hat poled a pirogue full of pineapples. A wispy-bearded man tossed a shrimp net. Half-naked children stared at us from rice paddies. No one waved. No matter. This was no pleasure trip. And all of us on the SS *Green Wave* were thinking the same thing. Let's make this run and unload this shit and get the fuck out of here.

We reached Saigon by nightfall, but there was no room at the cargo pier. We'd have to anchor just offshore in the river. For security reasons, there would be no water taxis to shuttle us ashore. The captain left by patrol boat to settle company business. The rest of us remained on sea watches.

It was about ten o'clock at night, and I was standing watch alone on the bridge. As the ship swung at anchor, I took compass bearings on the lights of the city to make sure we were not drifting, that the hook wasn't dragging. Suddenly, I saw someone dashing across the open deck. Then another. I looked over the side and saw a flotilla of small boats nosing up to the ship's hull. I caught a glimpse of someone scurrying up the Jacob's ladder. A surge of fight-or-flight adrenalin kicked in. I rushed into the wheelhouse and reached for the ship's whistle. But before I sounded the alarm, I heard laughter. Women's laughter. Then giggling. I went back out on the wing for a second look. I saw mini-skirts not fatigues. They were not Viet Cong sappers. They were do-mommies. The SS *Green Wave* was being overrun by hookers. And the crew was surrendering without a fight.

Toner was outraged. He was up on the bridge yelling "For gods sakes, man, this is a major breach of security! And it's happening on your watch! DO SOMETHING!"

"I can't leave the bridge," I told him. "Captain's orders."

"I'm in charge now," said Toner. "And I say get those sluts off the ship! That's an order, mate!"

The focsle — the crew's quarters — was pandemonium. In the narrow passageways, sailors with pants down to their ankles were chasing half-naked women who were squealing with delight. Bronzino was fornicating in the upper bunk of his cabin, the juxtaposition of limbs suggesting the most extraordinary sexual position. Meanwhile old Carroll Flowers was in the lower bunk, happily gumming two women at once.

The chief mate enlisted Fosdick to help me rout the boarders. "But how do we get them ... uncoupled?" he asked me.

"I don't know, Fosdick. Throw cold water on them." We had our work cut out for us. There were women laid out on hatch covers, in lifeboats, on lounge chairs and mess tables. And there was Beaucoup Love steering a girl towards the bosun's locker. Was no place sacred? Fosdick was right. They were dogs in heat. How do you separate them?

You don't. You sneak back up to the bridge — far from the rutting crowd — and hide in the dark until your watch is over. Foster relieved me at midnight. "Oh my oh my," he said, when I told him what was going on.

"It's all yours, Foster," I said and I headed for the sanctity of my cabin. There I discovered a young vixen in a pink nightie curled up on my bunk.

"Hello, mistuh," she said. "I love you too much."

By dawn's early light, the little boats and the things they carried were all gone. The men stood sheepishly before Captain Ragnar Dunderborg as he dressed them down. "What vere you t'inking?! Dose vomen could be the enemy for all ve know. Besides ... have you no shame?!" He shook his head in disgust.

We shifted to the dock at 1300 hours. Only the vehicles would be unloaded: the bulldozers, trucks and forklifts stowed on the weather deck. The explosive cargo would remain aboard. It would be unloaded in Cam Ranh Bay. Which meant another dangerous journey down the Saigon River and then, in the dead of night, a 150-mile run up the mine-infested coast. En route, heavy swells generated by a distant typhoon woke up an old acquaintance. BONGGGG.

We sailed past the hills of Binh Ba Island, and entered the chalk-green waters of Cam Ranh Bay. Numerous cargo ships were anchored in the inner harbor but we headed straight to the pier. A good sign, we thought. "Almost over," said Fosdick.

At the cargo dock, Fosdick and Beaucoup Love tripped over themselves in their rush down the gangway. The cadet and the fat man were so happy to be off the ship they did a little dance on the beach. Then speed-walked up the road — arms pumping as if on a workout — towards the strip of bars on stilts.

I was surprised to see the captain and chief mate also heading down the gangway. "Ship's business," said Mr. Toner. "Back soon."

Ee-yeah-royite.

But it would not be over for me. It was my turn for the cargo watch. Soon Army longshoremen were ambling up the gangway. They uncradled booms, rigged cargo falls, opened hatches. But there was something in their body language that I found unnerving. It was a vibe I couldn't quite put my finger on. They seemed to work with a smoldering resentment.

An hour or so later I was back aft watching them unload M60 machine guns from the number 5 hatch, when Carroll Flowers came up to me with his engines at Half Ahead. His normal speed was Dead Slow Ahead so I knew something was up.

"Lawdie, lawdie, mate. Da fools done burnt out da number t'ree winch. Yessuh! And dey dropping loads all over da place. Dey just dropped a jeep right on da pier. Wot hoppen when dey get to da bombs, eh? What hoppen den? Tell you one t'ing, mate. When I go ashore, I be stayin' ashore! Yessuh!"

I went up to the No. 3 hatch and saw the ship's electrician was already inspecting the burn-out winch. The GI's stood idly by watching him at work. Eyes on fire. I could smell the dope.

"Hey, Sparks," I said. "what do you think?"

"It's fucked," he said. "Can't do nothin' with this one."

Bursts of incongruent laughter from the GIs.

I found the Army stevedore in the ship's mess drinking coffee and told him they'd have to wrap the number three hatch. No winch. No work. "Affirmative, mate," he said with consummate indifference. Then he asked me where the sugar was.

I hurried back on deck to watch them unload the No. 2 hatch. This was the hold that was jam-packed with barrels of napalm and dozens of missiles and rockets and scores of one-ton bombs. I was hoping that this was the hatch that held our errant bomb.

When loading or unloading cargo, two booms are used. One hovers over the cargo hold, the other over the dock. Wire cables run up each boom to a block (or pulley) at the boom's end, then down to where they are married to a cargo hook. The hook is attached to a sling looped around a pallet holding the cargo. An operator controls both cables at the same time — a winch lever in each hand. He hoists the cargo up vertically then brings it horizontally over the deck, then straight down again to the pier. It takes a certain finesse.

Of which the GI on the winch at the No. 2 hatch had not an ounce. He yanked the cargo up from the hold too quickly, and it was a pallet-load of bombs. Then he paused too long, and the pallet swung in mid-air and slammed against the metal hatch coaming. He then lowered it off-kilter so the pallet landed hard on the pier at an angle and it broke apart, spilling bombs onto the pavement.

"What the fuck are you doing?!" I shouted. He looked at me with a mindless grin. Then shrugged.

"You gots to trow dem off da ship, mate." Carroll Flowers spit on the deck for emphasis. "Da cap'n's gone. Da chief mate's gone. You da onliest one dat can do it. You gots to trow dem off da ship, mate. Before dey kill us all. Yessuh."

Suddenly there was a loud eeech! We glanced up and saw the boom at the No. 1 hatch bent in half and twisted like a pretzel.

I threw them all off the ship.

In the morning, the captain asked me into his office. I expected a lecture, but all fight had gone out of the man. He simply told me we'd be shifting from the pier to the anchorage. There we'd await new winch motors and replacement booms. The boom at the No. 1 hatch was bent as well. The Old Man shook his head. "So ve yust sit out dere and vait. Yust sit and vait."

The crew was disheartened, and no one more so than Cadet Fosdick. Christmas was just a few weeks away and he'd hoped to be home for the holidays. For days he'd been talking about horse-drawn sleigh rides across frozen lakes and snowshoeing in the forests and drinking eggnogs around roaring fires. He'd bought a trunk full of presents for friends and family: feather slippers, rattan baskets, conical hats, silk shirts with dragons on them. I had this image of the Fosdick family sitting around the Yule log — mom, dad, gramps, grandma, big sis and baby bro — all wearing dragon shirts and straw cone hats.

The ship was at anchor for days. I thought of Langston Hughes' Sea Calm:

How still,
How strangely still
The water is today.
It is not good
For water
To be so still that way.

And it was still as death out there. We were back on sea watches. Back in limbo. We slept, we read, we stared at the heavens. The ship's only motion was an occasional roll caused by the wake of a passing freighter. BONGGGG.

It is not good to be so still that way.

17

THE BLUE DRAGON

War has the feel — the spiritual texture — of a great
ghostly fog, thick and permanent. ... Everything swirls.
The old rules are no longer binding, the old truths no
longer true.
— Tim O'Brien, *The Things They Carried*

The SS *Green Wave* received new orders from Naval
Headquarters. We were to sail for Da Nang. There the
cargo would be discharged using cranes on barges. It was
another hundred miles or so up the coast. And that much closer
to enemy territory.

Da Nang Bay is a big blue semi-circle ringed with green mountains. We dropped the hook in the anchorage area reserved for
ships carrying explosives. It was in the middle of the bay — out of
range of mortar fire, but within range of rockets fired from the
hills.

Captain Ragnar Dunderborg was on the radio telephone trying to find out when the barge and crane would arrive to discharge
the cargo. There were no barges and cranes available, he was told.
"Den vot der fock are ve doing here?!" No one knew. No one
knew why we'd been sent to Da Nang. No one knew how long

we'd be here. No one knew where or when — if ever — we'd unload our cargo of explosives. He looked over at me with those
pale blue eyes, the light drained out of them. This was his Hour
of the Wolf. He shook his head and muttered "Fock."

Water taxis nuzzled up to the ship, and everyone who was
not on watch scurried down the gangway like the proverbial rats.
Fosdick, Beaucoup and I were among them. It was a long bouncy
ride across the broad expanse of bay. But none of us minded because every bounce took us that much farther from the SS *Green
Wave.*

The water taxi dropped us off at a downtown pier on the Han
River. Da Nang is a port city with little of the colonial opulence
of Saigon. It was also under tight security. The US Military Police
and the *Canh Sat*, the Vietnamese National Police, were everywhere.

Beaucoup Love had set his sights on a place called the Moon
Bar, highly recommended by the bedroom steward who had
been "much pleasured there" on a previous voyage. Fosdick was
heading for the USO. The USO — the seaman's "home away
from home" — offered ping-pong tables, a paperback library, free
Bibles and "wholesome entertainment." Today they'd be singing
Christmas carols.

Myself, I wanted the ordinary, the mundane, the prosaic. I
strolled the busy road that ran along the Han River. And savored
the aromas from street carts: steamed shrimp, grilled beef on a
stick, black sausages, hot soups and stews. A barber cut a little
boy's hair — both were down on their haunches. The barber saw
me, smiled, and clicked his scissors — click click — would you like
a haircut too? "No thanks," I said in French, "I'm letting it grow
long."

On a tree-lined boulevard, I came upon a young man enter-
taining children with a kind of string game. One end of a string
was tied to a small pouch. The young man swung the pouch over
symbols chalked on the sidewalk, among them: a sun, a moon,
an eye, a hand. As he swung the pouch, he chanted what might

have been a children's rhyme. When he came to the last word of the rhyme he shouted: *Da khap noi!* and let go of the string. The pouch landed on the sun and a little girl clasped her hands in anticipation. The young man reached into a sack and stirred whatever was inside. The little girl jumped excitedly. He then handed her a coconut candy shaped like the sun.

A sudden shower came up. And I tilted my head back — face to the downpour. I wanted to break out into song. Or swing around a lamp post. Or jump in puddles. The locals took no notice of the rains. Old women remained squatting over their baskets, rain dripping from their conical hats. Rickshaw drivers forged through rivulets in the streets. Women carrying babies, food vendors ladling soup, boys playing soccer, all were drenched by the rains and simply went about their business. This was a lesser storm in their lives.

When I reached the riverfront, it was blowing like stink and wind-driven waves pounded the docks. Water taxis anchored in the river bobbed up and down like plastic fishing bobbers. I asked one of the boatmen when he'd make the next run out to the ships at anchor. "Too much wind," he said. "Too much wave."

Fosdick came walking up to the dock.

"So how was it, Fos?"

"It was beautiful, mate. Too beautiful. You should have heard 'em. Jingle Bells. Wow. And then they sang Tannebaum. Man, I almost cried."

Beaucoup showed up too, but he was bummed out. The Moon Bar was closed. Closed down by the military. An MP told him it had been serving as a front for the Viet Cong. The bar girls would lure seamen to somewhere out back where the VC would rob and kill them. "That really sucks!" said Beaucoup. "Guy just wants to get laid and they kill him. Aren't there rules against that kind of shit?!"

"You mean like a Geneva Convention for whoring. I don't think so, Beau."

"Well, there fucking oughta be."

Night fall. There was no let-up in the wind and we were stranded in the city. As the curfew hour approached, we checked into a hotel off the main boulevard. Vietnamese businessmen crowded the lobby. Posters of local pop-stars adorned the walls. I took a single room up on the second floor. Fosdick and Beaucoup took a room next to mine.

It was very spare — nothing adorned the walls. The place smelled like sardines. And springs poked up through the mattress on the bed. No matter. It would be good to sleep in a place that was unlikely to erupt in a violent explosion. Or so I foolishly thought.

Some time in the middle of the night, there was a loud commotion coming from down the hall. Pounding on doors. Yelling. Screaming. Sobbing. I got out of bed. Opened the door, and saw at the far end of the hallway men in black pajamas. Men with guns. A businessman was kneeling before them. I closed the door very quietly. "Da Nang is ours by day," an MP had once told me. "And the Viet Cong's by night. That's when the tax man comes."

I propped a chair under the door knob, then retreated to the balcony. Fosdick and Beaucoup were out on their balcony as well.

"Jesus fuck," said Beaucoup. "Did you see 'em?"

"Yeah. Did they see you?"

"No."

"Good. They didn't see me either."

"We tried to lock the door," whispered Fosdick, "but there isn't any lock."

"Prop a chair against it."

"There's no chair."

"Come on over then. We'll make a stand together."

Fosdick climbed over his balcony railing, then made the three foot step-over to mine. But for the portly Beaucoup Love it was more of a challenge. He kind of rolled over the railing — took the giant step to my balcony. But now with a foot on each balcony he was spread-eagled two stories above the empty street — his arms flailing for balance. He couldn't seem to bring the other leg over. Still it's amazing what a little fear will do. In a contorted move that any gymnast would envy he managed to grab onto the rail with both hands. Fosdick and I then hauled him over like a Hemingway tuna.

Moments later, we heard the pounding on the doors drawing closer. "They're almost here!" whispered Fosdick. More pounding. Closer still.

And now they were here. We heard them talking right outside my room. We waited for a knock on the door. But there was no knock on the door. Instead they were having a heated discussion among themselves. The words *chow-my* stood out. *Chow-my* means 'American.'

"Fuck, they know we're in here," whispered Beaucoup. The twenty-foot drop down to the street below now looked like a viable option.

Then the discussion was over. Something mechanical clicked. A pistol clip? Then ... nothing.

They moved on. The angels of death had passed us by. They continued on down the hall. Pounding on doors. Yelling. Someone — a businessman perhaps — wept out loud. Scuffling sounds. Shouted orders. Cause I'm the tax man. Yeah yeah, I'm the tax man. Then they were gone.

"Hey man, this has got to be against the fucking rules," muttered Beaucoup. Cadet Fosdick was shaking too much to say anything.

I wondered aloud why they had passed us by, why they'd left us alone.

"I bet this hotel brings in big bucks for the Cong," said Beaucoup. "They screw with us maybe the MPs shut the place down. Like the Moon Bar."

Fosdick shook his head. "Lamb's blood," he said. "Lamb's blood on the door." That was all he said for the rest of the night.

We decided to stay together for the night, though we doubted they'd come back. Soon the two of them were dozing off in my bed — shoulder to shoulder, heads touching. Laurel and Hardy in "Early to Bed." But I couldn't sleep. It was the Eldest Child Syndrome. When night is full of terrors — howling thunderstorms or raging parents — someone has to stand watch over the wee ones. I went back out on the balcony and sat down, legs dangling through the rails. Gazed up at the stars. Was that Pegasus up there, winging his way across the sky?

It was a long night's journey into day.

The city came alive with the first rays of light. Uniformed children trotted off to school, street vendors set up sidewalk stalls, pedicab drivers zoomed about ringing their bells, policemen directed traffic. It was a glorious morning. But it would be good to get back to the ship. Back to the devil we knew.

Anchor watch on the SS *Green Wave*. I took compass bearings on absurd things: pelicans, clouds, sampans — just for the hell of it. Entered them in the ship's log. 1000 hours: Bamboo log bearing 035 degrees. Dead fish bearing 185 degrees. Floating buffalo dung bearing 285 degrees. Maybe I was going crazy.

Then the bosun came rushing up to the bridge. "It's Fosdick," he panted. "He's hurt, mate. Hurt bad."

I found Fosdick in the No. 1 hold. Flat on his back moaning in pain, blood streaming from an ear, having fallen down the only open hatch. Beaucoup was with him, as was Ebanks and Flowers. Flowers held his hand, as one might a child's.

"Don't move him!" I shouted. Minutes later, I was giving him a shot of morphine.

"How you doing, Fos?"

"Couldn't be better," he said without a trace of sarcasm. He had this strange expression on his face. I couldn't tell if it was a smile or a grimace.

"The captain's put in a call to the Navy," I said. "They're gonna get you outta here." There was that look again. Was it joy? No, it couldn't be.

A Navy launch pulled up alongside, and medics came rushing up the gangway. Soon they were easing Fosdick onto a rescue basket. The bosun winched the basket up, and set Fosdick gently down into the waiting arms of medics on the launch. The ship's crew gathered at the railing: "Hang in kid."

"You'll be all right."

"Hey, man, think about it. You'll be home for Christmas!"

"Lucky bastard," someone muttered.

Cadet Fosdick saw me looking down at him and gave me a thumbs up. And yes, that was definitely a smile. I glanced over at Beaucoup Love and his sly wink said it all. Fosdick had jumped.

It was sundown and Beaucoup and I were up on the flying bridge, sitting on life jackets, waiting for the lightshow to begin. Monsieur Love had scored some Thai weed and he had laced it with "hocus" — with opium — and rolled it into a fat doobie. He lit up, inhaled deeply — choked and coughed — "very good shit" — and passed me the joint. The opium added just a hint of eucalyptus to the sweetness of the grass. The buzz kicked in as the sun disappeared behind the hills and the spectacle began.

Soon the distant hills were resounding with the fa-foom fa-foom of big guns, the whump-whump of artillery and the screeeee of tracers and rockets. A rocket landed near our circle of ships, and there was a new sound — ka-fwooosh! — as a geyser spurted up.

The hills and valleys were dotted with puffs of smoke. Helicopters darted in and out of clouds like luminous dragonflies. White phosphorous flares floated in air like miraculous visions. Explosions on earth threw off glowing red comets. The jungle flickered with flashes of mortar fire. The mountains trembled.

I propped the lifejacket against the ship's smokestack and leaned back against it. In the skies, tracers fired by the Americans crisscrossed tracers fired by the Viet Cong. Together, they created a stunning matrix against the twilight sky. Red smoke-trails against green smoke-trails. Rockets exploded like a meteor shower, prompting Beaucoup Love to burst into song: "and the rockets red glare ... the bombs bursting in air ... gave proof through the night ... that our flag was still there." He nah-nah-nahed the rest of the anthem since he was too stoned to remember more words.

A monstrous billow of dust and smoke rose up from the mountains like a mythical beast. Like a blue dragon. Its acrid, pestiferous breath wafted across the bay and burned the nostrils. Its horrifying shrieks and roars and hisses shattered the eardrums. Flames shot from its mouth. Searing a young maiden stirring a rice pot. An old man at a chess board. A little boy huddled on a sleep mat. An infant at her mother's breast.

Now a single rocket arced across the sky. Set free on the words of a children's rhyme — *Da khap noi*! It slowly curved towards the SS *Green Wave*. No matter. Should it land on us, there would be coconut candies shaped like the sun. For eternity.

18

CANOPIA

The sole cause of a man's unhappiness is that he does
not know how to stay quietly in his own room.
- Pascal, Pensées

The Doll Man was dead. As were Goldbug and the Neck
and a dozen other shipmates from Maritime. The victims
of shipboard accidents, explosions, collisions. We'd lost
Sunshine as well — a fine friend with a passion for soccer, the
clarinet, and the Torah — lost forever somewhere in the South
China Sea where he leapt from the stern of a ghost ship.

Others had simply vanished. Magpie was last seen in Tahi-
ti and the Mouth heading for the wilds of Alaska. Whiskey Joe
jumped ship in Vietnam and was presumed lost to the cathouses
of Vung Tau.

As for Maharrey, he simply went home.

The boys had skipped school a lot lately. Which was fine by
me; I enjoyed their company. We passed the days ice skating
in the pond or hiking in the woods or playing touch football on
the frozen lawn. "Just like the Kennedy brothers," said Garrett
sardonically.

At night, we would break out guitars and sing songs, many composed by Brian, the contemplative brother. Or we played Jeopardy, Scrabble, or Risk around the wobbly kitchen table. Risk is a board game in which the object is to conquer the world. Armies clash with rolls of the dice. Alliances are made and broken. The boys were skilled players and very competitive. Bright, creative, resourceful, they were living proof that no parents were better than bad parents.

Over countless cups of hot tea, I would tell them sea stories. About the dayman who went berserk and threw all the board games over the side, and the captain who spent the whole voyage hidden in his room, and the third mate who tapped Morse code on the radio operator's head. I would tell them about Philly and Beaucoup Love and Mr. King (and his wonderful jasmine tea.) They loved any story about old Carroll Flowers, especially about losing his teeth from eating "da sweetest fish in da sea."

But I said nothing about the booze and the bombs, the dope and the dragons, and the ship that was "bad from mornin'." I had not worked these things out in my own mind yet. As for that elusive *bonggg*, a loose 100 lb. bomb was found by Army longshoremen while I was ashore in DaNang. It was nestled like a sea lion in a raft of its brethren patiently awaiting its moment to roar. Which would now happen somewhere in the war zone instead of aboard the SS *Green Wave*.

On a crisp clear morning — cold as a witch's tit, as Guy would say — I ventured down to the pond with Kerry Ann in search of duck eggs. Kerry had taken this as her exclusive task. She was the family hunter-gatherer. We found a dozen eggs, tucked away here and there in patches of frosty brown grass. We fried them all up for breakfast. The whites were thick and viscous; the yolks were pumpkin orange and very "eggy" in flavor. Sopped up with Wonderbread toast and washed down with hot cocoa, we were fortified for adventure.

The boys and I tossed ice skates into the station wagon, and we and Shane O'Neill (the dog) piled in. Garrett took the wheel and drove the sputtering rig up Canopus Hollow Road. Soon the woods closed in and the blacktop turned to dirt, and we were thumping along an obstacle course of potholes and ice patches, boulders and tree limbs. The station wagon bottomed out now and then, and its sides were scraped and scratched by branches. "There goes the resale value," said Garrett. He was developing a deliciously dark sense of humor.

We pulled the wagon into a narrow turn-off, where hunters parked their rigs during deer and grouse seasons. We were on the private estate of a wealthy businessman who spent most of his time in the city. There was a hunting lodge right over the hill. The man owned thousands of acres of prime woods, lakes and streams. It was called the Field Estate. Except when the boys were here. They called it Canopia. And this day Canopia was all ours.

Crunch crunch crunch — we tramped over beds of dead leaves. It was the time of year when walking silently in the woods was impossible. Garrett leaned forward as he walked — a man on a mission. "Here's me head, me arse is coming," as Nanny Bridget used to say. She had passed away a few years ago, and we missed her wonderful stories, her generous spirit and her boundless love. Her wake was classic Irish: full of drinking and singing, laughing and brawling. Family feuds were rekindled (*There's good reason I was her favorite, you bitch!*), dark secrets revealed (*She's not your mother, Toots! You see that fat cow there? That's your real mother!*), and new animosities created, especially towards the Italian mourners (*Can you believe those dagos? Look at 'em: crying at a wake, for chrissakes!*). But by evening's end, all was forgotten and forgiven as they joined together in song, bellowing off-key (and in very bad Gaelic) Nanny Bridget's favorite: Cruiskeen Lawn — My Little Jug of Whiskey.

As we trekked through the woods, Brian lagged behind, taking in the surroundings: rabbit tracks on patches of snow, squirrels' nests in great oaks, black crows cawing at us. And there went Neal — "all wind and piss like a tanyard cat" — shinnying up a young maple tree. He reached up the slender trunk as high as he could, got a good grip on it, then jumped while still holding on to the tip of the tree. The tree slowly bent and he gently landed feet first on the ground. He was living Robert Frost's "Birches."

> *So was I once myself a swinger of birches;*
> *And so I dream of going back to be.*

We continued along the banks of Canopus Creek. The cold clear waters spilled over frozen fingers of ice. Then a rare sight: Countless silvery creatures — elvers, baby eels — were shimmying upstream.

"They've come all the way from the Sargasso Sea," I said.

"Where is that?"

"A thousand miles away. In the middle of the Atlantic Ocean."

"Cool."

"Have you ever been there?" asked Brian.

"Nope."

"Beat you there!" said Neal.

We studied the elvers; they were tenacious little things. Some took the easy way, squirming their way up tree limbs that had fallen in the stream. Others took the hard way and fought their way up tiny waterfalls. But all seemed determined to reach their destination.

"Where are they going?" asked Brian.

"The Green House," said Garrett.

Neal reached into the cold waters and caught one. He held up a wriggling elver by its tail.

"In Spain they call them *angulas*," I said. "They cook them up in this black oil and eat them with little wooden forks."

"Da sweetest fish in da sea," said Neal.

The source of Canopus Creek is a jewel of a lake tucked away in a narrow valley. The winter sun barely peeked over the hills. Clear Lake was frozen solid and was surrounded by naked trees with elegantly twisted limbs sheathed in ice. Where sunlight struck the trees, the branches twinkled as if covered with countless tiny Christmas bulbs.

We sat on snow covered logs and strapped on our skates. The ice groaned and crackled. Beckoning. There was an element of danger here. We had no idea how thick the ice was. We'd brought no augurs to drill down and measure it. No doubt it was thinner in the center of the lake. But that's also where the surface of the ice was as smooth as the face of a mirror. So that's where we headed. Boys do that.

Our blades cut fresh tracks in the virgin ice. We circled and spun and spiraled. But we were not Olympic prospects. More often we collided and fell and cracked heads against the ice. We laughed at ourselves as readily as we laughed at the world.

A breeze scooped up the powdery snow from the woods, and swept it across the lake and the white flakes swirled around us. It was a magical moment: like skating inside a giant snow globe. A god, holding up the globe in his hand, would see this idyllic scene of a picture-perfect family in a glittering crystal palace.

Later, as we skated back to shore, I was saddened by the thought that I'd be leaving them all once again. And one day, perhaps, forever.

That night the Green House — Never Land — was crowded with kids from the Valley. Among them, Birdsall, a skinny redheaded lad who lived in a house without indoor plumbing. And Mary O'Reilly, Garrett's witty girlfriend. And the Frump kids from up the road, hiding out from a violent father.

We sang folk songs: "Michael Rowed the Boat Ashore" and "Travelin' On."

I've laid around and played around,
this old town too long.

Then we picked up the tempo and rocked out to "Great Balls of Fire."

You shake my nerves and you rattle my brain!

Finally we segued into the Beatles. "Rain" "Nowhere Man." "In My Life." Our voices harmonized well.

The next day, I said goodbye to Maggie and the kids. Garrett drove me into the River Town. I asked him to take a short detour. We pulled up in front of the Old Man's apartment. For the longest while we simply sat there while I mulled over whether to knock on his door or not. But I had nothing to say to him. Nothing he would want to hear at least.

With a sea-bag slung over a shoulder, I boarded the New York Central southbound. The train hugged the Hudson River all the way to the City. I could see the Ghost Fleet across the river in the shadow of Dunderberg Mountain. Even now tugboats were separating another gray hull from the fleet. Soon the ship would be loaded with napalm and missiles and tanks and helicopters. And another ship's crew would be summoned to serve the Beast. Just the sight of it filled me with dread and despair.

That night, I stayed in a cheap hotel near Times Square. Cum-stained mattress. Black-and-white TV chained to the wall. I was thoroughly dispirited. Maybe the old man had it right. It is better to simply imagine the voyage than to actually go on it.

Early the next morning, I was in the Union Hall milling about with the usual suspects. The job board was full of postings for ships bound for Southeast Asia. Then I noticed a job as relief mate on a freighter bound for San Juan. No one seemed to want it, since they'd lose their position in the job line for what would be just a few weeks' work.

The ship was called the SS *Puerto Rico*.

PART THREE:

THE SWEETS OF LIBERTY

19

THE SS *PUERTO RICO*

Where lies the land to which the ship will go?
Far, far ahead is all her seamen know.
And, where the land she travels from? Away
Far, far behind is all they can say.
                    - H. W. Tilman, "Mostly Mischief"

I signed on the SS *Puerto Rico* in Port Newark, New Jersey. The ship — a small C1 freighter — was taking on a cargo of Pampers and Marlboros and Sears brassieres — the treasured produce of the Mother Country. Puerto Rico, it seems, is a U. S. Commonwealth. Its people are American citizens. They eat our Sugar Pops. They die in our wars. Whatever else I knew about Puerto Ricans came from music. The women were dark, fiery and sensuous or as Ben E. King sang in "Spanish Harlem":

With eyes as black as coal
that look down in my soul
And start a fire there
and then I lose control ...

As for the island itself, listen to María in *West Side Story:*

Puerto Rico,
You lovely island
Island of tropical breezes.
Always the pineapples growing,
Always the coffee blossoms blowing ...

To which Anita responds:

Puerto Rico,
You ugly island.
Island of tropic diseases,
Always the hurricanes blowing,
Always the population growing ...

We left Newark under steel gray skies. With Ambrose Lightship in the ship's wake, I went into the chartroom and spread out the pilot chart of the North Atlantic. And there was Puerto Rico: the easternmost of the Greater Antilles, an arc of islands that includes Jamaica, Cuba and Hispaniola. It is a near perfect rectangle 100 miles long and 35 miles wide. The island lies about 1,600 miles south by southeast of New York. About a six-day run at twelve knots.

The shuttle between Newark and San Juan was called a "gravy run." Every two weeks the crew was in their home port of Newark so there was little turnover in personnel. The mates and engineers were all permanent and had sailed together for years. They were like a family. But a dysfunctional family — this was, after all, the Merch. The captain and chief engineer bickered constantly like an old married couple.

"You know you could change your shirt once in while, Chief. The whole saloon smells like Bunker C."

"That was a hurtful thing to say, Captain. You can really be hurtful."

The other ship's officers were like rival siblings, vying for Captain Malone's attention and approval. As the relief mate, I was the odd man out. And that was fine with me. Things could have been worse. I could have still been on the SS *Green Wave*, still anchored in Da Nang Bay, still awaiting Apocalypse Now.

The Puerto Ricans on the ship worked mostly as cooks and bedroom stewards. They were an amiable lot. They hung out on the stern drinking India beer, salsa blaring from an eight track tape player, engaging in constant chatter, hands gesticulating wildly — everyone talking at once in a cacophony of Spanglish.

Saturnino Zapato was the ordinary seaman on my watch. He was from Utuado in the island's central highlands and had butterscotch skin and pale blue eyes. His ancestors were Corsicans who had come to the island a century ago to grow coffee. "The Papa — the pope — he say the Puerto Rican coffee is the best. The best in the world," said Saturnino. "But the American people doesn't like it. He like Sanka. So the coffee farms — *las finquitas* — they slowly disappear. Everything is sugar. Coffee is no more." Rather than work in the sugarcane fields — like a slave, he said, *un esclavo* — Saturnino went to sea. Still he kept a small coffee bush in his quarters. Every day he would bring it outside for some sun.

We entered the Gulf Stream, the water a deep indigo blue. In this part of the Atlantic, the current runs northeasterly at two or three knots. When winds blow from the northeast — and nor'easters are frequent here — the waves kick up fiercely. C1 cargo ships were small but they were beamy and known for their comfortable rides in heavy seas.

On the third day at sea we entered the dark, still waters of the Sargasso Sea. The air was thick and stagnant. Saturnino brought his coffee plant inside. It doesn't like the humidity, he said. We passed tangles of sargassum weed, enmeshed in huge rafts the size of football fields. Here, the flotsam of civilization — plastic toys and Clorox bottles and Styrofoam packing noodles were trapped in a vortex that swirled almost imperceptibly. We spotted a lone green turtle paddling furiously, as if desperate to escape this Limbo of the Lost.

In 1492, the *Niña*, the *Pinta* and the *Santa María* entered the Sargasso Sea from the east. "We saw much weed," wrote Columbus, "stretching to the north as far as you can see." The crew had heard rumors of just such a place. A windless sea where ships got trapped in the weed, only to be swallowed whole by sea monsters. "It caused them great apprehension," Columbus wrote, "because in some places the weed was so thick that it actually held back our ships."

For twenty-one days Columbus's fleet slowly plodded through it. "The crew is grumbling about the wind," Columbus wrote. "It is inconstant and that, along with the flat sea, has led the men to believe that we will never get back home." With the crew on the verge of mutiny, Columbus made them an offer: if they did not sight land in three more days they would turn back. "I also reminded them that the first man to sight land would be given a silk doublet as a personal token from me. Further, he would be given an annuity of 10,000 *maravedíes*." The men were pacified for the moment.

Day six on the SS *Puerto Rico*. Out on the bridge wing. I noticed on the horizon cumulus clouds hovering over what appeared to be mountains. I went into the wheelhouse, where Captain Malone sat in his chair pontificating to Saturnino about the need to master English if he wanted to succeed in life. "Your Spanish will only get you so far in life, Saturn." He had this habit of Anglicizing the Spanish names of the crew. Thus Pedro was Pete, Julio was Jules and Saturnino, Saturn. Saturnino Zapato. Saturn Shoe.

"I think I see land, Captain," I said.

"Clouds are what you see," said he.

"Sir, I'm pretty sure it's land. Take a look on the radar." On the radar screen, every sweep of the line revealed the glowing green contours of mountains. The captain refused to look.

"Sea clutter," he said dismissively. Fifteen minutes later, when I was off watch, Captain Malone announced that he had sighted land.

Alas, things were no different in 1492. It was a moonlit night on October 12 when a lookout on the *Pinta* saw what looked like high white bluffs in the distance. "*Tierra! Tierra!*" he shouted. The whole crew gathered on the deck for a look. It was indeed land. Captain Martín Alonso Pinzón ordered the cannons fired to signal Columbus on the *Santa María* trailing behind.

At day-break, the little fleet gathered together in the lee of a small Bahamian isle. The lookout beamed in anticipation of his reward. But Columbus announced that it was he himself who had been the first to spot land — some four hours before the lookout. "About 10 o'clock at night," he wrote later. "I thought I saw a light to the west. It looked like a little wax candle bobbing up and down. I now believe that the light I saw was a sign from God, and that it was truly the first positive indication of land." He kept his silk doublet.

The Great Discoverer was also something of a Great Exaggerator. Every place he set eyes on in the New World was an earthly paradise. Puerto Rico was no exception. Yet there is something alluring about the island when viewed from sea. To the east, I could see the Luquillo Mountains rising thousands of feet up into the clouds. To the west, clouds roiled dramatically over the narrow coastal plain. And dead ahead, great shafts of sunlight illuminated the old city of San Juan. It sits high on a bluff — a castle city out of a fairy tale. Even the seaside slum, La Perla — gaily colored shacks stacked tightly against the bluff, their tin roofs at odd angles — looked like a Cubist painting with a tropical palette.

With the pilot aboard, the SS *Puerto Rico* slowly steamed past the ancient Spanish fortress El Morro and entered San Juan Bay. To port was the Puerta de San Juan — San Juan Gate — a ten-foot-high wooden doorway set in the stone wall that surrounds the city. In the days of sail it served as the official entryway to the city. It is painted bright red. On a hill beyond the gate sits La Fortaleza, the Governor's Palace. Medieval towers — all white — rise above lush gardens. Now the ship turned east, past La Princesa jail and entered the San Antonio Channel. The customs house came into view: a pale pink building with an ochre edifice. The edifice is intricately carved with exotic symbols and topped with turquoise spindles. It looked like the palace of a Moorish prince.

The ship docked at a pier in Puerta de Tierra, the narrow spit of land that connects Old and New San Juan. The waterfront was lined with crude wooden bars with roofs of corrugated tin. One was painted a vibrant mango orange and bore a sign that read: "SAILOR BAR."

Saturnino and I headed there to await his family. Over Don Q rums, he confided in me that the Puerto Ricans in the crew had had enough of the captain. Especially his lectures on the importance of mastering English. In response, they'd Hispanicized his name. Captain Malone was now Capitán Cabrón. "Cabrón" being a male goat — or cuckold.

La familia Zapato showed up in a battered old Edsel. His brother, sister-in-law, mother, father, wife and kids all poured out of the car. Hugs and kisses for Saturnino; warm hand shakes for me. His brother Edgardo invited me to their home to join them for dinner but I politely declined. I was sure someone would have had to ride in the trunk.

Besides it was time to wander. I followed the street that hugged the waterfront. Just beyond the strip of bars were tenement buildings built in the fifties, perhaps. Faded pastel colors. Cement balconies. Laundry strung up everywhere. Shiny green shirts, lemon colored trousers, aquamarine skirts, purple bras and vermillion panties. Salsa blared from a boom box. Teenage boys tinkered with an old car. Teenage girls poured over a Latin fan magazine. Small boys chased a spunky dog with a baseball mitt in its mouth. No sign of Jets or Sharks.

I cut through the tenements to Avenida Ponce de Leon, a broad tree-lined boulevard that leads into the Old City. I walked west and soon came upon the Plaza de Colón, Columbus' square, which marks the entrance to Old San Juan. A marble statue of the man stands on a tall pinnacle. The Great Discoverer was covered with pigeon shit. He holds a crucifix in one hand, his hat in the other. He looks like he is asking for a hand-out. A bronze bas-relief at the base features Columbus in conversation with Queen Isabel on her throne. I could almost hear the words "earthly paradise" emanating from his lips.

In Old San Juan the streets are paved with *adoquines*, blue-black bricks made from smelter slag carried as ballast in Spanish galleons. I followed a narrow cobbled street to a little plaza — not much bigger than a courtyard. In the shade of mahogany and silk-cotton trees, old men played dominoes, while their *señoras* watched television on a set installed in the *plazuela* for those too poor to own one. It was bolted to a wall that was maybe 400 years old and tuned to a *telenovela* — a Latin soap opera. An aged street vendor sold oranges that he peeled on a rotating contraption. Another sold *piraguas* — ice cones — and school kids were gathered around him. He grated a block of ice, scooped the gratings into a snow ball, popped the ball into a paper cup, then poured lemon or mango or passion fruit syrup over it. The kids slurped down the ice cone, the syrup dripping all over their school uniforms.

I ordered up a lemon *piragua*, and the man said *"una peseta."* I held out a pocketful of change and he picked out a quarter. And I was reminded once again that Puerto Rico is part of America — or at least under its rule. But if the currency is American, it's been Hispanicized in a way that would certainly have offended Captain Malone. A nickel is *un vellón*, a dime *un vellón de diez*, a dollar is *un peso.*

Old San Juan was a bit down on its heels. The twin waves of renovation and gentrification were a decade away. The faded earth-tone walls of the buildings were mottled with black mildew. Masonry faces had sheered away, and one could see the crude red bricks that were fired in 16th Century kilns. Yet despite its shoddy appearance, San Juan was a living city with cafés, tobacco shops, pharmacies, groceries, churches and, yes, the bars and whorehouses that add a touch of naughtiness to all port cities. Balconies with dark mahogany railings hovered over narrow sidewalks. Many were festooned with flowers. Women shouted gossip from balcony to balcony. "*Y la boda de Yolanda! Qué maravillosa, verdad?*"

I entered a cafetería on Calle Luna — or Moon Street, as Captain Malone would say. The man behind the counter was an older gentleman in a pastel blue *guayabera*, an ornately pleated shirt. I ordered a hearty meal of rice and red beans and pork chops. Comfort food. *Tres pesos.* Three bucks. The service was leisurely; the counterman and other patrons were engaged in a spirited debate about Orlando Cepeda, the Puerto Rican outfielder for the St. Louis Cardinals and known on the island as El Peruchín — the Baby Bull. From what I could understand, they were weighing his skills against those of his father — Pedro Cepeda — El Perucho, the Old Bull. Because of the color barrier, Pedro had been denied the opportunity to play in the majors. The counterman turned to me abruptly, and said in English "He was like Baby Roooot! Baby Rooot!" Babe Ruth. There is nothing I love more than shooting the breeze about baseball. I just wished I could have joined in the conversation, but my Spanish was too limited, as was my knowledge of local *beísbol*.

Pleasantly sated, I moseyed on down Cristo Street, where working girls lurked in the doorways. "*Papi, ven acá!*" Air kisses. "*Ay, Papi, mira lo que tengo para ti!*" She hiked up her red leather mini-skirt, revealing, well ...

Directly across the street was the El Convento Hotel which for two hundred years housed the Carmelite nuns. The hookers lingering on the hotel's steps lent fresh perspective to Hamlet's words to Ophelia: "Get thee to a nunnery."

Church bells tolled. The call to afternoon novena. Old women dressed in black hobbled up the steps to the Cathedral of San Juan. I sat on a bench in the tiny park across the way. Wild parakeets screeched in the trees. There was the scent of gardenias in the air. The air was as soft and warm and enveloping as a baby blanket.

Richard Henry Dana, having endured his first year before the mast aboard the brig *Pilgrim*, wrote:

> I shall never forget the delightful sensation of being in the open air, with the birds singing around me, and escaped from the confinement, labour and strict rule of a vessel; of being once more in my life, though only for a day, my own master ... This day, for the first time, I may truly say, in my whole life, I felt the meaning of a term which I had often heard — the sweets of liberty.

I heard the sound of choral music coming from the cathedral, and ascended the steps to the entrance way. There I saw a choir of school girls. Dark hair, huge brown eyes, skin tones from amber to mahogany. The choir was led by a nun with pasty-white skin, pale-blue eyes. Irish, no doubt. I sat on the cathedral steps and listened to them singing in Latin, our shared tongue.

> *Tantum ergo Sacramentum*
> *Veneremur cernui*
> (Down in adoration falling,
> Lo! the sacred host we hail.)

Suddenly long buried emotions welled up inside me. I found myself fighting tears but I didn't know why. Maybe it was a Catholic thing. A wayward Catholic thing. The longing for a lost world of guardian angels and patron saints and a Heavenly Mother who loves and watches over you. A world of miracles and mercies. A world that was lost to me long ago and faraway.

I followed the cobbled Calle Las Monjas — the Street of Nuns — down to where it met the stone wall that encircled the old city. There, a group of friends, men and women about my age, had gathered to watch the sun set over the bay. One of them, a full bearded man with long hair, gave me a friendly nod. He held up a bottle of rum: would I like to join them in a drink?

Handshakes and introductions all around. His name was Alejandro, and he was an architect. As was the bookish-looking Nestor. Ramón was a schoolteacher; his wife Lourdes, a dance instructor. Iliana and Inés ran a boutique on Cristo Street that sold coconut lotions, massage oils and soaps of lime and papaya. Their own scents filled the air like night orchids.

We raised rum-filled paper cups to the sun as it slipped behind smoldering clouds. Shouts of *Salud!* and one Gaelic *Sleante!* The sky was streaked with lime and rose and magenta. "*Ay, qué bello!*" "*Qué rico!*" "*Qué hermoso!*"

It was strange. I felt like I knew this place, knew these people. Perhaps in another life.

Another couple joined us, and I was introduced anew as El Marinero. "*El trabaja en la marina mercante,*" said Alejandro. He works in the merchant marine. "*Como* Popeye, the sailor man." Good natured laughter all around.

The conversation was in a Spanish peppered with expressions like "*bien* groovy" and "*qué* freakout!" and "What a trip!" Most of them had spent some time in the States. Alejandro, Miguel and Aida attended colleges in the northeast. Lourdes studied ballet in Chicago. Iliana had a shop once in Greenwich Village. I asked if they had considered staying in the States but all said "Ay no." Too cold — the places and the people. Besides, said Lourdes, "Puerto Rico is home. Puerto Rico is family."

"And Puerto Rico is music," added Ramón.

Night fell and the music began. Ramón struck a pair of *palitos* or hardwood sticks. TOK-tik-TOK-tik-TOK-tik-TOK. TOK-tik-TOK-tik-TOK-tik-TOK. Alejandro added a bongo beat. Then conga drums appeared out of nowhere. Iliana shook maracas, her hips swaying to the beat. Inés too moved sensuously to the rhythm, her small breasts popping in and out of her tank-top. Someone scratched metal tongs against the ridges of a *güido* — or dried gourd. Another tapped out a rhythm with a cow bell. And now everyone was singing:

Aurelia Aurelia Aurelia
Mira el hombre que sube
Mira el hombre que sube
Sube sube por la ventana.

Alejandro shouted to me above the music, translating the lyrics. "Aurelia is a beautiful woman — and she is asleep at night — when her lover climbs up to her window. He calls to her. Wake up, *mi amor*. Wake up! I have something so sweet for you."

As the moon — a mere sliver — rose, they segued into another song and then another and then another. Someone handed me a pair of *palitos*, and, for a while, I added to the beat, but mostly I simply savored the moment: the seductive rhythms of the music, the warm glow of rum, and the new-found camaraderie.

On the island of Hispaniola, Columbus' men gathered around a bonfire on a white sand beach. The men smoked *cohoba* — a psychedelic seed — and watched entranced as Indian maidens danced before flames that licked the evening sky. *Palitos* and *güidos* and *maracas* — all native Taíno instruments — resounded in the night. Only the day before, Columbus's flagship, the *Santa María*, had run aground on a reef while exploring the coast. Because there was no room on the *Niña* and the *Pinta* for the return voyage home, Columbus asked thirty-six men to remain behind in the New World. None refused. And so savored their own sweets of liberty

On the island of Puerto Rico, we drank and talked, laughed and howled, sang and danced until the last star faded in the eastern sky and the tree frogs fell silent. But now I had to hurry back to the ship. It sailed at dawn. "What is your hurry?" Alejandro asked. "*Coje la próxima.*" Catch the next one. "It is like what we say about lovers," said Iliana. "*Si te pierdes una, cojes la próxima.* If you miss one, you catch the next one."

At first light, dockworkers cast the ship's lines from the bollards, and twin tugs nudged the SS *Puerto Rico* away from the dock. Soon she was heading into the broad expanse of San Juan Bay glittering in the morning sun. Gulls followed over the churning wake. It was a lovely sight.

Especially when viewed from the shore.

20

EL CUCO

One grain of rice equals one bead of sweat.
- Philippine proverb

If I was going to stay a while on the island, I'd need to earn some money. In American ports, including those in Puerto Rico, licensed deck officers were hired to stand watch for their shipboard counterparts. It was to give those who'd been to sea some shore leave, and, if it was their home port, to spend some time with their families. The port relief jobs would last as long as the ship was in port.

The Union Hall in San Juan was located near the Sailor Bar where I shared rums with Saturnino. A dozen Puerto Rican deck officers crowded around the job board. None were interested in going to sea. Like me, each was looking for a temporary gig as a port relief officer or "night mate." But today there were slim pickings. Among them, though, was a gig on the SS *Rice Queen* just in from San Francisco. I was surprised when I was the only one to bid on it.

The *Rice Queen* was located at a pier adjacent to a water-front slum named — with intended irony — Barrio Vietnam. The homes were the size of storage sheds — many of them constructed with rusted Marlboro or India Beer signs. Men sat on cardboard boxes drinking rum, women hung laundry on old TV antennas stuck in the ground, children played catch with balls of rags.

The SS *Rice Queen* was the only ship at the dock, and it was enveloped in a cloud of white dust. The chief mate greeted me at the gangway. Usually ship's officers resent night mates as shirkers and slackers, as Nancy boys not man enough to weather the fierce storms and raging psychopaths on the high seas. But the chief mate seemed glad to see me — which was not a good sign. He coughed up a pasty lunger and spit over the railing.

"Here. You might want to wear this," he said handing me a kerchief. "Wear it around your face. You know, like a bank robber." He hacked — a long jag this time. "Helps with the fuck-ing rice dust." Microscopically, the dust contained fine thorns dropped off from the outer sheath of the rice. Once inhaled, they became imbedded in the lungs and could trigger asthma attacks.

The chief mate went over the standing orders with me. The duties were pretty straightforward. I was to log the times when one hatch was emptied, and when unloading began on another; I was to check the mooring lines and record changes in the ship's draft. The hands-on management of the cargo operations was left to the stevedores who rode honcho over the longshoremen. "They know what they're doing (hack hack). Been doing it for years (spit)." If I had any problems, I was to go to the head stevedore. "But don't bug him unless you really need to. He is a piece of work."

The longshoremen, all Puerto Ricans, were swathed to the eyes in cloth like Bedouin herders. They guided a giant hose that vacuumed up the rice out of the hold. The hose ran up and over the ship's railing and extended across the pier to a granary. As the rice was sucked out of the hold, longshoremen — knee-deep in rice — swept it towards the mouth of the hose. It was grueling work.

The only one with his mouth uncovered was the head stevedore. Perhaps it was so the others could hear him shouting over the loud SHHHHH of the vacuumed rice. Mixed with sweat, the rice dust had formed a white paste over his dark face, so he looked like a New Guinean warrior. His rippling muscles, missing front teeth, and voice as deep as the netherworld created an intimidating persona. He also carried a cargo hook, curved like a scimitar. The longshoremen called him El Cuco, after the legendary bogeyman that kidnapped and tormented children.

He was shouting down into the No. 3 hatch where the longshoremen, standing on mounds of grain, shoveled rice towards the mouth of the vacuum hose. "*DAH-ley! DAH-ley! DAH-ley!*" *Dale*, literally "give it," but meaning "Keep it up! Let's go!" I approached him with temerity, and introduced myself as the officer of the watch. He sized me up and dismissed me with a shrug that said: who gives a roasted fart who you are? Then turned back to the crew: "*Dale, puñeteros!*" Let's go, you jerk-offs!

The *Rice Queen*, a converted T2 tanker, was one of a dozen ships that brought rice to the island. All rice consumed by Puerto Ricans was imported. They preferred the medium-grained varieties grown mostly in Central California. The *Rice Queen* had brought its cargo from Sacramento.

Rice is a major feature of Puerto Rican cuisine. There's *arroz con pollo* — rice with chicken; *arroz con cerdo* — rice with pork; *arroz con jueyes* — rice with land crabs; *arroz con gandules* — rice with pigeon peas; *arroz con garbanzos* — rice with chickpeas; *arroz con leche* — rice with milk. There are rice stews called *asopoas* — a cross between soup and *paella*. And rice desserts such as *arroz con dulce* — rice pudding made with coconut milk.

When not part of the main dish, rice is served as a side along with beans. Rice and beans are to the Puerto Ricans what potatoes are to the Irish, and what pasta is to the Italians — their "daily bread." The beans — or *habichuelas* — are red or pink kidney beans. They are slow-cooked in a tomato sauce flavored with *sofrito* — a blend of green peppers, garlic, cilantro, oregano and onions, suffused with chunks of squash. The cooked beans are served ladled on top of the rice. Together, rice and beans have a kind of protein-synergy effect — each bringing out the maximum nutritional benefit of the other.

When economic times were tough — as they had been for most of Puerto Rico's history — and as they certainly were for the people of Barrio Vietnam — rice and beans kept many an impoverished household from starvation. "Just make some rice and beans," the saying went, "and you'll get by."

The *Rice Queen* carried some 20,000 tons of rice, and, as it was unloaded, the ship would rise ever so slowly. It was time for me to check the ship's draft. The load lines that measure the draft are painted on a ship's hull. Walking along the pier to locate the markings, I passed directly under the cargo hose that led from a ship's hatch to the granary. Grains of rice sprinkled down on me from above. It was not much of a leak, but then I noticed another leak further down the hose — about halfway to the granary — and a steady stream of rice was pouring onto the pier. I went back aboard ship to report this to El Cuco. He was still at the No. 3 hatch, shouting at his minions. It took me a while to work up the nerve to interrupt him.

"Excuse me, uh ... *perdón. Perdón.* There's a leak. *Hay una* ..." I flipped through a pocket dictionary. "*Hay una gotera.*"

"*Gotera?*" he said.

"*Sí. Gotera.* Leak."

"*Gotera?!*" he said again, his eyes now bulging. I could see he was taking this personally.

"*Sí.* The rice — the, uh, *arroz* —. It is leaking from *el tubo* —. And it is spilling all over the pier."

"*Gotera?!*" He was livid now. "*Dónde? Dónde está?!*"

I went to the ship's rail and pointed out the leak. Only now it had been discovered by the people of the barrio as well. They were lined up on the dock, empty cans in hand, patiently awaiting their turn at the spill. There was a pregnant woman and a wiry old black man and children in rags and a line of destitute people that

stretched deep into the hive of wretched hovels that was Barrio
Vietnam.

I thought: Oh, man. What have I done? I've reported the
leak. I've squealed on these folks. And to El Cuco of all people.
Why did I say anything? It was not much of a leak really, a mere
trickle compared to the huge volume of rice gushing into the granary. But to these desperate people it was a bounty as rich as
the fishes and loaves in the Bible. Now I had quashed this little
miracle.

El Cuco was staring at them, methodically sucking in air like a
prizefighter before the bell, the veins on his neck about to burst.
He turned to me as if to say: Can you believe this shit?! I held my
breath awaiting the explosion. For a long while he took it all in,
counting every stolen grain, working himself up into a rage.

Then something happened. An old woman — patch on one
eye — tried to position her empty coffee can under the spill. But
she inadvertently stepped directly under the stream, and rice
poured over her like a shower of grain. She laughed and shook
her head: *Ay Dios mío!* And the others laughed along with her.
Then a young boy took her coffee can and held it under the spill
for her, while others brushed grains of rice from the old woman's
hair and dress.

I turned back to El Cuco fully expecting him to launch into
the mother of all tirades. But instead, he had this curious expression on his face. He seemed strangely conflicted. Something in
this little scene had touched him. It was as if part of him wanted
to hold the woman's coffee can for her, while another part wanted
to plunge his cargo hook into her heart. I don't know — maybe the
old woman reminded him of his mother.

"Is a small leak," he said at last. "*Verdad?*" He pawed his
head.

"Yes, it is a very small leak," I said.

"*Es casi nada.*" He pawed his head.

"You're right. It's almost nothing."

"Maybe we fix later," he said. He pawed his head.

"Sure," I said.

"*No problema.*"

"No problem at all."

El Cuco nodded, satisfied. "*Sí. No problema.*"

Then he simply turned away from the scene and walked back to the No. 3 hatch. There, he collected himself a moment. Took a few deep breaths. Looked out over his crew. Then bellowed: "*Dale! Dale! Maricones cabrones pendejos!*" Let's go! Let's go! You pussies — cuckolds — assholes!

21

TROUBADOURS

Calabaza, calabaza, cada uno pa' su casa!
[Pumpkin, pumpkin, everyone go home!]
        - Puerto Rican children's rhyme

I'd been staying in a small hotel in Santurce, the district known as New San Juan, the commercial hub of the city. Two busy avenues, Ponce de Leon and Fernandez Juncos, run its length. There was a faded art deco look to much of the architecture. Just off the main arteries were residential areas. Some were quite elegant, like Miramar where the actor José Ferrer was raised, but most of the neighborhoods had gone to seed. The middle class had abandoned the city for the suburbs.

In the evenings I wandered the livelier streets of the Old City, and now and then encountered Alejandro and the amigos in their sunset ritual.

"*Mira!* Popeye! You are still here!"

"Yep. Still here."

"We're going to have to make you an official Puerto Rican."

"I look forward to it."

"Have you applied for welfare yet?" said Nestor.

"No. Not yet."

"*Coño.* What are you waiting for?" he said with a laugh.

We would chat, sing, howl at the moon. I soon found myself drawn to Iliana, co-owner of the boutique on Calle Cristo. She was a dark haired beauty of Corsican descent. I hadn't been on a date since shipping out in the merch, and it took me a while to get up the nerve to ask her out.

I met her at her apartment on Calle Sol which she shared with Inés. She was dressed-to-the-nines in silks and hooped earrings and high heels. How she negotiated the cobbled streets in heels was beyond me. We took the eight-minute ferry ride across the bay to her favorite restaurant in Cataño. Our table on the veranda had a lovely view of Old San Juan. A sliver of moon was setting in the west. A piña colada for *la señorita* and a daiquiri for me and, yes, *la vida es buena.* Life is good.

I asked her about her boutique, and she spoke of the wondrous benefits of jasmine and lavender and vanilla. Her hands caressed the air as she spoke. Her favorite, she said, was coconut oil, incomparable for a long sensuous massage. "And when you are giving the massage, you can even lick the oil if you want. It is delicioso!" She kissed her fingers for emphasis. Countless rings sparkled.

Dinner came and Iliana attacked a whole grilled snapper with astonishing gusto. It was soon reduced to a mere skeleton, like the ribs of the hull of a beached boat. Then she picked up the fish head and sucked the eyes out of the sockets. "*Buenísimo!*" she said. "The best part of the fish." The island women, I was learning, were a delightful — if improbable — blend of elegance and earthiness.

To make ends meet, I took whatever night-mating jobs came along. I worked a few days on an auto carrier, the SS *San Juan*, which brought in hundreds of new and used cars for the traffic-choked highways of the island. Then I picked up a gig on the

SS *Seatrain New Jersey*, an odd-looking ship, stacked high with railroad cars. The railroad cars contained electric dryers, color TVs and hula hoops, all destined for Plaza Las Americas, the largest shopping center in the Caribbean. And then there was the SS *Mayagüez*. The *Mayagüez* would one day be captured by the Cambodian Navy and come to symbolize the ineptitude of U.S. policy in Southeast Asia. But now it simply delivered six hundred containers filled with meat deemed unworthy for the US market.

One day, the *Rice Queen* was back in port and once again I was the only one in the union hall to bid on it. I met the chief mate as he hurried down the gangway. He said I should check in with the third mate at the number one hatch. "He's a Maritime guy like you."

At first I didn't recognize him. His face was pasted white with rice dust, and with his flaming red hair and buck teeth, he looked like a tall, gawky circus clown. But there was no mistaking the Brooklyn accent.

"Hey, Maharrey! Maharrey, is dat you?"

I hadn't seen Filario since our chance encounter in Olongapo City in the Philippines, where we had commiserated over beers about life on the ghost ships. "This ship is no better," he said. "The rice dust will kill you." He coughed up white spittle. "And I tell you, Maharrey, dey got a crew chief working this ship, dat's real scary."

"*El Cuco*," I said. "The Crazy One. Yeah, I know him. He is pretty scary. But his bark is worse than his bite."

In any event, he said, it was only a temporary gig. After this trip he'd be back in the Union Hall; back to the ghost ships and the crazies that man them; back to the Land of the Blue Dragon.

"And what about you, Maharrey?"

I shrugged.

"You been here what —"

"About three weeks," I said.

"So what are you doin' here, Maharrey?"

"What am I doing here — what am I doing here. I have no idea."

"I mean you gotta ship out some time."

"Do I? Yes, I guess I do."

When my watch ended that evening, we took a taxi into the Old City. We wandered the cobbled streets.

"You like it here."

"Yes, I do."

I told him about Alejandro and the amigos and Iliana and the surprising benefits of coconut oil.

"I know you, Maharrey. I can't see you staying in any one place. It's not you. You're like dat song, you know. 'Oh de wayward wind ...'"

"I know it," I said, cutting him off. I wasn't sure I could handle a favorite country song sung with a Brooklyn accent. But, yes, the wayward wind is a restless wind, the lyrics go. A restless wind that yearns to wander. But was that still me? I wasn't so sure anymore.

We passed La Capilla del Cristo, the little stone chapel that overlooks the bay. Filario held his arms out as if trying to embrace the spiritual energy in the air. "It's all around us, Maharrey. The grace of God. You can feel it."

That's when we heard the music. Young boys singing a cappella. We followed the music up the street to Parque de Las Palomas, a secluded spot where hundreds of pigeons have nested in the stone walls. There, four young street kids, ages six to ten, were singing for hand-outs:

Chiri bi ribi
Po po pom pom
Chiri bi ribi
Po po pom pom

It was a popular song called "María Isabel" about a joyful day at the beach. But to Filario it was like an Ave María sung by angels.

"Wow. Listen to dem sing!"

To me, the boys were so off-key their singing grated on the ears. But Filario was impressed. "These kids are great, eh Maharrey?" He tousled the hair of the youngest, a little imp with big dimples. "Youse guys are really good. *Ustedes son buenos.*"

"These kids got talent, Maharrey. But nobody's giving dem money. Dat sucks." At two in the morning there were few people around to give them money. The boys encircled Filario, like wolf cubs nestling up to their mother's teats. He stuffed dollar bills in their cups and pockets and outstretched hands. "Hey, Maharrey. Don't be cheap."

We might have passed an enjoyable evening simply walking and talking had Filario not been stricken with this overwhelming philanthropic urge. "There's no money out here in da streets. It's like they're wasting their talent. And these kids could really use da bread, you know. I mean look at 'em. Skinny. Dressed in rags. These kids are hurtin', Maharrey."

"Come on, Filario. What are we gonna do? Adopt them? We gave them money, now let's go."

"I tell you what we're gonna do. We're gonna take 'em to where da money is. That's what we're gonna do. Take 'em to da money."

In the wee hours of a San Juan night there was only one place where da money was: the strip clubs. And that's where Filario intended to show off his young talent. At first glance, it seemed like a sensible plan. The bars, after all, were filled with Hookers with Hearts of Gold and Johns with Dicks of Silver. Surely the sight of four brown-eyed ragamuffins singing a happy song would move them to part with some coin.

Like a pied piper, Filario led the boys into a bar called El Canario where pulsing lights illuminated nude women gyrating on stage to a throbbing beat.

"Filario ... I don't know about this."

"Da money's here, Maharrey. It's here. Look around you." I looked around me and saw horny men transfixed by women on stage who were now dog-humping to "Hang On, Sloopy." The next thing I knew Filario was up there on stage with them. He whispered in their ears. The women had no idea who this man was, but he did seem to have an air of authority. And now with bewildered expressions they were leaving the stage.

"Can we cut the music?!" Filario yelled to the DJ. Surprisingly, the man potted down the music. "Dank you. Dank you."

He turned to the patrons. "We got a special treat for youse tonight." Men shifted in their chairs — this better be good. "We got some really talented kids here. And they want to sing youse something."

He called the boys up on stage and gave them an Ed Sullivan welcome: "These are really talented kids. Really really talented. Let's give 'em a hand." He applauded. I applauded. No one else applauded. The boys looked nervously to their mentor.

"Take it away, boys," said Filario. And the boys sang:

Chiri bi ribi
Po po pom pom
Chiri bi ribi
Po po pom pom

At first, the girls were receptive, pressing hands to their bosoms, cooing "*qué linda*" and "*qué* cute." But their maternal instincts quickly evaporated at the sight of male customers heading for the door. Who could blame the men? They'd been lured here on the promise of seeing naked women lathering each other with whipped cream and licking it off. And now they were being subjected to a scene out of the 1935 movie "Boys Town" with this tall red-headed loon playing Fighting Father Flannigan. The men slipped out the door in ones and twos, then whole tables emptied.

The women were now seething. When the song was over, Filario stepped back on stage, and one of them shouted: "*Vete pa' fuera!*" Get lost!

"Thank you. *Gracias.*" said Filario whose Spanish was weak on idiomatic expressions. "Let's give these boys another hand." He applauded. I applauded. The women shouted jeers and cat-calls.

"*Vete a hacer puñetas, coño!*" Go jerk off somewhere else!

"You want 'em to sing another song?" asked Filario. He turned to the boys who were now looking very nervous. "They love youse guys. You know another song? Uhh, *otra canción?*"

The boys shook their heads no.

"Okay, sing 'Chiri Chiri' again and I'll go round and col-lect the *dinero.*" The boys gamely sang on, as Filario circulated among the tables holding out an empty beer mug for donations. The whores stuffed the mug with coasters and crumpled napkins and tampons until one irate hooker — a huge mama in a day-glo lime-colored peek-a-boo outfit — rose up from her table like a dark cumulonimbus cloud, put her face to his and spat out: "*Vete pa' fuera pendejo pelirojo!*" GET LOST YOU RED PUSSY-HAIR!

We were back on the street, where Filario was celebrating our success tilting at the windmills of fortune. He reached into his pocket and pulled out a wad of bills. "Look at all the money we collected. Youse guys did really great." It was all his money, of course.

Then he turned to me. "Okay, Maharrey. Give 'em the mon-ey you collected."

"What money?"

He gave me a wink. "Maharrey ..."

"Jesus, Filario."

"Mahaaaaarrey ..."

"All right all right." I gave them my money. Then Filario gath-ered the boys in his long gangly arms.

"Youse guys got heart, you know. *Corazón!*" He tapped his heart. "*Y tienen mucho talento. Mucho mucho talento.* Don't ever forget that. I'm proud of you. *Tenemos mucho orgullo de ustedes.* We're both proud of you, right Maharrey?"

"Yep. Both proud."

"This town will be yours some day. Right, Maharrey?"

"Yep. It will be all theirs." There were hugs all around. Then the boys, free of their mentor, strolled back to the pigeon park singing their signature song.

It occurred to me that we no longer had taxi fare to take Filario back to the ship. It was a long walk back to the hotel.

As the morning sun peeked through the louvered windows, Filario curled up in a corner of my room and fell into the deep sleep of the pure at heart.

22

SERENITY

In a world of fugitives, the man going in the opposite direction will appear to be running away.
           -- T. S. Eliot

To understand Puerto Rico, Alejandro said, one must listen to its music, to its poetry. And to the poet José Gautier Benítez it was "an enchanted garden rising above the sea, a vase of flowers set between coral and mist." It was time to explore the island. I took off in a rented moped for the central highlands. If for no for other reason than to taste the coffee that the Pope — according to Saturnino — had called the finest in the world. For a guidebook, I brought along an anthology of Puerto Rican poetry that Alejandro had given me.

But first I had to negotiate my way through the traffic-choked city, and then the tar-paper slums and the cinder-block Levittowns that radiate like nuclear fallout from the most densely populated metropolis in the Caribbean.

Still, beyond the urban sprawl of San Juan lies another world. And yes, one might even call it an enchanted garden. The road led through sugar cane fields, described by Gautier Benítez as "a lake of honey waving in the wind, the fragile stalks swaying like the plumage of sea birds."

Then, higher up, was coffee country. Bushes with dark green leaves lined both sides of the road. The Pope's favorite coffee is brewed from Porto Rico Arabica beans which grow best in high altitudes under a canopy of trees. Now, the road curved sharply around the edges of steep mountains. Lush green vegetation hugged canyon walls.

I pulled off the road at a small *cafetín*. A hand-painted sign declared Aquí Me Quedo — Here I'm Staying. It was a rickety affair — open and airy — perched on a precipice that jutted out over the mountainside.

I took a seat at the outdoor bar under an eave of corrugated tin. In a glass case on the bar-top, a heat lamp warmed mashed potato balls stuffed with ground beef, and fried chunks of pork, and deep-fried plantains. Signs promised India Beer, Palo Viejo Rum and Coca Cola. The juke box was quiet. As was the pool table, its velvet cover torn and scuffed into an obstacle course.

The owner of Aqui Me Quedo was a fat cherubic man. When I asked him for a cup of real Puerto Rican coffee his eyes lit up.

"*Café Rico. El mejor del mundo.*" The best in the world. "*Con leche?*" he asked. With milk?

"*Sí.*"

"*A sus órdenes.*"

Country folk — *jíbaros* they are called — rode up on horseback. The horses were small *paso finos*, bred by the Spanish colonists for riding in the mountains. Their gait is so smooth, it is said, one can ride holding a glass of rum and never spill a drop. Like the cowboy in America, the *jíbaro* is seen as the embodiment of rugged individualism. Instead of a six-gun he wields a machete.

The *jíbaros* ordered a round of beers. The owner of the *cafetín* nodded towards me and told them I'd come all this way for some "*café criollo.*" They looked my way and smiled shyly. *Jíbaros* are a quiet, reserved people. With the milk now warmed in the pot, the owner proceeded to make my cup of brew. But wait. That's not instant is it? Ah, yes. He was spooning dark granules from a jar of Café Rico Instant Coffee into the cup of warmed milk. I had to smile. There was something about the island that conspired against any attempt to romanticize the place. I took a sip.

"Good. *Bueno*," I said. The owner gave me a thumbs up. Then he turned back to the *jíbaros* and their own conversation. Something about *gallos* — fighting cocks — but that was about all I could understand. They clipped their consonants and spoke with a high nasal twang. It sounded like the secret language of cats.

I took the Pope's coffee out on the veranda to savor the view: the spectacular peaks of Petronila, Doña Juana, Maravilla — all ringed with mist. The mountains were impossibly steep and deeply creased. Gushing cataracts cascaded down verdant walls.

Just below me, there was a little blue cottage that clung to the wall of the mountain. A woman was out on a wooden balcony hanging laundry. She had long dark hair and high cheekbones, the legacy perhaps of Taíno Indians. The woman glanced up from her laundry to take in the view. She watched entranced as a pair of tiny emerald-green birds danced on air. It was like a scene out of the poem "Vida Criolla" by Luis Llorens Torres.

Oh, how pretty is my cottage
and how joyful the palm forest!
How fresh the banana plants
on the little river's bank.

Except for the brief American invasion in 1898, this is a land that has never known war. And at longitude 60 degrees west I was almost exactly on the other side of the world from the ultimate conflagration in the Land of the Blue Dragon. This year alone, hundreds of thousands of bombs rained down on North Vietnam as Operation Rolling Thunder intensified. In response, Vietcong and NVA troops launched the Tet offensive surging into the towns and cities of South Vietnam — and blowing a hole in the American embassy for good measure. A little more than a month later, U.S. troops massacred a hundred Vietnamese peasants — men, women and children alike — in a little hamlet called My Lai.

Meanwhile on the home front, Martin Luther King Jr. was assassinated, igniting race riots in more than 100 U. S. cities. In Eastern Europe, Russian tanks crushed thousands of Czechs marching for a free bourgeois society. While in Paris, 600,000 Frenchmen rioted to bring down the bourgeoisie. In China, a million Red Guards, brandishing little Red Books, went on a deadly rampage of destruction to rid their society of "monsters and ghosts." All over the world, people had taken to the streets to protest the madness of our times — or to ignite it.

"Each man must take part in the passion and action of his times," wrote Oliver Wendell Holmes, "or be in peril of being judged never to have lived." Inspiring words indeed, but then so are the words of the poet Luis Llorens Torres: "What happiness not to know about letters and the stars ..."

This is a good place, I thought. I could spend some time here. For I had seldom spent more than a few days in any one port. Even my visits home were measured in days not weeks. As much as I loved my siblings, home was still the place where, when you have to go there, they have to take you in. I was living the life of sketches and vignettes foreshadowed during that long-ago sail on Manhasset Bay. "You see I usually find myself among strangers," said Jay Gatsby. "Because I drift here and there ..." It had been a serendipitous life that seemed to fit my restive spirit. Wayward wind, restless wind. But I could feel myself losing that youthful yearning for the novel, for the ephemeral. It wasn't so much a desire to put down roots, but rather a longing for deeper, richer, more resonant life experiences. Or as Carroll Flowers would say: "De stranger don' know, where da deep water lies." And I relished the prospect of spending a little more time in a place.

And yet ... and yet ... through clefts in the mountains, I could see royal blue waters beyond, glimmering in the sun. And off in the distant horizon a freighter steaming towards San Juan Bay.

Pitching and rolling in a sea of whitecaps. And I thought of all the places the merchant marine had taken me. I was twenty-two years old and had already crossed the world's oceans dozens of times, explored countless far-off places and met innumerable endearing, if eccentric, people. Hell, I'd even been "married" once — if only for a few hours, and, yes, to a Portuguese hooker. No place on the island is more than fifteen miles from the ocean, and its nearness was a reminder of where I'd come from and where, one day, I'd be returning once again.

For the call of the running tide is a wild call and a clear call that may not be denied.